Exploratio.
Theology and In.   .ion

Michael Austin

Explorations in Art, Theology and Imagination

Michael Austin

Equinox Publishing Ltd

London   Oakville

Published by

UK: Equinox Publishing Ltd., Unit 6, The Village, 101 Amies St., London SW11 2JW
USA: DBBC, 28 Main Street, Oakville, CT 06779

www.equinoxpub.com

First published 2005

Cover image: *Madonna and Singing Angels* by Botticelli
Staatliche Museen zu Berlin – Preußischer Kulturbesitz, Gemäldegalerie
Photo Jörg P. Anders

Library of Congress Cataloguing-in-Publication Data
A catalogue record for this book is available from the Library of Congress

ISBN   1 84553 027 6   (hardback)
         1 84553 028 4   (paperback)

Typeset by Forthcoming Publications Ltd
www.forthcomingpublications.com

Printed and bound in Great Britain by Antony Rowe Ltd, Eastbourne

For John Armitage Hey

friend, teacher, scholar

Contents

Preface

These are explorations along very well-trodden paths. However, familiar paths occasionally offer perspectives perhaps not noticed (in this book very rarely) or differently interpreted (often) by those who have walked them before.

There have been many Christian interpretations of art from a variety of theological perspectives. The direction of these critiques has invariably been from theology to art. Theological (even dogmatic) presuppositions have determined the way in which art in general or movements in art or particular works of art have been interpreted. There is a need now for an understanding of art which affirms the crucial importance of art for theology. The direction of the critique must be from art to theology rather than from theology to art. Christian theologians must at the very least appreciate and affirm the value of art for the religion of the Incarnation.

This book sets out some steps towards such an appreciation. It has three broadly interconnecting themes: embodiment and incarnation, similarities and differences, faith and imagination.

Embodiment and Incarnation

'Art rests on the fact that deep feelings pattern themselves in a coherent way all over our life and behaviour', wrote Richard Wollheim (*Art and Its Objects* [1980], p. 112). Religion rests on the same fact. Art and religion arise from our need to express these deep feelings. Through religion as well as through art we are able, as Wollheim says, 'to compensate for how little we are able to say by how much we are able to do'. Art as embodiment of meaning has much to teach, and to learn from, the religion of the Incarnation.

Similarities and Differences

Given this common spring the book studies the similarities in the ways that art and religion work, noting the extent to which each can act as a critique of the other. Taking Christianity as its example, the book argues that the

Church's attitude to the arts has been ambivalent. While being a great patron of the arts, Christianity has in the past (particularly though not exclusively in its reformed and evangelical traditions) tended to over-value the word of Scripture and of dogma such that the non-verbal arts of painting, sculpture, music and dance have been at best ignored and often feared. On their side, artists (particularly in the modern period) have asserted their autonomy and have generally rejected notions of responsibility to social, ethical or religious principles or ideals. While respecting the autonomy of each there is a need for artists and theologians to listen to and learn from each other.

Faith and Imagination

If Christians can be courageous enough to see their religion in the light of art their understanding of the Bible will be greatly enriched and their (often complacent) reliance upon dogma be challenged by a much needed aesthetic corrective—a corrective which is much more searching than rational analysis because it reaches to levels of feeling and awareness which are beyond words.

The book attempts to explore these themes in two parts. The four chapters on Part I are, in the main, descriptive and survey what a few artists, philosophers and psychologists have had to say, or imply, about the relationship of art and religious believing. The seven chapters in Part II are largely speculative. They are not logically connected, but rather interpret the relationship of art and religious believing by following different paths.

I am indebted to Edward Bailey, founding director of the Centre for the Study of Implicit Religion and Spirituality, for his active support and encouragement. For over thirty years Edward has made a most significant contribution to the study of contemporary religion. I am grateful to the editors of *The Journal of Aesthetic Education*, *The British Journal of Aesthetics* and *Modern Believing* for permission to draw on articles of mine previously published by them.

Finally, I am deeply grateful to my friend John Hey with whom much of this book has been discussed and to whom it is dedicated, to Ann for her unfailing support, to Angela Lane who read the book in draft, and to Duncan Burns for his editorial skills and advice. Any mistakes of fact and errors of judgment are, of course, mine. In particular I apologise very readily for any inadvertent plagiarism and unacknowledged quotations. Sometimes the striking ideas and turns of phrase of others are absorbed into my own thinking such that I believe them to be mine!

Introduction

'Art Hidden in the Depths of the Soul'

So it was that Immanuel Kant characterised the imagination[1]—a significant concept for this most sharply rational of thinkers. The imagination is, he said, 'the blind but indispensable function of the soul'.[2] A comprehensive examination of the role of the imagination in Kant's philosophy is far outside the scope of this book and I mention him here simply to make a point. It is that any mental process that seeks to make some sense of the ways we understand and interpret our experience of each other and the world—and theology is certainly at least that if it is nothing else—is greatly impoverished if it relegates the imagination to a kind of footnote, or, worse, leaves it out of account altogether. For Kant the imagination provides the frame of reference or what he called the 'general condition', the pattern or shape or form without which we cannot make sense of what we experience. He uses the example of the triangle. No one *image* of a triangle can do justice to the infinite number of different kinds of triangle that we see in a lifetime. Yet we say 'that's a triangle' of a triangle that we have never seen before, or, to use another example of Kant's, we say 'that's a dog' when we have never been confronted by that particular animal before. The (and this is Kant's word) *schema*, the unifying principle of triangle or dog can exist nowhere else but in thought. It is the product of the imagination, working unconsciously, this 'art, hidden in the depths of the human soul, whose true modes of action we shall only with difficulty discover and unveil'.

This book is about some connections and correspondences between art and Christian believing. Our imagination sees those connections and makes those correspondences. It does this intuitively. Through the imagination we recognise connections and form unities. It uses the material provided by our experience of life and of the world in creative ways that pre-date our rational attempts to explain the connections and unities that (to again use Kant's word) our soul intuitively *sees*.

1. Immanuel Kant, *Critique of Pure Reason* (London: Dent, 1993), p. 144.
2. Kant, *Critique of Pure Reason*, p. 84.

This is a truth of which theology has largely (though perhaps not completely) lost sight.[3] Many years ago John Baillie, in his seminal book *Our Knowledge of God*, took theology to task for ignoring the imagination. Theology, he said, 'has been too much ruled by intellectualist preconceptions'.[4] The same rule has prevailed in much writing about art. John Berger takes to task those who 'mystify' art: 'Mystification has little to do with the vocabulary used. Mystification is the process of explaining away what might otherwise be evident'.[5] That is what intellectualism does. It so often substitutes the narrow perspective of reason for the rounded vision, the 360-degree panorama, of the imagination.

But what *is* the imagination? Following Kant we might say that it is the way in which our minds work in particular ways to make sense of our experience. I say 'to make sense' because the imagination is most certainly not to be identified with the untrammelled, ill-disciplined, irrational part of us. The imagination is not opposed to the intellect—it does not work in ways that are irrational or alien to our reason. Our true imagination does not, as we so often say, 'run riot'. Rather, it works in *different* ways. These different ways have been attractively and sympathetically analysed by John McIntyre.[6] Our imagination, he says in a brilliant summary, is our mind working in ways that lead to perception, selection, and integration; in ways that are creative and constructive, cognitive and interpretative; that are empathetic and sustaining and truly communicative; that make the absent present and distance of little consequence. Let us note in passing that McIntyre distinguishes the imagination from images. Images are what the imagination uses when it functions as it does. We will have more to say about this later in the book.

Professor McIntyre may have come close to falling into the hole that theology's conceptual, rational, ways of working have placed in our path, for to analyse (his word) the imagination is to subject it to reason. The ways of reason have to do with analysis, argument, and conceptualising; with establishing causal connections and with the drawing of conclusions based upon verifiable evidence. The exercise of my *reason* leads me to construct systems and employ arguments to bring order (hopefully) out of my experience. The exercise of my *imagination* compels me to paint pictures and tell stories and create myths, to recognise and value apparent disorder, and above all to draw upon the golden treasury of the art of those before me

---

3.   Those who want much more scholarly and sophisticated studies of the role of the imagination in theology should read, for example, David Tracy, *The Analogical Imagination* (London: SCM Press, 1981); John McIntyre, *Faith, Theology and Imagination* (Edinburgh: Handsel Press, 1987); David H. Kelsey, *The Uses of Scripture in Doctrine* (Philadelphia: Fortress Press, 1975); John W. Dixon, *Art and the Theological Imagination* (New York: Seabury Press, 1978).

4.   Quoted in McIntyre, *Faith*, p. 1.

5.   John Berger, *Ways of Seeing* (London: Penguin Books, 1977), p. 15.

6.   McIntyre, *Faith*, p. 160-68.

and around me and through which I interpret the *significance* of my experience—an experience which, strangely and paradoxically, is itself shaped by
my imagination and by that art. My imagination and the images of true art
seem to go before me, leading me through my life. Imagination leads
reason. Art goes before philosophy.

These words 'art', 'consciousness', 'theology' and not least 'imagination',
together with our notions of objectivity and subjectivity, are all inevitably
defined by our current uses of them. The meaning that we attach to a word
owes less to its etymology and past use and much more to the use to which
we put it and the context in which we place it. But we need to release the
word 'imagination' from its connection with make-believe and restore it as
the basic instrument of our true understanding. The principal tool and
weapon of the reason is *argument.* The paint-brush of the imagination is
intuition. It is intuition, not rationality, that is the first imperative that leads
to true art as, I believe most profoundly, it brings us to art's twin sister—
true religion.

That is a landscape painted with a very broad brush. Intuition is of great
interest to philosophy, while rational argument and careful analysis are in
no way anathema to the arts. Philosophers are intrigued by the evident fact
that one can move intuitively from A to E without apparently passing—logically and causally—through B, C and D. For their part true art and true
religion use rationality to protect them from degenerating into magic or
mere fantasy or sentimentalism or irrational speculation. Philosophy, the
arts and religion seem alike to have self-critical functions, intrinsic to themselves, which in the end prevent them from becoming too self-regarding,
self-contained and self-delusory, though for each of them that end may be
a long way off.

Nevertheless reason and imagination, argument and intuition, philosophy
and the arts do work in identifiably different ways—ways which cannot be
satisfactorily explained in terms of the other's ways of working.

This book is a modest plea for a full recognition of these truths for theology. It tries to do this by asking theology to pay serious attention to the
ways of working of the artist and thereby to recognise and value its own
deeply imaginative heart at a time when the churches seem to be becoming
ever more enclosed within their canonical definitions, dogmatic prescriptions
and regulatory systems. It attempts to do this by encouraging its readers to
escape the border police who patrol the boundaries of self-regarding religion and self-defining art and to meet in the no-man's land that lies between
them, a country clothed with what Hugh Kenner so perceptively described
as the whispering forest of all traditional poetries 'where the very words to
which millions of minds respond have helped to form the minds that respond
to them'.[7] The territories of the orthodoxies of religion and art are, however

7.   Hugh Kenner, *The Pound Era* (London: Faber & Faber, 1972), p. 521, quoted in
John Ashton, *Understanding the Fourth Gospel* (Oxford: Clarendon Press, 1991), p. 3.
Ashton rightly claims that with John's *Gospel* we are deep in that forest.

much their heartlands are disputed, well-mapped and signposted. Between those territories lies this whispering forest of the imagination.

What I suggest here are some imaginative connections between art and religion, some pathways that open up through the whispering forest which lovers of art and religious believers might explore together. In a book as brief as this on a topic so wide I have necessarily had to be very selective. In art I have restricted myself to the work and thoughts of the pioneers of the modern movement in painting. In aesthetics and in the psychology of art I have relied on a few of those who, in the second half of the twentieth century, made influential and lasting contributions. The fathers of Western philosophy from Kant to Nietzsche have unavoidably been subject to the most perfunctory of surveys. Theologians are represented by the four major figures who made significant contributions to an understanding of the rela- tionship of art to theology in the twentieth century. No attempt has been made even to survey the very considerable literature bearing on this topic.

There is here no preaching of what some Christians will assert is the 'full gospel' or any presentation of the so-called 'biblical truths' of neo-ortho- doxy. It is most certainly not an exercise in christological orthodoxy. I make no apology whatsoever for those omissions. It is not a book with these intentions. All it seeks to do is to make a very modest contribution to open- heartedness and to act as a small flag marking one way to the deep and universal truths to which true art and true religion are witness.

Philosophers and theologians have spoken in their own ways about the imagination. Artists must now send us into the whispering forest in their way. Almost exactly half-way through the *Purgatorio*, and therefore at the very heart of *The Divine Comedy*, Dante tells of the imagination. In Italo Calvino's paraphrase, Dante, in two tercets or terzinas in Canto XVII.13-18, describes the imagination as that which has 'the power to impose itself upon our faculties and our wills, stealing us away from the outer world and carrying us off into an inner one, so that even if a thousand trumpets were to sound we would not hear them'.[8]

We are confronted here by what Calvino calls 'high fantasy', that is, 'with the loftier part of the imagination as distinct from the corporeal imagina- tion, such as is revealed in the chaos of dreams'. Fantasy here is not some far-fetched notion or a day-dream, or even imagination unrestricted by reality as the word is commonly employed to mean in English. It is rather what Mark Musa in his translation of the *Purgatorio* speaks of as 'inner visions'. With that word 'vision' too we will also have to deal in the pages that follow. Whence does this imagination, these inner visions, come if, as Dante says, 'the senses show you nothing'? He proposes two possibilities: 'By will maybe of Him who sends it down, or else self-wrought?', as Dorothy

---

8.   Italo Calvino, *Six Memos for the Next Millennium* (London: Random House [Vintage], 1996), p. 82.

L. Sayers renders it so beautifully.[9] Is the imagination the instrument of God or the product of the material universe? Dante leaves this question unanswered as will we.

Let us begin an exploration of that ancient and whispering forest (on his ascent Dante is to enter 'the heavenly forest thick with living green'), there perhaps to have our imaginations transformed into Dante's nightingale, 'the bird that lives to sing'![10]

9.   Dante Alighieri, *The Divine Comedy*. II. *Purgatory* (trans. and ed. Dorothy L. Sayers; Harmandsworth: Penguin Books, 1974), Canto XVII.16-18.

10.   Dante, *The Divine Comedy*. II. *Purgatory*, Canto XVII.21.

Part I

Chapter 1

Art for Whose Sake?

The Question of Art

We begin with some questions about art, though at the very outset we must heed Paul Cézanne's caution that 'all chatter about art is almost useless'. Some chatter is inevitable however, not least about what it is that we mean by the word 'art'. We cannot hear Cézanne's warning unless we first plunge into the question: What is art?

This is a question that would hardly have been asked until the eighteenth century. Only then did the notion of 'the fine arts' as the separate disciplines of painting, sculpture, music, poetry and architecture united by some kind of common aesthetic become distinct from craft skills on the one hand and the scientific disciplines on the other. The notion of 'Art' is therefore of recent invention. This will become important for our discussion later. That art, religion and science are discrete fields of human concern and endeavour having little or nothing in common with each other, and indeed opposed to each other, is therefore a comparatively modern idea, yet we can see its appeal fading rapidly. The use of the words 'beauty' and 'beautiful' is not confined to art and aesthetics. Questions of meaning and value are no longer regarded as the concern of religion alone. Science is no longer seen as providing the only valid account of the world. Postmodernism is marked by the dissolving of pretentious distinctions and arrogant claims. However, the question of what art *is* persists, and that is where we will begin.

A Question of Criteria

What has something got to be for it to be called a work of art? Has it got to be the imitation of something, or the expression of some thing's 'essence' for it to be called art? Or is a work of art so defined in terms of factors internal to itself as an object such as symmetry or proportion or the balance of the elements that comprise it, that is its formal qualities? So diverting and difficult has this question become that some have given up the attempt to define art against any set of criteria external to an artist and an artwork.

The painter Francis Bacon said once that 'there is no such thing as art—only artists'. In Bacon's view artists and no one else determine what it is that they do. It is not for the beholder to say 'this is art—but that isn't'.

That point of view has its attractions if only because defining art in an objective way is well-nigh impossible today. As we will see, not only do fashions in art change (and therefore the criteria against which art is judged) but a powerful tendency in contemporary philosophy would have us question whether there is such a thing as objective truth at all. If there is no such thing as objective truth then one opinion about a work of art, and indeed whether it *is* a work of art is as good as any other. As Rudolf Arnheim points out, 'one can hardly blame the artist for proclaiming that art is anything he chooses to call art if the very people who are supposed to supply the standards by which to judge what is and what is not art assert that there are no such objective criteria'.[1]

This is a crucial matter, and not merely for art of course, and we will return to it again. But even assuming that objective criteria do exist by which we can judge what is art and what is not, trying to answer the question 'What is art?' would still be very difficult. If we wanted to attempt a definition the process might go somewhat along the lines of this interrogation set out by Richard Wollheim:

> 'What is art?' 'Art is the sum or totality of works of art'. 'What is a work of art?' 'A work of art is a poem, a painting, a piece of music, a sculpture, a novel…'. 'What is a poem? a painting? a piece of music? a sculpture? a novel?'… 'A poem is…, a painting is…, a piece of music is…, a novel is…'
>
> It would be natural to assume that, if only we could fill in the gaps in the last line of this dialogue, we should have an answer to one of the most elusive of the traditional problems of human culture: the nature of art.[2]

But, as Wollheim points out, matters are nowhere as simple as that. If they were then works of art would be of merely secondary consideration. If there *were* a set of clear and universally accepted and therefore authoritative criteria which determined not only whether a painting or a sculpture or a novel *was* in fact a painting or a sculpture or a novel but also whether given examples of each were or were not art then all found objects or created artefacts which people thought might qualify as works or art would be assessed according to those externally imposed canons. And were this the case the criteria would be more important than art itself. Artworks accepted as such by those who determined or interpreted the criteria would then serve no other function than to demonstrate the supposed validity of the criteria. Some works of art would be allowed into the cathedrals of accepted

---

1.   Rudolf Arnheim, *To the Rescue of Art* (Oxford: University of California Press, 1992), p. 6.
2.   Richard Wollheim, *Art and its Objects* (Cambridge: Cambridge University Press, 1992), p. 1.

dogma, the great galleries and prestigious exhibitions and collections, and everything else rejected as either poor art or not art.

A Question of Acceptability

And that of course is very much what has happened in the past and still happens now. Each period in art criticism determines the criteria of acceptability. As T.S. Eliot observed: 'our criticism, from age to age, will reflect the things that the age demands'.[3] The process of criticism is circular and self-contained. In each historical period, and in every centre of art, there is a prevailing art establishment with an inner group of distinguished *cognoscenti* who debate and eventually determine, if not what is and what is not art, then certainly who are and who are not the exemplars of what is acceptable in current art. Writing, in 1965, of the Paris art market John Berger noted that 'it has become an accepted idea amongst nearly all French intellectuals...that art is the natural blessing of France... In France it is believed that there are no questions about art which have not already been fully answered there.'[4] So, at one time abstract art prevails and representational art is out of favour. At another so-called 'realism' is in the ascendancy while what might be regarded as more imaginative or expressive art is given little attention.

In fact critics and historians of art are much more knowledgeable and sophisticated than to be influenced by mere fashion, even the fashion they themselves create. They, and we, now recognise as great artists men who, like Vincent van Gogh and Paul Cézanne, sold few pictures in their lifetime and who were castigated by most of the influential critics of their day. That underlines a point that I wish to make. Except in the short term the criticism of art follows art, it does not lead it or determine it. In 1911 Wassily Kandinsky said that 'in real art theory does not precede practice, but follows her'.[5] Indeed the very nature of art criticism suggests that there can never be one authoritative and 'correct' interpretation and evaluation of any work of art because there can never be a universally accepted set of criteria to which to appeal.[6] Thus, as Anne Sheppard points out, the so-called 'laws' of single viewpoint linear perspective are not laws at all but conventions which any painter is free to ignore, as Manet and the Impressionists did. So it is too with the established 'rules' of musical composition, or the Renaissance requirement that the time covered by the action of a play should be the

---

3.   Quoted in Peter Ackroyd, *T.S. Eliot* (London: Penguin Books, 1993), pp. 196-97.
4.   John Berger, *Success and Failure of Picasso* (London: Granta Books, new edn, 1992), pp. 177-78.
5.   Wassily Kandinsky, *Concerning the Spiritual in Art* (New York: Dover Publications, 1977), p. 35.
6.   Further to this see Anne Sheppard, *Aesthetics: An Introduction to the Philosophy of Art* (Oxford: Oxford University Press, 1987), pp. 78-93.

time taken by the performance—a condition ignored by Shakespeare. There are no canons, codes and criteria in art. Artists, certainly great artists, lead. Theories, canons and criteria follow.

A Question of Authority

Now, to mention here briefly and in passing an important theme for development later, this points to an important distinction between art and religion, certainly between art and the Christian religion. If, as I will argue, religion is *at least* a kind of art, then the argument seems to fall on this ground alone for Christianity *does* possess criteria universally accepted by the Church. The three-fold test of catholicity by which truth and falsehood is determined is 'what has been believed everywhere, always, and by all'.[7] These criteria determine credal orthodoxy. Any theological claim or proposition which fails the test of credal orthodoxy is not by definition Christian doctrine. What is and what is not Christian truth is thus capable, so it might be assumed, of being determined by recourse to the defining authority of the universal Church. Yet clearly this is not the case in practice, else why is the Church divided not merely on matters of order but over fundamental questions of faith? And even if the Church was not divided, and all Christians submitted to its authority, what of those outside the Church? Quite properly they would ask (as they do ask) upon what *independently* verifiable grounds these truth-claims and this authority rests. For them it is not enough to lay claim to special revelation, because that claim is itself formed by, and lies within, the structure of the faith. The fact is that all orthodoxies, be they in art or in religion or even in science, are closed sets of criteria that allow for no development and adaptation beyond the limits they themselves have established, until, that is, they change in the face of overwhelming evidence. As Richard J. Evans has said of history and historians, 'arguments and theories, however dominant in the intellectual life of their day, have to be assessed on their own merits, not accepted uncritically simply because they are espoused by a majority'.[8]

Of course, as with thoughtful seekers after truth outside the Church who cannot accept the Church's truth-claims, those of us moved by art can choose to dissent from the critics. We can trust our own judgment and declare that the kings of the art world have no clothes. Or, much more likely, as with those who while not belonging to the Christian community have an uneasy suspicion that those who do may be right, we can look at a calf cut in half and pickled in formaldehyde and, struggling with our own sense of inadequacy and lack of knowledge, try to work out why the experts consider the poor animal a work of art.

---

7.   The Vincentian Canon laid down by St Vincent of Lerins in his *Commonitorium* (II, 3).

8.   Richard J. Evans, *In Defence of History* (London: Granta Books, 1997), p. 14.

A Question of Common Sense?

There is no easy way out of the dilemmas this discussion raises. A seem-ingly common sense approach to a work of art, particularly, say, a so-called 'modern' painting or sculpture or piece of music that we say that we do not 'understand', might be to ask some obvious questions about it: 'What is it?', or 'Has it got a purpose?', or 'What does it mean?', or 'How can I judge whether it is good art or not?', or 'Am I supposed to feel anything?' Even the critics have asked those questions when faced with art outside their frames of reference, or at least have been driven to some outspoken and commonplace reactions. When Whistler's painting *Nocturne in Black and Gold: The Falling Rocket* was exhibited in 1877 the world's foremost art critic John Ruskin famously wrote that 'I have seen and heard much of Cockney impudence before now, but never expected to hear a coxcomb ask two hundred guineas for flinging a pot of paint in the public's face'—a comment that led to a notorious libel action at the end of which Whistler won a ruinous one farthing's damages. And even great artists can be wrong about art. A few years later Leo Tolstoy in his *What is Art?* launched a bitter attack on what we now know to be the greatest masterpieces of Impres-sionist and Symbolist art. He admitted that he did not understand these paintings but went on to argue that as, by his definition, good art is art understood by the masses, and this was not, then Impressionist and Symbolist art was therefore bad art. But, he said,

> people may habituate themselves to anything, even to the very worst
> things. As people may habituate themselves to bad food, to spirits,
> tobacco, and opium, just in the same way they habituate themselves to
> bad art—and that is exactly what is being done.[9]

Thus did Tolstoy dismiss the contemporary painters Manet, Monet, Renoir, Sisley, Redon, Pissarro and Puvis de Chavannes—just as, a page or two later, he was to castigate the 'composers of the new school' who employ 'strange loud sounds' produced by 'perspiring and agitated' performers who 'just throw hands and fingers wildly at the keyboard in the hope that you fall into the trap and praise [them]'. Tolstoy named these decadent com-posers. They were 'Liszt, Wagner, Berlioz, Brahms, and (newest of all) Richard Strauss'![10] To be fair to Tolstoy, in applying his criteria of aesthetic value (that is, that good art is that which is understood by the masses) he rejected, along with Beethoven's Ninth Symphony, most of his own literary output!

We will return to Tolstoy's judgment in Chapter 5.

---

9.   Leo Tolstoy, *What is Art?* (London: Walter Scott, 1898 [Ward Lock Reprints, 1970]), pp. 95-101.
10.   Tolstoy, *What is Art?*, p. 97.

Questions the Artist Asks

The history of art criticism produces ample evidence that asking the so-called common sense questions about an artist or a work of art rarely if ever produces an answer that can stand a second hearing. The reason, certainly so far as great art is concerned, is that it is not merely for us, the viewer or listener, to ask questions of art. The artist, whether consciously or not, asks questions of *us*. The artist can and does often confront us with truths to which we would prefer to be blind and compels us to pay attention to them. Seen in this way art is for our sake. It has a moral dimension. Art can widen our perceptions of ourselves and of others and of our responsibilities and duties. If we respect art the possibility is that we will respect other people and the natural world.

The reason why artists can perform this prophetic role is that they see where so often we are blind and hear when we are deaf. And artists possess eyes and ears not merely into nature but above all into the inner world of their, and therefore of our, true self-hood—the world of our most intimate feelings and emotions. Artists give expression to those emotions and feelings in ways that we are not able to do, for we may not even have identified these feelings and acknowledged their power. Henri Matisse was once asked in a radio interview one of our common sense questions: 'What then of the artists? Of what use are they?' He answered:

> They are useful because they can augment colour and design through the richness of their imagination intensified by their emotion and their reflection on the beauties of nature, just as poets or musicians do. Consequently we need only those painters who have the gift to translate their intimate feelings into colour and design.[11]

The argument here is that artists enable us to have a wider perception of the possibilities that the world offers and therefore can enhance our awareness of truth, value and freedom. Artists can do this because, Matisse goes on to say, an artwork is much more than a mere expression of the artist's inner feelings and unrecognised emotions. It has a life of its own independent of the artist. It is for this reason that it can also speak to and for my feelings and emotions. Michelangelo's great uncompleted series of slaves or prisoners, the famous *Prigioni* now in the Galleria dell'Accademia in Florence, figures that are still, as it were, captured in the blocks of marble yet struggling to emerge, speak for and to all those of us striving to escape from any one of a million prisons *whether or not this was Michelangelo's intention*. D.H. Lawrence said of the wonderful naked *David* by Michelangelo in the same room in the Accademia that he stands forth 'stripped and exposed and eternally half-shrinking, half-wishing to expose himself'. To the unrecognised emotions of how many does that great figure and that remarkably perceptive comment speak?

11. Jack D. Flam, *Matisse on Art* (Oxford: Phaidon Press, 1973), p. 92.

A Question of Meaning

It seems that a great artwork is great because it has an existence independent of its creator. In this independence is its meaning. For Matisse a
painting by him 'is not a mirror reflecting what I experienced while creating
it, but a powerful object, strong and expressive, which is as novel for me as
for anyone else'. At the age of eighty-two Picasso said: 'Painting is stronger
than I am. It makes me do what it wants.'[12] Although the painting had its
origin as an expression of his emotions and feelings the completed work
has an independent existence. In Picasso's case so independent is it that he
claimed that his art controlled him. This relationship between the artwork's
origin in, but independence of, the artist is, Matisse himself observed, 'the
eternal question of the objective and the subjective'.[13] In a work of art
objective and subjective are united.

Now here we touch on a fundamental fact about art—perhaps *the* most
fundamental. It is that art *communicates* and thus, at a deep personal
level, *unites*. This has rarely been better expressed than by George Heard
Hamilton:

> Because each work of art originates in the mind and feelings of a human
> being, it reaches its destination in the mind and feelings of another. A
> work of art, therefore, is a fact of consciousness quite as much as it is an
> object existing beside us in the physical world and an event in the
> chronology of the historical past. A history of art is therefore a history of
> consciousness...[14]

Developing this we might say that this profound communication as 'a fact of
consciousness' in my mind and feelings is of the nature of an *incarnation of
meaning*. The meaning of an artwork finds its *destination* in my experience
now.

There is much in these observations for the theologian to ponder. It is a
key theme of this book that the way in which a work of art is an *embodiment* of meaning (as Louis Arnaud Reid argues) speaks powerfully to what
it is claimed is the incarnation of God in the person of Jesus. George Steiner
in his remarkable lecture *Real Presences* says that

> Where we read truly, where the experience is to be that of meaning, we
> do so as if the text (the piece of music, the work of art) *incarnates* (the
> notion is grounded in the sacramental) *a real presence of significant
> being*... To be 'indwelt' by music, art, literature, to be made responsible,
> answerable to such habitation as a host is to a guest—perhaps unknown,
> unexpected—at evening, is to experience the *commonplace mystery of a
> real presence.*[15]

12. Quoted in Berger, *Success and Failure*, p. 29.
13. Berger, *Success and Failure*, p. 90.
14. George Heard Hamilton, *Painting and Sculpture in Europe 1880–1940* (New
Haven: Yale University Press, 1993), p. 19.
15. George Steiner, *No Passion Spent* (London: Faber & Faber 1996), p. 35.

Similarly, the notion of an artwork as a fact of the artist's consciousness existing in and through his artwork and reaching its destination in me, the viewer or listener, has much to say to the way in which the Gospel is heard as 'good news' and the sacraments are received. Christians who have become preoccupied with the communication of the Word through propositions and have been dismissive and even fearful of the non-verbal arts, or who may have come to treat the sacraments (whatever they may say to the contrary) as mechanical grace and have lost sight of their relation to metaphor would do well to consider the theological implications of art carefully. The kind of Christianity which, while professing faith in the incarnation of God, can knowingly restrict the Gospel to dogma or to mechanical actions has to ask itself how much of God it knows. The religion of the Word made flesh has all too readily re-made the flesh into the words of proposition and dogma.

A Question of Value

Those brief and inadequate observations suggest an answer to another basic question about art: Why bother about it? For very many people the word 'art' is about what people do in their spare time. Well—what do they do? They read novels, they read poetry, they go to the theatre or to concerts, they watch television, they go to art galleries or visit buildings or walk in the country. Now these are all aesthetic activities as Anne Sheppard has noted.[16] For me going to church is very much an aesthetic activity. It may be, and must be, more than that (whatever that 'more' is), but I would find it very difficult to attend church regularly if worship was not a richly sensuous experience of eye and ear. But why indulge in aesthetic activities? As Anne Sheppard says,

> People engage in these activities from choice and for their own sake. Reading a novel will not help me earn my living... Going to an art exhibition will not cure me of any physical ailment. A visit to a beauty spot will not make my house any warmer.[17]

And, we could add, going to church does not, of itself, either solve my problems or make me good. So why do people seek out aesthetic experiences? One straightforward answer is that they give them pleasure. But why seek this particular kind of pleasure? What is it about reading novels or looking at pictures or listening to music or walking in the Lake District which makes these particular pleasurable activities worthwhile and other pleasurable activities not? This is a huge question in aesthetics to which we cannot here do justice, but we have already suggested one of several answers. It is that art (certainly great art) engages both our emotions and our intellect. It

16. Sheppard, *Aesthetics*, p. 1.
17. Sheppard, *Aesthetics*, p. 1.

makes demands of us intellectually, morally, emotionally and, I am certain, spiritually—demands which we need to accept in order to develop our powers of imagination and understanding. More than that, at least for me in those arts which move me above all others—painting and sculpture and music (significantly the non-verbal arts)—art excites me, thrills me, heals me, judges me, touches me at a depth which nothing else can reach. Art, for me, is salvific.

A Question of Understanding?

It is certainly beyond rational understanding. This raises another of those common sense comments (and implied questions) about art, particularly so-called 'modern' art, and one we have already touched on: 'I don't understand it. What does it mean?' But why do we need to 'understand' art? Picasso said this:

> Everybody wants to understand art. Why not try to understand the songs of a bird? Why does one love the night, flowers, everything around one, without trying to understand them? But in the case of painting people have to *understand.* If only they could realise above all that an artist works of necessity, that he himself is only a trifling bit of the world, and that no more importance should be attached to him than to plenty of other things that please us in the world, though we can't explain them.[18]

Here Picasso echoes Claude Monet who once said that he wished to paint as the bird sings. As John Berger comments, Picasso is here in part voicing a protest against the pretentious intellectual constructions that has surrounded so much art in the modern period, and is in part also affirming his own genius. Berger, echoing Monet, says of Picasso's comment: 'He makes art like a bird sings. Understanding has nothing to do with it—indeed understanding is a hindrance, almost a threat'.[19] Thoughtful Christian believers may detect a resonance here with their feeling that there is an intellectual pretentiousness about much theology such that it can hinder, and even threaten, Christian believing. For them the Christian faith is instinctively felt to be both an expression and a response to that absolute truth revealed 'as the bird sings'. This in turn hints at the fundamental importance of the art which is liturgy and the art which is the Bible in carrying and expressing and directing to their true origin these feelings of absolute worth. We should note here that the religiously orthodox will condemn this notion as mere romanticism possessing no intellectual rigour. But what lies beyond the mind? To what ultimate goal are our inchoate yearnings no less than our intellectual speculations directed? If, as many neuroscientists are now maintaining, such speculations are merely the expressions in consciousness of the activity of our neural pathways, the function of which is solely to

18. Berger, *Success and Failure*, p. 29.
19. Berger, *Success and Failure*, p. 29.

further our biological ends, then notions of objective intellectual rigour are as subjective as romanticist ramblings.

The Question of Beauty

To speak of art as salvific and of liturgy and scripture as art brings us within sight of another wide range of questions about art, two of which we have already touched upon. These have to do with the relationship of art to Christianity. On the basis of Old Testament texts, notably Exod. 20.4,[20] the early church Fathers were inclined to iconoclasm, though there is a wealth of evidence to show that this was far from universal. For those who sought to destroy art the argument was that the senses—all the senses—distract us from God. Iconoclasm has its roots in the fear of the sensual attractiveness of art.[21] Loveliness, beauty, forms and shapes were liable to distract the soul from its search for God and to tempt one into the grievous sin of, as Augustine put it, 'the gratification of the eye'. However, St Augustine, a great literary artist himself, confessed to God that 'the beautiful things of this world kept me far from you and yet, if they had not been in you, they would have had no being at all'.[22] In that passage Augustine expresses a Christian dilemma as old as Christianity itself. The beautiful things of the world are of God, yet they can replace God. As George Pattison summarises it: 'Here we can see the ambiguity of [Augustine's] attitude towards material beauty. It is a sign of the divine Beauty—but woe to him who keeps his eyes fixed on the sign and fails to pass on to that which it signifies'.[23] It was a dilemma which John Calvin and those who have followed him did not recognise. For Calvin there is no place for art in Christianity at all, and although he was not, he said, 'gripped...by the superstition of thinking absolutely no images are permissible', his rigid position led to the waves of iconoclastic destruction that marked and marred the Reformation and which still disables many evangelicals from giving its God-given place to the sensuous and the aesthetic within and outside their Christian faith. On the other hand, the Church (or, rather, wealthy churchmen) has for many centuries been among the greatest of art's patrons. One could not hope even to summarise the work commissioned from Giotto, Leonardo, Donatello, Michelangelo, Raphael, Rubens and other immortals among the painters

20. 'Thou shalt not make to thyself any graven image, nor the likeness of anything that is in heaven above, or in the earth beneath, or in the water under the earth. Thou shalt not bow down to them nor worship them.' This would seem to allow decorative or non-representational or non-imitative art, as in Islam.

21. Though, as Arnheim points out, the church fathers were worried most by three-dimensional art. Paintings tended to be accepted as non-verbal means of spreading the word of God (*To the Rescue of Art*, p. 91).

22. St Augustine, *Confessions* (London: Penguin Books, 1961), p. 231.

23. George Pattison, *Art, Modernity and Faith* (Basingstoke: Macmillan, 1991), p. 15.

and sculptors. And what of the composers? Think of Johann Sebastian Bach whose two great Passions and the *B minor Mass*, the *Magnificat* and the Christmas and Easter Oratorios to say nothing of what might be regarded as the lesser works of his genius, composed weekly for his choir in Leipzig, express such profound spiritual realities, or Palestrina—and what can one say of Wolfgang Amadeus Mozart or of Handel or of Verdi, the confessed agnostic who composed an incomparable *Requiem*? These extraordinary artists received commissions from the Church or wrote for the Church as paid employees. What is now so revealing is that the liturgical music they composed is performed almost exclusively outside divine worship. The sheer power not only of the beauty of the work of these men, but their capacity to touch us so deeply, carries us above the dogmas which separate us to unite us through a shared experience which is beyond words to describe.

The fundamental Christian dilemma about art and the Church, which can best be summarised in the two opposed propositions: 'It is beautiful so we must destroy it to the glory of God' and 'It is beautiful so we must possess it for the glory of God' has not been fully resolved by theologians. In fact very few have engaged with the question of art directly. In the next chapter we will consider four contrasting twentieth-century theologies of art.

Chapter 2

Art and the Theologians

Karl Barth: Mozart's Music as Parables of the Kingdom

Paradoxically, Protestant theologians have not been able to ignore art even though they have distrusted it profoundly. Art has thrust itself upon them. Even Karl Barth could not escape art. Barth was the twentieth-century theologian who has most rigorously denied that man can know God other than by God's revelation of himself in Christ. In the 1920s, in sharp reaction to what he regarded as the trend to place man and man's achievements at the centre of theology, he voiced a totally uncompromising *Nein!* against any tendency in Christianity which would suppose that God was other than wholly other. He was thus inflexibly iconoclastic. Nevertheless he was compelled to find a place in his life as a theologian for art. As a boy he was captivated by music and devoured the aesthetic philosophy of Schiller. As a young pastor he conducted performances of, among other works, Mozart's *Ave Verum* corpus. Throughout Barth's long life the work of his beloved Mozart exercised a profound influence upon him. He took part, as a viola player, in performances of Mozart's string quartets. The sound of Mozart accompanied the writing of his huge and definitive *Church Dogmatics*, and, revealingly, he inserted a special excursus on Mozart in the section in volume III,3 on 'Nothingness'. Here he says of Mozart that

> He has heard, and causes those with ears to hear, even today, what we shall not see until the end of time—the whole context of Providence. As though in the light of this end, he heard the harmony of creation to which the shadow belongs but in which the shadow is not darkness, deficiency is not defeat, trouble cannot degenerate into tragedy and infinite melancholy is ultimately forced to claim undisputed sway... Mozart causes us to hear that even on the latter side, and therefore in its totality, creation praises its master and is therefore perfect.[1]

And this from a theologian who rejected any claim of natural theology and who maintained that

1. Karl Barth, *Church Dogmatics*, III, Part 3 (Edinburgh: T. & T. Clark, 1978), pp. 298-99.

> The world with its sorrow and its happiness will always be a dark mirror
> to us, about which we may have optimistic or pessimistic thoughts; but
> its gives us no information about God as the Creator. But always, when
> man has tried to read the truth from sun, moon and stars or from himself,
> the result has been an idol.[2]

It seems almost that Mozart was Barth's theological Achilles' heel. Whereas,
for Barth, the Protestant Johann Sebastian Bach had an affected 'desire to
preach' the Catholic Mozart had no such presumptions and simply 'plays
and does not cease to play'. Most compelling of all, in his lecture *Mozart's
Freedom*, the elderly Barth said:

> I am not a man with particular artistic gifts or an artistic education, nor
> am I inclined to confuse or to identify salvation history with any part of
> the history of art. But the golden sounds and melodies of Mozart's music
> have always spoken to me—not as gospel, but as parables of the king-
> dom revealed in the gospel of God's free grace, and they continue to do
> so with the utmost freshness. Without it I could not think of what moves
> me personally in theology, in politics. There are probably few theologians'
> studies in which the pictures of Mozart and of Calvin can be seen side by
> side at the same level.[3]

One is bound to ask how Barth could distinguish theologically between the
gospel on the one hand, and 'parables of the kingdom revealed in the gospel
of God's free grace' on the other. By Barth's own confession, and notwithstanding the abiding rigour of his theological position, the 'utmost freshness'
of Mozart's music, it seems, was so revelatory of God's free grace that
Barth could not have written theology without it.

How do we explain this ambivalence, indeed apparent contradiction?
Barth came later to regret the polemical stridency with which he expressed
his position in the 1920s. The famous watchwords of Barth's polemicism—
the notion of the 'wholly other' breaking in upon us 'perpendicularly from
above', and the concept of the 'infinite qualitative distinction' between God
and man—were, he was to say in 1956, only 'partially right in the sense in
which all preponderantly critical–polemical movements, attitudes, and positions, however meaningful they may be, are usually only partially in the
right'. Barth acknowledged that he and those who believed as he did had,
in those turbulent years, laughed derisively at their opponents rather than
greeting them with a sad and friendly smile.[4] Barth came fully to acknowledge that God's deity does not exclude his humanity, 'since it is God's
freedom for love and thus His capacity to be not only in the heights but also
in the depths, not only great but also small, not only in and for Himself but
also with another distinct from him, and to offer Himself to him'. Indeed, in

2.   Karl Barth, *Dogmatics in Outline* (London: SCM Press, 1949), p. 52.
3.   Karl Barth, *How I Changed my Mind* (Edinburgh: St Andrew's Press, 1969),
pp. 71-72, quoted in Eberhard Busch, *Karl Barth* (London: SCM Press, 1976), p. 410.
Other references *passim*.
4.   Karl Barth, *The Humanity of God* (Atlanta: John Knox Press, 1960), pp. 41-42.

Jesus Christ 'the fact is once for all established that God does not exist without man'.[5] It follows that human culture (including art evidently) expresses man's attempt to be man and thus 'to hold the good gift of his humanity in honour and to put it to work'.[6] God, Barth was to say, 'is always free to produce even in human activity and its results...parables of His own eternal good will and actions'. Then comes a key admission: 'It is more than ever true, then, that with regard to these [human activities] no proud abstention but only reverence, joy, and gratitude are appropriate'.[7]

However, even given this proper recognition of the gift of the love of God expressed in human culture, Barth could never find in his theology the place for the visual arts that he could find for music. There is, he said, 'no theological visual art. Since it is an event, the humanity of God does not permit itself to be fixed in an image'.[8] Perhaps here Barth's incipient iconoclasm betrays itself. Be that as it may this statement quite misunderstands the nature of the dynamic, continuing, event which is the relationship of the viewer of a painting or a sculpture with the artwork. But not all great music passed Barth's test by any means. Not only does Bach merely preach to us, Barth said, but the theologian who does not proceed first from God's relationship with man lacks 'the skylight and hence serenity' and remains 'a gloomy visitor upon this earth of darkness, an unpleasant instructor of his brethren, whose teaching, at best, compares with the sombre music of Beethoven and Brahms!'[9] Barth's ambivalence to the arts remains and was never adequately resolved.[10]

Paul Tillich: The Expressionists and Art as Disclosure

Barth's great contemporary, long-time acquaintance but outspoken critic, Paul Tillich, gave a quite different place to art in his systematic theology. Although Tillich wrote no major work on the philosophy of art or in aesthetics, his essays on the subject of art and theology have been very influential. The nature of art and its relationship to religion lay at the heart of his central preoccupation as a theologian. This was his 'theology of culture'.

The formative influence on Tillich's religious thought—indeed on his whole life—was his bitter experience as a chaplain in the German army during the first world war. During this time, art, and particularly painting, gave him a measure of escape from the horrors that he had witnessed and in the midst

---

5.   Barth, *The Humanity of God*, pp. 49-50.
6.   Barth, *The Humanity of God*, p. 54.
7.   Barth, *The Humanity of God*, p. 55.
8.   Barth, *The Humanity of God*, p. 57.
9.   From Barth's 1953 address 'The Gift of Freedom: Foundation of Evangelical Ethics', in *idem*, *The Humanity of God*, pp. 70-96 (89).
10. Further to Barth's theological reflection on Mozart see his *Wolfgang Amadeus Mozart* (Grand Rapid: Eerdmans, 1986).

of which he ministered. He wrote that 'my delight even in the poor reproductions obtainable at the military bookstores developed into a systematic
study of the history of art. And out of this study came the experience of
art...' Just before the war ended Tillich visited the Kaiser Friedrich Museum
in Berlin. As he walked through the door he was immediately confronted by
Botticelli's *Madonna with Singing Angels*, the so-called *Raczinski Tondo*,
painted in about 1477. For the remainder of his life Tillich would describe
his encounter with the picture as, he said, 'a revelation' which placed him in
'a state approaching ecstasy'. In that one moment, he was to say, Tillich
came face to face with 'something of the divine source of all things'.

On his return from the trenches Tillich found, he said, 'a deep gap
between the cultural revolution and the religious tradition in central and
eastern Europe'.[11] He outlined two ways in which the gap might be closed.
The first was through Christian political action. The second, which concerns
us here, was through a recognition of the profound influence that, in any
age, culture and religion have upon each other. In this regard Tillich departed
radically from Karl Barth. Whereas Barth asserted that data about God
could come only from God himself, that is, that divine revelation was not to
any degree conditional on man's historical circumstances or his understanding or wisdom, Tillich held that man's grasp of God's revelation of
himself was necessarily dependent on the historical and cultural circumstances in which men and women find themselves and of which they are
the product. We can only grasp the truth by the means with which we are
equipped to grasp it. The self-revelation of God is thus effectively subject to
man's contingent, culturally conditioned capacity to receive it. Thus religion
is inevitably intimately related to culture however rejecting it might be of
prevailing cultural attitudes towards it. This very distancing, even perhaps
to the point of almost complete indifference the one of the other, witnesses,
paradoxically, to the intimacy of the connection between religion and culture. It is a condition of the current relationship that, other than in excep-
tional circumstances, they are perceived to be so far apart.

Tillich's theology of culture stressed the vital role that art could play in
bridging the gap between religion and the secular world in the extraordinary and crucial period which followed the first world war—a period which,
incidentally, saw both the rise to dominance of the modern movement in
art and also the acceleration of the decline of formal religious observance in
western Europe.

The key to Tillich's aesthetic is his understanding of what constitutes the
religious in 'religious art'. What makes his reaction to the *Raczinski Tondo*
so fascinating is that it belonged to a style which Tillich later rejected as

11. Paul Tillich, 'Religion and Secular Culture', *The Journal of Religion* 26.2 (1946),
pp. 79-86 (79), quoted in Michael F. Palmer, *Paul Tillich's Philosophy of Art* (Berlin:
W. de Gruyter, 1983), p. 33. Palmer's excellent book is a definitive critical study of
Tillich's aesthetics. Other references *passim*.

non-religious[12] primarily because it was so remote from life. Botticelli portrayed the madonna and child surrounded by angels carrying flowers. Above the madonna a crown signifies her heavenly status. Few images could portray a subject so apparently divorced from everyday life than the *Tondo*. For Tillich truly religious art speaks from, of and to the realities of ordinary life—the life with which a properly incarnational religion is concerned. Thus Tillich viewed with suspicion any art that contained such overtly traditional religious subjects and symbols as those in the Botticelli *Tondo* for these spoke of an ideal world remote from the everyday world of human experience. The only art that could be regarded as truly religious was art which dealt with the actuality of the real. For Tillich Expressionist artists did this and their art could thus alone be regarded as religious art. He found in the work of artists such as van Gogh and Cézanne, Picasso and Braque, Nolde and Rouault a concern for the human situation, a commitment to the world of the everyday and a consciousness that the artist had a prophetic and critical role to play in social and political life.

Of course, Expressionist art is more than an art which is concerned with the everyday. The same could be said of realism and impressionism. All art is expressive, but that art which, as Norbert Lynton puts it, 'is intended to move us through visual gestures that transmit, and perhaps give release to, emotions and emotionally charged messages'[13] and, one should add, of which *the artwork is itself the embodiment* is properly called Expressionist. This is a significant clue to Tillich's perception of Expressionism as truly religious art. What the Expressionist artist does and what he seeks to communicate are of a piece. The symbol is the actuality. In this sense the symbolism of an Expressionist artwork is intuitive in that it cannot be separated from the artist's method of working. C.E. Gauss said that

> This intuition is a consciousness of life which is of the nature of a religious attitude. They [Expressionist artists] make no distinction between their consciousness of life and their manner of expressing it. The work of art is thus a sample of the feeling it expresses. It is only the rendition of that feeling in concrete form. The work of art is thus a symbol in a special sense.[14]

We can see here why Tillich was so attracted to Expressionist art. It seemed to confirm, indeed perhaps it gave rise to, his theory of religious symbolism. For Tillich religious artistic forms are 'primary-immanent' religious symbols; that is, as Michael Palmer says, they are 'the finite media of revelation in the aesthetic sphere, through which [is] revealed the mystery of being, God

12. Further to this see Palmer, *Paul Tillich's Philosophy*, p. 7 and *passim*.

13. Norbert Lynton, 'Expressionism', in Nikos Stangos (ed.), *Concepts of Modern Art* (London: Thames & Hudson, 1994), pp. 30-49 (30).

14. Charles Edward Gauss, *The Aesthetic Theories of French Artists from Realism to Surrealism* (Baltimore: The Johns Hopkins University Press, 1949), p. 63, quoted in Flam, *Matisse on Art*, p. 33.

as being-itself'.[15] Expressionist art is religious art for Tillich because it is disclosive of the ultimate ground of reality. It is symbolic in that it points to that which is unconditioned and beyond itself.

Let us take an example. Vincent van Gogh painted two pictures of cafés in Arles in the autumn of 1888. Tillich said of *Café Terrace at Night* that it portrays 'in beautiful colours...the horror of emptiness'.[16] Van Gogh himself wrote to his brother Theo about this painting that 'it represents the outside of a café, with the terrace lit up by a big gas lamp in the blue night, and a corner of a starry blue sky'. He went on: 'The problem of painting night scenes and effects on the spot and actually at night interests me enormously'. For Tillich this painting is a social statement. For the artist it is an experiment in technique. The two interpretations are not mutually exclusive. Van Gogh was fully aware of the profound social statements that he was making through his art. Of the second café painting, *All Night Café*, van Gogh wrote to Theo that 'I have tried to express the terrible passions of humanity by means of red and green', and

> I have tried to express the idea that the café is a place where one can ruin oneself, go mad or commit a crime. So I have tried to express...the powers of darkness in a low public house, by soft Louis XV green and malachite, contrasting with yellow-green and harsh blue-greens, and this in an atmosphere like a devil's furnace, of pale sulphur.[17]

Tillich's reaction to *Café Terrace at Night* shows how his philosophical and theological presuppositions controlled his appreciation of art. Van Gogh's interpretation of his *All Night Café* suggests that Tillich's could match that of the artist. Yet Tillich dismissed much great art because it did not fit his theological criteria. They may have resonated with this Expressionist artist's own inner feelings, but the presuppositions controlled the interpretation.

However, other Expressionist artists seemed to confirm Tillich's belief that their work was deeply religious. For Matisse and Cézanne, Expressionist artists *par excellence*, the process of painting, as Jack Flam says of Matisse, had 'an almost religious significance because it involves a restructuring of time and space, a penetration into Reality itself'.[18] Commenting on Matisse's *Notes of a Painter*, published in 1908, Flam says that for Matisse the act of painting was 'an act of belief'. For Matisse, art, rooted in everyday experience, is a medium for 'the elevation of the spirit above and beyond'. It is 'the transfiguration of experience into a state of what might in the past have been called 'the sublime'.[19] As early as 1908, Matisse could write that the human figure 'best permits me to express my almost religious

15. Palmer, *Paul Tillich's Philosophy*, p. 193.
16. Quoted and cited in Palmer, *Paul Tillich's Philosophy*, p. 6.
17. Numbers 533 and 534 in the 1958 edition of van Gogh's letters quoted in Lara Vinca Masini, *Van Gogh* (London: Thames & Hudson, 1967), p. 29.
18. Flam, *Matisse on Art*, p. 35.
19. Flam, *Matisse on Art*, p. 34.

awe towards life'.[20] For his part Cézanne pursued what Kurt Badt described as 'the One which is permanent in the changing world'.[21]

The process by which this 'penetration of Reality' is achieved is one of *realisation* (Cézanne) or *condensation* (Matisse). From an intuitive apprehension of the truth or the Real in the everyday (in Cézanne's case the Provençal landscape) the artist develops a motif (for Cézanne, say, Mont Sainte-Victoire) which is in turn the vehicle for his articulation of the structures and thus the meaning behind and beneath the landscape—the pictorial absolute—which made a painting, for Cézanne, a 'coloured state of grace'. What Tillich did was to translate these Expressionist perceptions of *au dela* into the categories of a particular Christian theological system and it is for this that he must perhaps be criticised. Artists must be allowed to speak for themselves and in their own terms. Any theology (if that is what it is) is done by them implicitly. Theologians make art manageable by translating it into the categories of religious dogma. Theologians resist reductionism, but they succumb to its temptations themselves. Many, for example, manage the imaginative extravagance of scripture by making it subject to the categories of dogma.

Not surprisingly Tillich had little time for impressionism, though in this he (and, one has to say, near-contemporary Expressionists) both misunderstood what Manet and those who followed him were trying to achieve (and succeeded in achieving) and perhaps also displayed an anti-French bias.

That Tillich should have been so moved by the Botticelli *Tondo* and yet also find in, say, Rouault's harshly revealing clowns and prostitutes and portrayals of Jesus a true art of the incarnation demonstrates how complex were the springs of his theological aesthetics. No further analysis can be attempted here, but it is worth underlining that Tillich's own theological presuppositions, formed within the Lutheran traditions of the Germany of his youth and young manhood determined his intellectual understanding of the role of art and enabled him to find in Expressionist painting a model which confirmed his presuppositions. Whatever was the impact of the Botticelli *Tondo* on his emotions and sensitivities as a young man experiencing the horrors of war it was as a systematic theologian that he came to interpret art. The Botticelli painting may have been a revelation to him, but, when he later recalled his ecstatic state, he was careful to observe 'that no artistic experience can match the moments in which prophets were grasped by the power of the Divine Presence'. His experience, however profound, was, he now says, only analogous to revelation as religion understands it. Tillich is here measuring his extraordinary personal experience against architectonic theological and metaphysical criteria. Similarly, it was against

20. Quoted in Flam, *Matisse on Art*, p. 38.
21. Kurt Badt, *The Art of Cézanne* (London: Faber & Faber, 1965), p. 217, quoted in Flam, *Matisse on Art*, p. 159.

these criteria that Tillich valued Expressionism. He was incapable, as Michael Palmer points out, of theologically valuing an artwork for its own sake and in its own terms. Works of art, for Tillich, are cited as evidence for a theological argument the truth of which he had already accepted, rather than evidence upon which a theological argument could subsequently be built. In this regard, paradoxically, Karl Barth's anecdotal, non-dogmatic, sensuous appreciation of Mozart is more likely to reach the heart of the religious significance of art than is Tillich's definition of religious art derived from placing it within a theological system. Nevertheless Barth's exclusion of art from his dogmatic theology and Tillich's inclusion of it in his systematic theology alike strip the world, as George Pattison says of Barth's attacks on natural theology, 'of all theophanous possibilities'[22] because both Barth and Tillich tested art against predetermined theological criteria and refused to allow it to speak for itself.

Hans Urs von Balthasar: Beauty, Form and Revelation

Roman Catholic theologians have been less reticent than Protestant religious thinkers in their assessment and appreciation of art, though their general view of the role of art for religion has developed along somewhat similar lines. By far the most significant figure in this regard is Hans Urs von Balthasar, described by Karl Barth, whose work greatly influenced Balthasar, as 'the shrewd friend from another shore'[23] thereby gently indicating both Balthasar's indebtedness to Barth and his radical criticism of him.

Balthasar's is by far the most comprehensive, sustained and systematic study of theological aesthetics yet produced and only the briefest note of it is possible here. In the first of two essays at the conclusion of a *Festschrift* in honour of his eightieth birthday Balthasar set out his simple theology of the Church's mission:

> The meaning of Christ's coming is to save the *world* and to open for the whole of it the way to the Father; the Church is only a means, a radiance that through preaching, example, and discipleship spreads out from the God-man into every sphere.[24]

'Radiance' is a significant word for Balthasar. What the Church must radiate is 'the glory of the Lord'. This is the title of the several volumes of his great work *The Glory of the Lord*, sub-titled *A Theological Aesthetics*. What these volumes offer is 'a typology of the relationship between beauty and revelation' which demonstrates 'that there neither has been nor could be any

---

22. Pattison, *Art, Modernity and Faith*, p. 72.
23. Barth, *The Humanity of God*, p. 44.
24. John Riches (ed.), *The Analogy of Beauty* (Edinburgh: T. & T. Clark, 1986), pp. 194-95.

truly great and historically fruitful theology which was not expressly conceived and born under the constellation of beauty and grace'.

In a crucial passage Balthasar describes the nature and *locus* of beauty
thus:

> The beautiful is above all a *form*, and the light does not fall on this form
> from above and from outside, rather it breaks forth from the form's
> interior... The content [*Gehalt*] does not lie outside the form [*Gestalt*] but
> within it... In the luminous form of the beautiful the being of the existent
> becomes perceivable as nowhere else, and this is why an aesthetic ele-
> ment must be associated with all spiritual perception as with all spiritual
> striving.[25]

Balthasar does not mean by 'beauty' and 'the beautiful' what is meant by
these words in, he says, 'the modern or even the philosophical (transcendent) sense, but the surpassing of beauty in "glory" in the sense of the
splendour of the divinity of God himself manifested in the life, death, and
resurrection of Jesus and reflected, according to Paul, in Christians as they
look upon their Lord'.[26] Christians thus radiate the glory of the beauty of
God as it is seen in Jesus.

This disarmingly simple thesis is argued at great length and with great
penetration and is supported throughout by rich and very wide-ranging
reference to theology and the arts. What Balthasar bids us do is to contemplate the essential reality, or meaning, of a thing as it exists in the world
and as it is revealed in its beauty. John Riches sums up Balthasar's programme thus: 'His whole theological endeavour is directed to learning to
see things as they are in themselves, whole and entire, and in so seeing to
perceive the reality of being in all its variety and concreteness'.[27]

In passing we may discover here a clue to the apparent paradox of
Tillich's 'revelation' when confronted by the *Raczinski Tondo*. Despite the
life-changing extra-ordinariness of this event Tillich was to reject this kind
of art as not 'religious' in the sense in which he was later to define the
term. He perceived the essential beauty or reality of a work of art later to
be condemned by his own theological system. Though not referring to
Tillich, John Riches interprets Balthasar as saying that

> Where theology no longer sees the beauty, however paradoxical, of the
> revelation-figure, it not only loses the power to attract and to convince
> but it also loses sight of its very centre and can listen only to the echoes
> of the divine word in its own self-consciousness. It ceases to be concrete,
> attracted to the particular *Gestalt* in which the divine glory is to be seen,

25. Hans Urs von Balthasar, *The Glory of the Lord*. I. *Seeing the Form* (ed. J.
Fessio and J. Riches; trans. E. Leivà-Herikakis; Edinburgh: T. & T. Clark, 1982),
pp. 151, 153.

26. Riches, *The Analogy of Beauty*, p. 224.

27. Section on Balthasar in D.F. Ford (ed.), *The Modern Theologians* (2 vols.;
Oxford: Basil Blackwell, 1989), I, pp. 237-54 (240).

and concerns itself with the abstract, that which is perceived as the condition of the possibility of any perception at all.[28]

We might add that theology's 'self-consciousness' is created by the results
of its philosophical methodology, namely the construction of metaphysical
systems and the formulation of dogma. The concern for metaphysics and
ethics has led the modern church, in both its Protestant and its Catholic
manifestations, to ignore, in Balthasar's view, the 'third transcendental',
beauty, which is the concern of aesthetics. Yet 'more than either metaphysics or ethics, aesthetics tends towards an immanental self-transfiguration
on the part of the world, even if it is only for the moment when the beautiful
catches the eye'.[29] Such language speaks of the immediacy of the incarnation, or what de Caussade called 'sacraments of the present moment'.

Balthasar issues two warnings. The first is that our contemplation of
beauty should not lead us to confuse this-worldly beauty with the revelation
of God. There is indeed an 'analogy between God's work of formation and
the shaping forces of nature and of man as they generate and give birth'
but we must, he says,

> never subjugate and subordinate God's revelation with its own form [that
> is] to the laws not only of metaphysics and of private, social and socio-
> logical ethics, but also of this-worldly aesthetics, instead of respecting
> the sovereignty which is manifested clearly enough in God's work.[30]

However, the boundary between the two is never clear, for

> the beautiful brings with it a self-evidence that enlightens without media-
> tion. This is why, when we approach God's revelation with the category
> of the beautiful we quite spontaneously bring this category with us in its
> this-worldly form. It is only when such a this-worldly aesthetics does not
> fit revelation's transcendent form that we suddenly come to an aston-
> ished halt and conscientiously decline to continue on that path.[31]

The second warning arises from the first. It is that there is a clear distinction between theological aesthetics and aesthetic theology. Theological
aesthetics is 'the attempt to do aesthetics *at the level and with the methods
of theology*'. Aesthetic theology results from 'betraying and selling out
theological substance to the *current viewpoints of an inner-worldly theory
of beauty*'.[32] But what theology is to be accepted as definitive in the first,
and, in the second, how are these current viewpoints to be theologically
evaluated?

Balthasar, unlike Tillich, does not attempt a detailed critical evaluation of
any movement in the visual or plastic arts, or any specific work of art, in

28. Ford (ed.), *The Modern Theologians*, I, p. 241.
29. Balthasar, *The Glory of the Lord*, I, pp. 34-35.
30. Balthasar, *The Glory of the Lord*, I, p. 37.
31. Balthasar, *The Glory of the Lord*, I, pp. 36-37.
32. Balthasar, *The Glory of the Lord*, I, p. 38 (my italics).

the light of these, for him, crucial distinctions, yet he freely acknowledges the difficulty of so doing. How are we to categorise what we claim to be a revelation from God? And were we to be confident that an experience we have had *is* a divine revelation how can we distinguish between the revelation and the part played in it by the means by which we perceive it? In a defining passage in which the three transcendentals of truth (metaphysics), goodness (ethics) and beauty (aesthetics) are brought to bear on his overarching theme of 'glory' and related to the visual arts Balthasar says:

> What is manifested in a given manifestation is always, at the same time, the non-manifest. The soul expresses and represents itself in the living organism, and yet, precisely in so doing, it has its being 'behind' the manifestation and, through this manifestation, it builds for itself a cell, a husk, a containing cavity. To beauty belongs not only the 'measure, number and weight' of the organised material, but also the 'energy' of the organising agent, which expresses itself in form without losing itself to the external, and the 'glory' proper to being free and, still more deeply, proper to the ability to squander itself in love. Along with the seen surface of the manifestation there is perceived the non-manifested depth: it is only this which lends the phenomenon of the beautiful its enrapturing and overwhelming character, just as it is only this that insures the truth and goodness of the existent. This holds both for the beauty of nature and the beauty of art, and for the latter even in those abstract constructions which reduce the dimension of depth to a minimum by attempting to express everything at the horizontal level of surface, colour and rhythm.[33]

So it is (and here Balthasar speaks of what are claimed to be revelations of the divine in other religions) when people 'bring a unique expression of Being to the full maturity of a valid symbolic form (in stele, myth or dramatic action), what right do we have to relativise this construct from the perspective of any typology whatever, thus necessarily robbing it of its believing soul?' for what the artist ('a Michelangelo, a Goethe, a Keats') does is 'to see such gods with their inner eye' and *we* know this, for 'many of their figures presuppose such encounters'.[34]

In Balthasar's *Glory of the Lord* we have a magisterial statement of the worth of art for 'the believing soul'. Yet it is a theology of art rather than an aesthetic which allows art to inform theology *in its own terms*. Notwithstanding that Balthasar acknowledges that a work of art which is a unique expression of Being must never be relativised 'from the perspective of any typology whatever' (not even a Christian typology) nevertheless Balthasar's theologically conservative conception of God is the sole truth in terms of which his superbly articulated concept of beauty, and therefore his evaluation of art, is constructed.

33. Balthasar, *The Glory of the Lord*, I, p. 442.
34. Balthasar, *The Glory of the Lord*, I, p. 500.

Hans Kung: Art and the New Question of Meaning

Kung begins his short book about modern art, *Art and the Question of Meaning*,[35] by affirming that however difficult art is to define, it has unquestionable reality. But what kind of reality is it? For very many today contemporary art is 'functionless, meaningless, pointless as for many belief in God is also futile'.[36] Is art to die, and art galleries to become museums of dead art, as churches have become, for so many, tombs of a long dead God? Has modern art destroyed art by rejecting its religious origins? Kung fully acknowledges and affirms man's post-Renaissance autonomy. As man has claimed autonomy, so his art is autonomous. It is an art 'brought under man's responsibility and control and withdrawn from the direct influence of the churches, of theology and of religion'.[37] Yet it is also an art which has proved supremely capable of giving form to 'sacral materials' and 'sacral places', and here Kung cites portrayals of the crucifixion by Corinth, Gauguin, Ensor, Beckmann, Schmidt-Rottluff, Arp, Malevich, Baumeister and Buffet, Le Corbusier's chapel at Ronchamp and Matisse's in Vence, Leger's and Bazaine's windows at Audincourt and Courfaivre, and Chagall's biblical cycles in Zurich, Jerusalem and Nice. He could have added to his list: what of Mark Rothko's extraordinary *The Entombment* from the mid-1940s or the cycle of paintings for the chapel in Houston? Indeed, Rothko's abstract 'colour field' paintings have frequently been described in mystical, spiritual or religious terms.[38]

This raises for Kung what he calls the 'new question' of art and meaning. Art has an 'immanent sense' but it has no purpose or use in itself. Works of art, as such, are not means to an end. 'They count as art only if the element of the nonfunctional, disinterested, useless-playful is dominant'.[39] This modern definition of art as having an 'immanent sense' but no extraneous function, that it is created 'simply to be, to please, to reveal', does not deny that it has a sociopolitical dimension, whether this is acknowledged or not. That is to say, art has a 'public character'. It can (though this is not its ostensible purpose) enlighten, emancipate, derestrict, democratise.[40] The 'new question of art and meaning' is raised by setting art's immanent sense and its socio-political function in the wider context of art and the meaning of life, art and total meaning. Because there are today so many people for whom the great questions of meaning remain unanswered it follows that

35. Hans Kung, *Art and the Question of Meaning* (trans E. Quinn; London: SCM Press, 1981).

36. Kung, *Art and the Question*, p. 14.

37. Kung, *Art and the Question*, p. 17.

38. See Anna C. Chave, *Mark Rothko* (New Haven: Yale University Press, 1989), p. 1, and her Chapter 5.

39. Kung, *Art and the Question*, p. 22.

40. Kung, *Art and the Question*, p. 24.

this 'crisis of orientation on the grand scale' has profound political implications and it would be strange if art (this 'delicate seismograph of the
social condition') did not reflect it. The issue is, 'can art itself, visual art,
make any contribution to overcoming this crisis of meaning?' Kung argues
that art cannot provide a final answer unless it becomes again what it once
was, a kind of religion. For a long time it was seen as possessing 'an uplift-
ing, redeeming, reconciling function, as redeeming from life and reconciling
with life'. But the twentieth century amply demonstrated that art does not
possess redeeming, reconciling power. Far from art 'absorbing man into the
divine world' it has been a graphic expression of man's futility, his estrangement, his isolation in the world.[41] Kung argues that it is this fact that
enables us to raise the question of art and meaning in a wholly new way.
Can works of art be meaningful in an age of meaninglessness? Can there be
meaningfulness when meaning itself is meaningless?[42] Theodor Adorno
(and Hans Rookmaaker) argued that an artwork can symbolise meaninglessness in a way that is aesthetically meaningful. This is what Adorno calls
'the affirmative lie'. An artist for whom the world and his own existence is
futile can express this futility in his art. Hans Rookmaaker believed that this
was the case with all the undoubted masters of the modern movement in
art. They were true to a lie.[43]

Hans Kung asserts that an artist *can* do this, but he need not. He has an
alternative. He can 'hold fast to a fundamental value and meaning of his life
and of the world as a whole'. It is not for the viewer and the critic to
determine whether the artist is being true to a lie for

> what is apparently absurd may have a deeper meaning. Even the meta-
> phors of a broken world, even the mechanical-surrealist human dolls of
> Giorgio de Chirico, the erotic drawings of Hans Bellmer or the 'Vienna
> School', Francis Bacon's caricatures of popes, can certainly be expressive
> of an ultimately affirmative attitude.[44]

Despite all appearances the artist can have a basic trust in reality. He can
'assent to *a ground of meaning of this reality*, which as primal reason,
primal support, and primal meaning secretly justifies, sustains, and guides
this reality of our life and of our world.'[45] This assent to the ground of
meaning cannot be demonstrated or evidenced (it may not be known to the
artist) but it can, Kung says, be rationally justified. It is an assent which
thousands of artists in thousands of images for thousands of years have
assented to—and it is an assent, Kung asserts, which is fundamentally
grounded in the religion from which art emerged in the distant past. So, he

41. Kung, *Art and the Question*, pp. 28-29.
42. Kung, *Art and the Question*, pp. 30-31.
43. Hans Rookmaaker, *Modern Art and the Death of Culture* (London: Intervarsity
Press, 2nd edn, 1973), p. 132. On Rookmaaker see Chapter 10, below.
44. Kung, *Art and the Question*, p. 32.
45. Kung, *Art and the Question*, p. 35.

argues, 'the fact [is] that in the great breakthrough of modern art not only were merely questions of form involved, but also spiritual impulses, the great questions of meaning—questions of the meaning of art, of colour, of life, of man as such'.[46] Modern art, even the most despairing, even that art which portrays man and his existence as absurd, may be fundamentally religious. A work of art can be a great symbol, a great meaningful sign:

> a symbol which, despite all difficulties and opposition, can remind us human beings of the great heritage of the past, the future still to be won, of the meaning, value, and dignity of our life here and now;

> a symbol that can arouse our passion for freedom and truthfulness, our hunger for justice and love, our yearning for fellowship, reconciliation, and peace;

> a symbol which may perhaps enable us to perceive something of what 'involves us unconditionally', the still hidden, incomprehensibly great mystery in us and around us: that is, the suprasensible ground of meaning of all our reality in the midst of the world of sense.[47]

Is this 'suprasensible ground of all our reality' God? For the Christian theologian surely the answer is 'Yes'. In true art, great art, we can detect traces of this transcendence. In a later, equally brief, book on Mozart Kung tells of the ineffable mystery of great music:

> Truly, more than any other music, Mozart's music—though it is not heavenly music but completely earthly music—seems to show in its sensual yet unsensual beauty, power and clarity, how wafer-thin is the boundary between music, which is the most abstract of all arts, and religion, which has always had a special connection with music. For both, though they are different, direct us to what is ultimately unspeakable, to mystery.[48]

Art and a Self-Effacing Theology

Kung opposes Balthasar in significant respects. For Kung art anticipates 'the still-awaiting humanizing of man'. This has a salvific ring to it and leads George Pattison[49] to say that 'art anticipates—perhaps in a fuller sense than that intended by Kung—the messianic kingdom itself, the return of the world to that created fullness in which we may declare, with God, that it is all "very good"'. In fact Pattison argues that a contemporary theology of art 'should not be content to find a place for itself within the field of natural theology but should instead see itself in terms of a theology of redemption'. He suggests that what art compels us to do is to be drawn into the world by the 'unsurpassable meaning and value' to be found in the pursuit of those

---

46. Kung, *Art and the Question*, p. 36.
47. Kung, *Art and the Question*, pp. 54-55.
48. Hans Kung, *Mozart: Traces of Transcendence* (London: SCM Press, 1992), p. 33.
49. In Pattison, *Art, Modernity and Faith*, p. 153.

desires which 'enable and inspire us to affirm the goodness of the world'. Art, for Pattison, reveals the 'structural grace of things' (the phrase is Umberto Eco's), a grace 'revealed to the rightly desiring heart and which we appropriate in our own acts of seeing and of shaping the visible things of this visible world'.[50] Pattison does not develop in any detail quite what this means for an understanding of both art and for theology. And, for all Pattison's call for a theological appreciation of art which does not force art into a pre-determined theological system but which rather allows it to speak for itself, his own approach is still primarily theological as he himself admits.[51] He necessarily addresses art from the side of theology. Even Don Cupitt's much more radical approach[52] is essentially theological and philosophical.

Theologians must be on their guard against commandeering art for religion,[53] must allow artists to speak to them in their own language, and must try to make what they can of what they hear. What they will hear will tell of correspondences and connections, of similarities, of interactions and of parallel interpretations and perceptions which will suggest a far closer relationship of *essence* between art and religion than many theologians have been prepared to acknowledge. As the churches at the beginning of the twenty-first century become more fearful and therefore more conservative there may be fewer theologians prepared to take the risks that embracing a truly incarnational religion demands of them. In particular what they hear may suggest to them that their many (often contradictory) understandings of God and redemption and salvation in Christ need to be radically reconsidered if a new world is to be made.

50. Pattison, *Art, Modernity and Faith*, pp. 153-54.
51. Pattison, *Art, Modernity and Faith*, p. xi.
52. Don Cupitt, *Radicals and the Future of the Church* (London: SCM Press, 1989), pp. 19-31.
53. The warning is Hans Kung's (*Mozart: Traces of Transcendence*, p. 31).

Chapter 3

Making New Worlds

In 1907, at the age of 38, Henri Matisse went to Italy. Soon after he returned to France he published his first theoretical statement about the nature of art, 'Notes of a Painter', in *La Grande Revue.* In it he wrote this:

> What interests me most is neither still life nor landscape, but the human figure. It is that which best permits me to express my almost religious awe towards life. I do not insist upon all the details of the face, on setting them down one-by-one with anatomical exactitude. If I have an Italian model who at first experience suggests nothing but a purely animal existence, I nevertheless discover his essential qualities, I penetrate amid the lines of the face those which suggest the deep gravity which persists in every human being. A work of art must carry within itself its complete significance and impose that upon the beholder even before he recognises the subject matter. When I see the Giotto frescoes at Padua I do not trouble myself to recognize which scene of the life of Christ I have before me, but I immediately understand the sentiment which emerges from it, for it is in the lines, the composition, the colour. The title will only serve to confirm my impression.[1]

What experience did Paul Tillich the theologian have when he was confronted by Botticelli's *Madonna with Singing Angels*? As we have noted, he described it as a 'revelation'. He came face-to-face with 'the divine source of all things'. Face-to-face with the human figure Matisse the artist expresses his 'almost religious awe towards life', that 'sentiment' which he immediately and intuitively recognises in the Giotto fresco cycles in Padua. Were Tillich's 'revelation' and Matisse's 'almost religious awe' two quite different experiences? Although Tillich was later to say that his revelation could not match the experience of the Divine recorded by the Old Testament prophets, and while Matisse adds the qualifying 'almost' when he tells of the sense of religious awe he feels when confronted with the human figure, nevertheless the religious terms employed by Paul Tillich the philosopher and theologian and Henri Matisse the painter do need to be noted and explained. In any case, of what value are the qualifications? Did Tillich come face-to-face with the divine source of all things or did he not? For

1. Reprinted in Flam, *Matisse on Art*, pp. 35-40.

Matisse does the word 'almost' indicate that what he experienced was *not quite* religious awe? We need to look into this question further.

We begin our exploration by considering some apparently superficial connections between the experience of art and the experience of religion.[2] This will be a very small-scale and superficial exercise because the relation between art and religion, even restricting the enquiry to the Christian religion, is important and complex and far beyond the scope of this book. All we will try to do here is simply to ask the question: Why is it that those who claim to have aesthetic experience and those who claim to have religious experience so often speak of their experiences in remarkably similar ways? Answering that lesser question may provide some pointers towards an answer to the much greater question of the relationship of art and religion—a relationship which is far closer than either the theorists of aesthetics or students of theology commonly suppose.[3] Friedrich Schleiermacher was both a great theologian and a teacher of aesthetics. He wrote, early in the nineteenth century, that 'Religion and art stand beside each other like two friendly souls whose inner relationship, if they suspect it, is still unknown to them'.[4]

We will tackle our question under four headings: first, in terms of knowing (or what philosophers call the epistemological question), asking 'Are aesthetic and religious ways of knowing the same or at least similar?'; secondly, in terms of being (the ontological question), asking 'Do art and religion tell of the same fundamental or absolute truths?'; thirdly, the theological question, 'Do they provide the same, or at least similar, routes to personal integration or salvation?'; and finally, in terms of ethics, asking 'Do art and religion modify human behaviour in the same or similar ways?'

Art and Religion and Knowing

Those who have aesthetic experience and those who have religious experience claim that they experience *something*. As most of those who make such claims are clearly not the victims of some abnormal psychological state, we must assume that they *do* experience something. This being so it is worth asking the lover of art and the religious believer what it is that they experience and how they experience it. The philosopher of art and the theologian each provide answers which suggest that what each experiences is specific to art or to religion and that neither answer can be reduced to the categories of the other. Orthodox and conservative Christian theologians might say that the religious experience they have is, in the final

2. This chapter draws in part on material I first published in *The Journal of Aesthetic Education* 14.3 (1980), pp. 18-35.

3. Further to this similarity of ways not treated here see especially H.D. Lewis, *Our Experience of God* (London: Collins, 1970), pp. 239-54.

4. Quoted in Eliot Deutsch, *Essays on the Nature of Art* (Albany, NY: State University of New York Press, 1996), p. 89.

theological analysis, an experience of God the Father Almighty revealed in Jesus Christ through the mediation of the Holy Spirit in the light of scripture and Christian tradition. They may qualify this assertion to a greater or less extent, but in substance they interpret their experiences (and the religious experiences of others) such that that interpretation is consonant with acceptance of the claims of a credal formula. Paul Tillich may speak of the 'Ground of Being' but he is a Christian theologian because he identifies the Ground of Being with the God of Christian faith. However and under whatever circumstances God is encountered, it is nevertheless God as Christian tradition understands him who *is* encountered.

The theories of knowledge advanced in answer to the question of *how* God is encountered range, classically, from reason to revelation, at the extreme from the near humanism of natural theology to the antihumanism of conservative dogmatic theology. At one end of the spectrum, the exponent of natural theology might argue that human experience provides data from which the existence of God can be inferred. At the other end of the spectrum the neo-orthodox theologian will not only vigorously deny this but will assert that even the capacity to apprehend God's revelation of himself in not innate to man but is given him by God, for God is both the source and the means of knowledge of God. But whatever their view theologians *qua* theologians will agree at least that God *is* and is ultimately the source of their experience of him.

When religious experience is investigated under other than specifically Christian categories a very extensive range of experiences claimed to be religious is revealed. This was clearly demonstrated by the Alister Hardy Research Centre working first in Oxford and subsequently in Nottingham. So extensive was the range of experiences reported that the researchers did not attempt to define 'religious', they allowed their informants the freedom to decide for themselves that a particular experience *was* religious. What united the very wide spectrum of experiences was that each was claimed to be a *religious* experience.

Restricting ourselves to some major twentieth-century figures, theorists of art show a similar range of permissible opinions as the nature and mode of what is claimed as aesthetic experience. On the one hand there is what we might call the metaphysical or transcendental view. This was criticised by John Dewey when he attacked those philosophies of art that locate art 'in a region inhabited by no other creature, and that emphasize beyond all reason the merely contemplative character of the esthetic'. He continued: 'For many persons an aura of mingled awe and unreality encompasses the "spiritual" and the "ideal" while "matter" has become...something to be explained away and apologized for.'[5] Towards the other end of the spectrum

---

5.   John Dewey, *Art as Experience* (New York: Capricorn, 1934), p. 10, quoted in S.K. Langer, *Feeling and Form* (London: Routledge, 1953), p. 36. Langer quotes Roger Fry as saying in *Vision and Design* that aesthetic experience is 'disinterested intensity of contemplation' (pp. 37-38).

there are those who would argue that the experience of art is nothing more than the experience of the physical world organized in a pleasurable way. This seems to be the view of Herbert Read when he characterizes plastic art as

> an attempt to create pleasing forms. Such forms satisfy our sense of beauty and the sense of beauty is satisfied when we are able to appreciate a unity or harmony of formal relations among our sense perceptions.[6]

Aesthetic experience, at least the experience of the plastic and visual arts, is thus 'a pleasurable sensation' deriving from 'certain arrangements in the proportion of the shape and surface and mass of things' which 'are present to our senses'.[7] These 'arrangements' excite 'a pleasurable sensation' because they are beautiful. Thus Read can say that although

> there are a dozen current definitions of beauty...the merely physical one I have already given (beauty is a unity of formal relations among our sense-perceptions) is the only essential one.[8]

For I.A. Richards this experience is not fundamentally different from other experiences, and indeed he seems to suggest that aesthetic experience serves a functional biological purpose.[9]

Halfway along this spectrum lies the aesthetics of Susanne Langer. She attempts to define art in a way that serves to connect creativity, feeling and expression and so to preserve an extrapersonal element in art. Thus she says that 'art is the creation of forms symbolic of human feeling'.[10] She qualifies this general definition when she says that

> the true connoisseurs of art...feel at once that to treat great art as a source of experiences not essentially different from the experiences of daily life...is to miss the very essence of it, the thing that makes art as important as science or even religion, yet it sets it apart as an autonomous, creative function of a typically human mind...

and

> the aesthetic experience is different from any other, the attitude towards works of art is a highly special one, the characteristic response is an entirely separate emotion, something more than common enjoyment—not related to the pleasures or displeasures furnished by one's actual surroundings, and therefore disturbed by them rather than integrated with the contemporary scene.[11]

Given this wide variation of definition, what *is* the experience of art? The answer seems to be that as 'art' is impossible to define precisely so it is

6.   Herbert Read, *The Meaning of Art* (London: Faber & Faber, 1951), p. 18.
7.   Read, *The Meaning of Art*.
8.   Read, *The Meaning of Art*, pp. 18-19.
9.   Quoted in Langer, *Feeling and Form*, p. 38.
10. Langer, *Feeling and Form*, p. 40.
11. Langer, *Feeling and Form*, p. 36.

impossible to define aesthetic experience precisely. E.H. Gombrich, at the beginning of his influential *The Story of Art*,[12] echoing Francis Bacon, argues that art is impossible to define because 'there really is no such thing as Art. There are only artists.' This being so, 'I do not think that there are any wrong reasons for liking a statue or a picture' though 'there *are* wrong reasons for disliking a work of art'.[13] It follows that it is as difficult to define what it is to experience art as it is precisely to define the experience of religion.

Yet this difficulty is not explained by saying that art (or religion for that matter) is concerned with merely subjective emotions and feelings. This is far from the case. The production of a work of art is a most demanding matter. Gombrich notes that the artist never gives way to his feelings in a process of almost unconscious self-discovery. The great artists have invariably sought to solve problems rather then merely to give expression to their personalities. He quotes van Gogh writing to his brother about the 'work and cool calculation', the 'complicated calculus' of painting. Yet what is this complicated calculus? Gombrich writes:

> it is precisely the desolation of aesthetics that we cannot formulate it with the same precision we can formulate the problems of science or the rules of a game. Even if we had the artist here to explain his aim of fitting colours or shapes into some complex configuration of contrasts or consonances, there would be nothing but your sense of courtesy to prevent you from saying 'so what?—We can see that it is hard to do and to get it all as you want it, but is it worth it, is it a value, is it art?'[14]

We may know what a scientist is attempting to do but what an artist is *for* (or what religious believing is for) is far more difficult to understand.

Thus both the philosophers of art and the theologians, as well as men and women who claim to be neither, agree that the experience of art and the experience of religion are real experiences of *something*. The difficulty is defining what this something is. Those who occupy positions at the ends of the aesthetic-experience and religious-experience spectrums seem to agree either that experiences of both kinds are experiences of transcendence or that they are not. And they seem to agree along each spectrum as to how these experiences come to them. Does aesthetic experience require for its reception an 'intensity of contemplation' (so Roger Fry), or merely a certain degree of sensitivity in the central nervous system, such that the experience *is* that degree of sensitivity (so I.A. Richards, and a number of contemporary neuroscientists[15])? Does religious experience depend for its

12. E.H. Gombrich, *The Story of Art* (Oxford: Phaidon Press, 15th edn, 1989).
13. Gombrich, *The Story of Art*, p. 3.
14. E.H. Gombrich, 'Art and Self-Transcendence', in *idem*, *Ideals and Idols* (Oxford: Phaidon Press, 1994), pp. 123-30 (126).
15. See, for example, V.S. Ramachandran, 'Sharpening Up "The Science of Art": An Interview with Anthony Freeman', *Journal of Consciousness Studes* 8.1 (2001),

reception entirely upon the divine initiative (so Karl Barth) or upon a capacity in man to test a so-called experience of God against objective rational criteria, such that the experience is, effectively, a cerebral activity (so, for example, Brand Blanshard who asks, 'What is the difference, after all, between one who takes reason as the guide of life and one who, accepting revelation as the guide, imposes the test of reason on the candidates to revelation?'[16]). Leaving aside for the moment what aesthetic experience can be said to be a revelation of, *is* it revelation (so Langer[17])? Is it 'transfiguration' (so Hannah Arendt[18])? Is it 'embodiment' or 'incarnation' of meaning (so Louis Arnaud Reid[19])? Is the nature of what is experienced such as can properly be said to produce 'exhilaration' (so Langer[20]) or 'exaltation' (so André Dunoyer de Segonzac[21])? Is the precondition for the production of a work of art a state of being which can only be described as a 'state of grace' (so de Segonzac[22])? Is art a way of entering a 'coloured state of grace' (attributed to Paul Cézanne[23])? Is religious experience an experience of the objectively transcendent or the perception of something that wells up from the subjective self and therefore of the self alone? Is aesthetic experience of the nature of the physical or the spiritual or, because they are interrelated in some way, of both? Or is it the experience of what Karl Popper has called a 'third world...of objective contents of thought especially of scientific and poetic thoughts and works of art'—a world which, as E.H. Gombrich puts it, 'is neither the world of things or facts nor the world of subjective feelings'.[24] Is the canon of art based not upon, say, reputation or fashion but on absolute, unquestionable, self-transcending value?[25] And if that is the case what is the absolute and

pp. 9-29, and the article 'The Science of Art' by V.S. Ramachandran and William Hirstein in *JCS* 6 (1999), pp. 15-51, and the criticisms of it in subsequent editions (*JCS* 6.6-7 [1999] and 7.8-9 [2000]).

16. Quoted in Basil Mitchell, *The Justification of Religious Belief* (London: Macmillan 1973), p. 144.

17. Langer, *Feeling and Form*, p. 405.

18. Hannah Arendt, *The Human Condition* (California: University of California Press, 1958), p. 168.

19. L.A. Reid, *Meaning in the Arts* (London: Routledge & Kegan Paul, 1969), Chapter 4, esp. p. 78.

20. Reid, *Meaning in the Arts*, p. 395.

21. Quoted in M. Milner, *On Not Being Able to Paint* (London: Heinemann Educational, 1971), p. 106.

22. Milner, *On Not Being Able to Paint*.

23. Milner, *On Not Being Able to Paint*, p. 25.

24. K.R. Popper, *Objective Knowledge: An Evolutionary Approach* (Oxford: Oxford University Press, 1972), p. 106. Quoted in Gombrich, 'Art and Self-Transcendence', p. 125.

25. As Quentin Bell interprets the position of E.H. Gombrich in the latter's *Ideals and Idols* (see 'Canons and Values: A Correspondence with Quentin Bell', pp. 167-83 [168]).

ultimate source or sanction or critique for this self-transcending value? Is this absolute what Paul Tillich calls the 'Ground of Being', and if it *is*, is art what in religion would be called sacramental? Are both religious experience and aesthetic experience experiences which, fundamentally related to the material though they are, are nevertheless transforming, transfiguring, transcendental, ontic experiences?

The similarity of the questions which philosophers of art and students of religion ask themselves as to the *how* of what is claimed to be experienced and the (at least verbal) similarity of the answers which they advance prompt the question whether, leaving aside their respective assertions as to the source of these experiences, *they are not each speaking of the same way of knowing*. The difference between aesthetic experience and religious experience would then become no more than the difference between the conceptual schemes of explanation or frames of reference of the philosopher and the student of religion respectively. Both appear, superficially at least, to share an epistemology. They seem to know in ways which each describe in terms of intuition and faith.

Yet clearly both the lover of art and the religious believer would claim that their respective experiences are specific to themselves. Both dispute that each has very much in common with the other.[26] Thus from the side of art S.K. Langer, while making much use of the word 'revelation' in *Feeling and Form*, takes a line in *Problems of Art* which clearly and decisively distinguishes religion from art. She agrees that artistic perception is intuitive and that it takes place 'spontaneously and immediately, without benefit of logic'. She acknowledges that, for some lovers of art at least, 'a special power of intuition leads the art connoisseur to knowledge of an inner reality' which is 'a metaphysical contact with the real'. Yet she is aware also of the dangers of

> this sort of mysticism, mixed with every degree of philosophical irrationalism and transcendentalism on the one hand, and on the other with sheer sentimentalist and romantic fancies.[27]

Artists themselves have been seduced by this 'sort of mysticism' but the question remains to be answered: What kind of experience is the experience of art such that artists very often speak of it in mystical terms? S.K. Langer retrieves intuition from this metaphysical jungle by linking it to rationality. She calls it 'an act of understanding', a kind of 'immediate reasoning'. It is 'perception', and it is immediate; but this intuition is no different from that which 'enters into ordinary understanding and forms the basis of discursive reason'. Art is thus 'both a product and an instrument of human insight'. By definition it is not religion.

26. See further Lewis, *Our Experience of God*.

27. S.K. Langer, *Problems of Art* (London: Routledge & Kegan Paul, 1957), pp. 60-61.

Similarly, a Christian philosopher with a deep knowledge and appreciation of art asserts that religion is not art. In his *Our Experience of God*, speaking for many orthodox theologians, H.D. Lewis argued that what distinguishes religion from art is precisely that religion is not the product and instrument of human insight. Religion derives its meaning and purpose 'from an unconditional source quite different in nature from finite being'.[28] Religion, but not art, understands the universe as a finite entity. For Langer art is 'natural light'. For Lewis religion is divine light. The one is not reducible to the terms of the other.

Yet surely direct awareness of that which is categorised as the aesthetic or as the religious is so categorised because of the prior existence of a theory or system or conceptual scheme or habit of thought in terms of which the claim can be defended.[29] Those who believe in God are liable to interpret extra-ordinary experience, and even heightened ordinary experience, in terms of a conceptual frame of their religious belief. So it is, too, with those who have profound experiences of art and who are not religious believers and for whom rational explanations of their experience are more sensible. It is quite possible for a religious believer and a rationalist both to be moved deeply by the same work of art and to interpret that shared experience very differently. Susanne Langer does not need to postulate 'any mysterious factor in the mind or in the world to admit that artistic perception is directly intuitive'.[30] H.D. Lewis does need to postulate an 'unconditioned source' to account for the experience of religion. At this point I take no position on one side or the other. What is at least worth discussing is whether what both the lover of art and the religious believer experience is at root the same thing, known and explained in two different and sometimes mutually exclusive ways. The epistemologies of both art and religion seem to be very similar, even to the extent of the language symbols which both use. Is a religious way of knowing intrinsically different from knowing through art? And if it is not, what is it that is known?

Art and Religion and Being

These are profoundly important questions to which the greatest figures in Western philosophy gave their attention—Kant, Schleiermacher, Hegel, Kierkegaard and Nietzsche—but for the moment we will confine ourselves to what those who have aesthetic and religious experience say that it is that they experience.

What is the essence of aesthetic experience? André Malraux speaks of 'the admiration and other less definable emotions conjured up in us by the

28. Lewis, *Our Experience of God*, p. 245.
29. Further to this, see Mitchell, *The Justification of Religious Belief*, p. 115, where he so argues with respect to claims to direct awareness of God.
30. Langer, *Problems of Art*, p. 69.

first great poem we encountered; they stemmed as from a revelation, not from any reasoned judgment'.[31] What is revealed to us is 'another world',[32] not an idealised world or a dream world, but a 'fantastic world', fantastic 'in the sense that its elements are not those of reality; but its fantasy is intrinsic and fundamental, quite other than the wayward imagining of the day-dream...'[33] This other and fantastic world which we enter when we contemplate great art is, like the real world, a 'creation' or, rather, a series of creations couched in a language peculiar to itself.[34] It is a creation or universe compared to which

> the most self-evident reality is merely an appearance, a mask, a lure, or, as compared with the noble aspirations of the soul which only the highest art can satisfy, an earth-bound solace of the eyes.[35]

Malraux argues that this universe of meaning has the artist both as its master and its servant; its master insofar as it is the artist who imposes on 'the uncharted scheme of things' a 'meaning' or 'coherence', and its servant inasmuch as the artist approaches his work with awe, knowing that he must obey his vision. Thus,

> the relationship between the artist and art is of the order of a vocation. And the religious vocation, when authentic, is not felt as the result of choice, but as the answer to God's call.[36]

It is a vocation which compels the artist to choose between true and false values;[37] which compels him to subordinate himself to nothing outside his art;[38] which demands of him a faith which stakes a claim on eternity;[39] which enables him to have a dialogue with God;[40] which gives him victory and liberation and 'the gratitude of coming generations for victories which seem to promise their own';[41] which compels him to 'bear witness' [42] and to 'revolt against man's fate'.[43] I quote Malraux at length, well knowing his controversial status, yet he is not so controversial that what he sees as the essence of art is not echoed by others, not least artists themselves. Henri Matisse and Paul Cézanne both wrote of the vocation and single-mindedness of the artist being parallel to that of the priest. Cézanne speaks constantly

31. André Malraux, *Voices of Silence* (St Albans: Paladin, 1974), p. 312.
32. Malraux, *Voices of Silence*.
33. Malraux, *Voices of Silence*.
34. Malraux, *Voices of Silence*, p. 121.
35. Malraux, *Voices of Silence*, p. 356.
36. Malraux, *Voices of Silence*, pp. 317, 324.
37. Malraux, *Voices of Silence*, p. 530.
38. Malraux, *Voices of Silence*, p. 494.
39. Malraux, *Voices of Silence*, p. 495.
40. Malraux, *Voices of Silence*, p. 473.
41. Malraux, *Voices of Silence*, p. 464.
42. Malraux, *Voices of Silence*, p. 460.
43. Malraux, *Voices of Silence*, p. 639.

in his correspondence of the need for the artist to remain close to and be true to nature, yet this 'strong feeling for nature' must express itself not in the imitation of nature but in its *realization*, by which he means that the artist must discover nature's true reality, for 'nature for us men is more depth than surface'; it is 'the show which the *Pater Omnipotens* Aeterne Deus spreads out before our eyes'.[44] It is little wonder that Cézanne's genius in realising the depth of nature could call forth from his friend Joachim Gasquet the comment that the 'noble forms' which Cézanne evoked 'fill us with a sense of religion'.[45]

A hundred others, artists and critics, could be quoted in support of a theory of aesthetic experience which sees its essence as an experience of what in religion would be called the divine. André Dunoyer de Segonzac speaks of the state of exaltation, of communion with life, nature, and his fellow beings which enables the artist unconsciously to exalt, re-create and transcribe the world about him.[46] Paul Cézanne is said to have remarked that one is 'revivified' by a painting, and

> born into the real world... To love a painting one must first have drunk deeply of it in long draughts. Lose consciousness. Descend with the painter into the dim, tangled roots of things, and rise again from it in colours, be steeped in the light of them.[47]

Here is what in the Christian religion would be called an experience of death and resurrection. It is a veritable baptism. Samuel Palmer cried:

> How does an animate and inanimate creation, all the range of high arts and exquisite sciences proclaim the immortality of the soul, by exciting, as they are intended to excite, large longings after wisdom and blessedness which three-score or three hundred years would be too short to realise. We are like the chrysalis asleep, and dreaming of our wings.[48]

Here is death and resurrection again. At a quite different point in relation to the felt essence of art stands Paul Klee who lived near ' "the dead and the unborn" at an almost cosmic distance from the world'.[49] Andy Warhol's paintings of images of popular culture powerfully remind us of the transience of life and the imminence of death and serve as powerful contemporary religious allegories.[50] Marc Chagall said that 'art seems to me

44. John Rewald (ed.), *Paul Cézanne: Letters* (Oxford: Bruno Cassirer, 1976), p. 301.

45. Rewald (ed.), *Paul Cézanne*, p. 265.

46. Quoted in Milner, *On Not Being Able to Paint*, p. 106.

47. Milner, *On Not Being Able to Paint*, p. 25.

48. Quoted in David Cecil, *Visionary and Dreamer* (London: Constable, 1969), p. 75.

49. C.J. Jung, *Man and His Symbols* (London: Aldus, 1964), p. 270.

50. See Zan Schuweiler Daab, 'For Heaven's Sake: Warhol's Art as Religious Allegory', *Religion and the Arts* 1.1 (1996), pp. 14-31.

to be a state of soul, more than anything else. The soul of all is sacred...'[51] For Paul Gauguin 'a picture is basically of psychic significance; it mirrors the innermost being of the painter'[52] In van Gogh's work 'God is hoped for... rather than unmasked through his creation'.[53]

What is being expressed here by so numerous and so diverse a group of painters (and I choose only painters for reasons of space) is that the essence of their art is at least nonrational. What they say may be dismissed as 'the religion of aestheticism' as Gombrich describes it, a pseudo-religion that 'lacks that awareness of distance that his religion gave to Dante'. Yet Gombrich is not prepared is dismiss as mere 'metaphysical sentimentalism' what the artist has to say, even in ways such as these, about the springs of his art. For Gombrich art transcends the self-centredness of the artist. Art seeks perfection and absolute value. Although Gombrich has no time for religious or quasi-religious justifications for art he is compelled to wonder 'if we need this kind of metaphysics to justify a more than subjective theory of art, one that explains and accepts the demand for self-transcendence and some notion of perfection'. This search for self-transcendence, this 'feeling for the existence of values', indeed of absolute values, always transcends the artist's skill but it has been the compelling influence of the Western tradition of art.[54] This may not be a religious justification for art but it establishes it on some kind of metaphysical base and may explain why so many artists resort to religious language when trying to tell us what drives them. They eschew logic. Whether they assert that painting is an outburst of emotional turmoil as Vlaminck does when he says that 'when I have colour in my hands, I couldn't care less about anyone else's painting. Life and me, me and life',[55] or whether they express their conviction of the interiorness of the source of their artistic perception in less extravagant terms as does Gauguin when he says, 'I am content to search for my own self and not nature',[56] artists, at least modern artists, affirm that their art is not the result or the creation of some conscious, rational endeavour. Paul Valery expressed the experience of many artists when he said that 'there are functions which prefer the shadow to the light...that is that minimum of conscious awareness which is necessary and sufficient to make these acts come about or to bait them...', and 'Sometimes I think and sometimes I am'.[57] Nicholas de Staël confesses,

> I lose contact with the canvas at every instant, find it again and then lose it... It has to be like this because I believe in the accidental. The only way

51. R. McMullen, *The World of Marc Chagall* (London: Aldus, 1968), p. 55.
52. M.-C. Jalard, *Post-Impressionism* (London: Heron, 1968), p. 29.
53. Jalard, *Post-Impressionism*, p. 42.
54. Gombrich, 'Art and Self-Transcendence', p. 128.
55. Jalard, *Post-Impressionism*, p. 83.
56. Jalard, *Post-Impressionism*, p. 29.
57. Quoted in R. Arnheim, *Picasso's 'Guernica'* (London: Faber & Faber 1964), p. 1.

> I can advance is from one accident to another—as soon as I feel logic is
> becoming too logical I am unnerved and that drives me naturally to
> illogicality.[58]

Picasso said famously:

> I see for the others. That is to say I put down on the canvas the sudden
> visions that force themselves on me. I don't know beforehand what I
> shall put on the canvas, even less can I decide what colours to use.
> Whilst I'm working I'm not aware of what I'm painting on the canvas.
> Each time I begin a picture, I have the feeling of throwing myself into
> space. I never know whether I'll land on my feet. It's only later that I
> begin to assess the effect of what I've done.[59]

Now, admittedly, these are vague and ill-defined indications of the essence
of what is perceived in and through art, yet they are *necessarily* vague.
This is so if only because, as Rudolf Arnheim says, 'artists...have learned to
tread cautiously when it comes to reporting the internal events that produce their works. They watch with suspicion all attempts to invade the
inner workshop and to systematize its secrets.'[60] It follows that these 'internal events' can be explained other than in the categories of religion. The
psychologist of art will rightly assert that 'there is no reason to assume that
whatever presents itself "out of the blue" is therefore sent by the gods'.[61]
Long dead, at least in the philosophy and psychology of art, is the belief
that works of art are produced by those who have a touch of the Muses'
madness in their souls. Arnheim and Anton Ehrenzweig and many others
would argue that what expresses itself in a work of art wells up from within
the artist *per se*. Yet psychologists of religion explain religious experiences
in precisely the same way. It depends entirely upon the conceptual frames
which interpreters of aesthetic and religious experiences find adequately
explains for them the nature and essence of these experiences. My point
about the essence of these experiences is that they appear to belong to the
same fundamental ground of seriousness or at least, as Gombrich would
say, of 'absolute value'.

It is worth noting further that for both the religious believer and the
lover of art the essence of their experience is no alien and otherwordly
thing. It belongs to the world in which they live but transcends that world.
Charles Gore, writing in the late nineteenth century at a time when, as we
will see later, many artists were seeking religious inspiration and validation
for their work, could speak of the doctrine of the Holy Spirit in words that
find an echo in the writings of artists and lovers of art, albeit without the
references to God:

> Where life is most penetrating, profound, invincible, rational, conscious
> of God, there is fullest freedom of operation of the Holy Spirit. Thus,

58. Douglas Cooper, *Nicholas de Staël* (New York: W.W. Norton, 1961), p. 76.
59. Quoted in Berger, *Success and Failure of Picasso*, p. 136.
60. Arnheim, *Picasso's 'Guernica'*, p. 1.
61. Arnheim, *Picasso's 'Guernica'*, p. 9.

> obviously enough, the doctrine of the Spirit is no remote or esoteric
> thing; it is no mere ultimate object of the rapt contemplation of the
> mystic; it is the doctrine of that wherein God touches man most nearly,
> most familiarly, in common life.[62]

The essential this-worldliness of the experience seems to hold true for the
lover of art and for the religious believer whether or not they regard the
source of the experience as external or internal to themselves. It is well
known how, following Paul Tillich, Christian theologians have often replaced
'out there' analogies with 'depth' analogies when speaking of God. Yet both
classes of analogies do no more than assert that there is a fundamental
truth which gives meaning to life. Though Samuel Palmer can speak of the
source of aesthetic experience in transcendental terms and while Paul Gauguin speaks of it basically in mystical-psychological terms, Gauguin is doing
no more than exchanging an 'out there' analogy for a 'depth' analogy of the
same experience.

So it seems that if we take seriously what artists and religious believers
say there is little difference of substance between aesthetic and religious
experience. Profound differences lie between the various conceptual theories which are advanced to explain or interpret these experiences, but it is
the interpretative schemes which are in opposition not the experiences they
seek to explain. Henri Matisse, summing up his aims and fulfilment as an
artist, said that

> Most painters require direct contact with objects in order to feel that they
> exist, and they can only reproduce them under strictly physical condi-
> tions. They look for an exterior light to illuminate them internally.
> Whereas the artist or the poet possesses an interior light which trans-
> forms objects to make a new world of them—sensitive, organized, a living
> world which is in itself an infallible sign of the Divinity, a reflection of
> Divinity.[63]

Matisse here is not merely borrowing the language of religion to express a
truth about which religion has nothing to say. He is using language common to both religion and art to express the nature of an experience common
to both.

Art, Religion and Wholeness

We can pursue this question further if we turn—daringly for the Christian
believer—to ask whether art as well as religion offers wholeness or, in the
Christian vocabulary, salvation. When artists and lovers of art speak of
'revelation' or 'joy' or 'transfiguration' they seem to be speaking of the life-
changing, integrating, enriching effect of art upon them. Is this experience

62. Charles Gore, 'The Holy Spirit and Inspiration', in *idem* (ed.), *Lux Mundi*
(London: John Murray, 1889), p. 231.
63. Flam, *Matisse on Art*, p. 61.

in any sense analogous to what Christians mean by salvation? As the Greek word *sōzein* in the New Testament may properly be rendered as 'to make whole' as well as 'to save', we may rephrase our question: Do works of art make us whole? It seems that they do in at least three ways:

1. They provide the feeling and the fact of permanence and give stability to the lives of men and women. In a sense our art gives us a kind of immortality. Hannah Arendt wrote that 'because of their outstanding permanence, works of art are the most intensely worldly of all tangible things'. The 'human artifice' therefore becomes 'a home for mortal men, whose stability will endure and outlast the ever-changing movement of our lives and actions'. Men and women require the help of *homo faber* in his highest capacity, that is, the help of artists, of poets and historiographers, of monument-builders or writers, because without them the only product of their activity, the stories they enact and tell, would not survive at all.[64]

2. They provide us with a means to wholeness, integration and oneness with ourselves and the natural order. Thus D.H. Lawrence wrote that 'art is a form of religion, minus the Ten Commandments business which is sociological. Art is a form of supremely delicate awareness and atonement—meaning at-one-ness, the state of being at one with the object.'[65]

3. They provide us with an opportunity at least to taste freedom. The emancipation of art is both a means and an end, the cause and the product, of modern man's emancipation. Herbert Read says that 'the theories of art…agree in stressing the freedom of the artist—the artist is not a slave to Nature, or to the science of nature. His mind is emancipated—free to express, not himself (for that would still be a kind of slavery) but a new vision, a new order of reality, an ideal beauty'.[66] As we will see this contention has been vigorously attacked by conservative evangelical and catholic critics alike, yet Read makes a case. The artist's independence of nature gives him 'the possibility of creating a reality through the means of art' and is 'one positive method of vindicating the individuality of the person. Art in this sense becomes the most precious form of *freedom*'.[67]

We could add to this such fundamentally Christian concepts as forgiveness, acceptance and reconciliation, fundamental to the doctrine of salvation. Perhaps it would be extravagant to claim that a work of art can be redemptive, but it cannot be denied that it may be a means of redemption. In his

---

64. Arendt, *The Human Condition*, p. 173.
65. D.H. Lawrence, *Selected Essays* (London: Penguin Books, 1950), p. 304.
66. Herbert Read, *The Philosophy of Modern Art* (London: Faber & Faber 1964), pp. 76-77.
67. Read, *The Philosophy of Modern Art*, p. 102.

Ethics Dietrich Bonhoeffer held that the experience most expressive of man's true condition is the experience of shame. He wrote that shame is man's ineffaceable recollection of his estrangement from the origin; it is grief for this estrangement, and the powerless longing to return to unity with the origin. We strive to cover this intrinsic shame:

> The covering of shame conceals everything nascent that proceeds from man's yearning for the reattainment of the unity which he has lost. The secrecy of shame remains outspread over the creative power of man which comes to him in the self-sought union of the disunited. It is the memory of the disunion from the Creator, and of the robbery from the Creator, which is here disclosed. This is true of the coming into being of a work of art, of a scientific discovery, and indeed of any creative work which arises from the union of man with the world of things. Only when life is born, when the work is perfected, is the secret broken through by jubilant open joy. But the secret of its coming into being it bears within itself for ever.[68]

Art, Religion and Ethics

If art and religion both rest on the same fundamental ground and if their ways of knowing and their grasp of reality are at least parallel, do they share an ethic? I leave until a later chapter the questions of what it means to speak of a work of art possessing moral beauty and of the implications of saying of an artist that his work displays obedience to a vision and that it has integrity. Here we will refer only to the supposed ethical effect on the observer and compare this with the ethical dimension of religion.

Most religions have an ethical dimension. Faith implies morality. Artists do not make the same assumption. The *is* of art does not imply *ought*. Yet art does have ethical consequences.

First, art possesses instrumental moral value. An American philosopher, Joseph Kupfer, argues that aesthetic experience is an essential ingredient of responsibility. This is so because a work of art becomes an 'aesthetic object' because of the discriminating and organising response of the viewer or listener. Thus 'aesthetic apprehension includes, in addition to the relations which make up the aesthetic object, the relation of the interpreter, the critical audience to it. We stand in a *free* and *responsive* relation to the aesthetic object.'[69] In other words, art needs its observers. We, the audience, are actively involved in a work of art. We participate in the creative process begun by the artist. But in so doing we are changed by the work of art. Our participation was expressed by Dewey as a balance between doing and undergoing. Kupfer says that 'what we do is conditioned by what we

68. Dietrich Bonhoeffer, *Ethics* (London: SCM Press, 1955), pp. 20-23.
69. Joseph Kupfer, 'Aesthetic Experience and Moral Education', *Journal of Aesthetic Education* 12.3 (1978), pp. 13-22 (14).

are taking in and what we perceive is shaped by our active involvement'.[70] Our activity is shaped 'to contours not of our choosing in order to form the unified independent entity' of the work of art. Art changes us in a moral direction. So it is that art can be morally educative. Art springs from and is given to a human community. Kupfer says that as the different parts of a work of art exist in mutual dependence and benefit, so our response to and participation in the unity in diversity which is an artwork prepares us for responding to and working with others in the human community. This may sound a little far-fetched. Many would want to counter it by saying that many great works of art, especially the art of the modern period, mirror the *dis*unity, the *dis*location, the corruption of human society. In any case the private valuations put on his contemporaries by moral man find great difficulty of expression in an immoral society. Nevertheless the words most often used to describe a great work of art—words like 'unity', 'wholeness', 'harmony', 'integration'—may well carry ethical force for those of us who, sufficiently moved by a great work of art, resolve to be better people. And if much of the art of the twentieth century *does* reflect and interpret modern man's disunity and dislocation, is not this the truth?

Finally, Kupfer argues that art criticism resembles moral dialogue insofar as 'directing, discriminating, redescribing, and highlighting are common to both aesthetic and moral communication'.[71] He points out that the criticism and interpretation of art proceed, like moral dialogue, by example as well as by speech. This is most clearly seen in the performance arts but it can also be found in the plastic arts and painting. The art critic, by developing in us the capacity to discriminate and synthesise, 'can inform our dispositions in morally valuable ways'.[72]

Here we have a functional view of art which sees it as possessing instrumental moral value. It will be quickly rejected by those who would assert that an artwork is an end in itself and should not be either produced or justified by any external factor. Yet there is a resemblance between experiencing a work of art and the taking up of ethical positions. It would be dangerous for the lover of art and the theologian to labour these similarities. The fact that art and religion seem to have the same personal and social ethical effects is no argument for the identification of art and religion, but it may suggest again that they spring from the same fundamental ground.

But can it be said that art is capable of effecting moral change because of its intrinsic nature rather than merely because it can be used instrumentally as a moral guide? Is art *of necessity* ethical? Is an ethical quality a quality which a great work of art possesses *a priori*? Artists are very reticent on the subject. Yet one or two intimations exist that such may be the case. In his

70. Kupfer, 'Aesthetic Experience', p. 15.
71. Kupfer, 'Aesthetic Experience', p. 20.
72. Kupfer, 'Aesthetic Experience', p. 22.

Lines: Tintern Abbey, Wordsworth wrote of the 'beauteous forms' of the Wye valley as having 'no slight or trivial influence' on 'a good man's life'. Can it not also be said that the 'noble forms' of Cézanne's landscapes have a similar effect? Am I not made a better man, as I am also frequently made a chastened man, by the experience of great art? Art certainly enables me to catch a glimpse of the 'life of things' as the natural landscape did for Wordsworth. Here one passes from speculation to confession and from perception to prayer.

What conclusions can we draw thus far? It is clear that art and religion are not identical. Notoriously difficult as it is to define religion, any adequate definition would have to take account of features common to many (though by no means all) religions: a body of doctrine, a code of ethics, a religious community and forms of worship. Art would not qualify as religion against these criteria. But these criteria derive from the nature of religion as social. At the level of intuitive perception, where both art and religion engage us as persons, art shares much with religion. Indeed, at this level it is difficult to see where the distinction lies. They both, as Thomas Martland says, 'display the swatches of "reality" by means of which men see what "is" and from which they create their world'. Echoing Matisse, Martland says that 'rather than serving as illustrations which describe men's world, art and religion contribute the fabric of new worlds which men now come to see and understand as their world'.[73]

It seems that what are seen to be the differences between the experience of art and the experience of religion are in fact differences between the conceptual frameworks by which these experiences are interpreted. Because of the assumptions we bring to our experiences, the experiences themselves are given their distinctive interpretation. We experience what we expect, or want, to experience. We will return to this crucial question of the *experience* of art and religion later. But we need now to address that fundamental question: Do religion and art rest on the same ground? We need to test this contention and look further into the claim that art and religion—art and Christianity—reveal their origin in the same fundamental seriousness, the same Ground of Being, the same God.

73. Thomas Martland, *Religion as Art* (Albany, NY: University of New York Press, 1981), p. 1.

Chapter 4

Art and the Philosophers

So, while religion and art are not identical, the contention is that they do seem to stand upon what we have called the same fundamental ground of seriousness. *If* they do, then what is that ground? If ultimately, as Christians claim, that ground is God then very important conclusions follow. The Christian claim is that God showed himself uniquely to humankind in the person and the work of Jesus. We say that he did so 'for us and for our salvation'. If that is true then art, and everything else in God's redeemed creation that is good and true, is, as we have noted, potentially salvific, that is it is capable, by God's grace, of making us what we were created to be as sons and daughters of God. That is a huge claim and has always raised extremely important philosophical questions. Even assuming its truth, before we can ask *how and in what ways* art is salvific we still have to ask what the evidence is that art and religion stand upon the same ground and, ultimately, reveal the same truths. Is this view merely a hopeful extrapolation from the *belief* that everything ultimately rests in God or is there some philosophical argument, and indeed any empirical evidence, that it is so? This is a question that has engaged the greatest philosophers in the West and we must now pay attention to their very demanding ideas.

Before we do it is worth reminding ourselves that, as we noted in the last chapter, many artists speak of the significance of their work in religious or philosophical terms. However, as R.G. Collingwood pointed out many years ago, artist-aestheticians may know all about art but may not be able to avoid talking philosophical (or for that matter theological) nonsense. So, what do the philosophers have to say about our question—bearing in mind, as Collingwood also went on to say, that 'philosopher-aestheticians are admirably protected against talking nonsense: but there is no security that they know what they are talking about'![1] We must let this serve as a kind of philosophical health warning as we now step into a world of demanding ideas.

---

1. R.G. Collingwood, *The Principles of Art* (Oxford: Oxford University Press, 1938), p. 3.

It is impossible in a few paragraphs to do other than sketch the main lines of the aesthetics and philosophies of art of but a few of the major Western philosophers who have addressed the question of art. Sketches inevitably give a very incomplete and often distorted view—but we must make the attempt. We begin with the most influential European philosopher of modern times, Immanuel Kant (1724–1804). We will spend rather longer with Kant than with the other philosophers we will consider because the fundamental philosophical questions that Kant considered, and in the light of which he developed his aesthetics, concerned them all and we must give some time to outlining these questions.

Immanuel Kant: Art, Nature and Beauty

The range of Kant's interests as a philosopher were very wide, his thinking changed quite radically, and his ideas are often very difficult to follow for those of us who, like me, are not professional philosophers. However, the main focus of his attention is clear enough. It has to do with rejecting traditional speculative, rational, metaphysics and seeking to answer the questions metaphysicians ask by relying, not as they did, on human reason but on an alternative way of understanding human experience. In doing this Kant created his own metaphysical system. But what is 'metaphysics'?

The word was first coined to refer to some of Aristotle's writings. In the collection of his works these came after those on physics. These ideas were therefore, in the catalogue, 'beyond Physics' (in Greek *ta meta to phūsika*) in the place they came in the collection. Today the word is usually (but unsatisfactorily) defined as the theoretical philosophy of being and knowing.

It has been said that metaphysics is the most abstract and 'high-falutin' part of philosophy.[2] It grapples with the ultimate questions. Among the most important of these are: What is it that we experience? How can we be sure that we know anything outside ourselves? What really exists and what makes existence possible? Can we have freewill in a universe governed by scientific laws? Is abstract thought possible in a material world in the constant flux of change? Are values and norms possible in such a world? What is reality? Such questions as these prompt another, namely: Are these very questions sensible? Are the questions, let alone the answers, illusory? This is where Kant made his contribution.

Kant's first published works dealt with issues in physics—the nature of fire, volcanoes, the causes of earthquakes, the orbits of the planets and questions like that—but he came to these questions primarily as a philosopher rather than as a scientist. He wanted to know upon what ground the physical properties of the cosmos rest. If nothing happens without a

---

2.   D.W. Hamlyn, 'History of Metaphysics', in Ted Honderich (ed.), *The Oxford Companion to Philosophy* (Oxford: Oxford University Press, 1995), p. 556.

sufficient reason, then what is the ultimate reason why everything exists? In other words, what are the metaphysical presuppositions for science?

Kant was dissatisfied with the answers to these questions offered by contemporary metaphysicians. These were largely derived from principles in formal logic.[3] They were, he said, 'castles in the sky'. He was also unconvinced by the theories of their opponents: those who believed that the basis for all knowledge was to be found in the human mind (the rationalists) and those who held that all knowledge of the world came only through the senses (the empiricists). Kant went part of the way with both the rationalists and the empiricists in that he held that when we engage with the world we use our senses and our reason—we receive information through our senses but process it, analyse it, codify it, through our reason, or what Kant alternatively and sometimes confusingly called our 'understanding'. The question is, whence comes this understanding? It must be more than a mere inference from our senses for we not only deduce so-called scientific laws from what our senses tell us but we also ask the ultimate questions about the *meaning* of what our senses tell us, and ask to what fundamental truth about the world these laws point. Inference or deduction is a matter of logic and immanence and temporality and is based upon experience of the knowable world. The answer to the question of ultimate meaning or purpose lies beyond the knowable world and is an issue for metaphysics and transcendental reality. Kant believed that we can only construct these laws and ask these questions because we possess what he called 'synthetic *a priori* knowledge'. We bring order to the chaotic, random, sensations we receive because we have inherent (but not innate) within us certain concepts (what Aristotle called 'categories') which enable us to synthesise our experience of the world and which, Kant said, 'the understanding contains *a priori*'. *A priori* knowledge is knowledge which is, literally, prior to experience, that is, it does not depend for its authority upon any evidence from our experience. These categories (twelve in number in Kant's scheme) enable us to recognise, say, that space and time and causality belong to the mind and not to experience. Without this *a priori* (or, Kant says, 'transcendent') knowledge we could not live as human beings. Indeed, we are different from animals only because we inherently possess this given knowledge.

By a series of what he called 'transcendental deductions' from his *a priori* categories Kant was led to the idea of God. His argument had three strands. First, he argued that if everything in the natural world depends for its existence on some other thing that causes it, then we are forced to go outside this world to explain how everything began—to some uncaused Cause. Second, if everything we observe is a synthesis, that is, if it displays a fundamental unity, this can best be explained by it having been formed

3.   Notably the so-called law or principle of contradiction that something cannot simultaneously be and not-be.

by a wise creator who had a purpose for his creation. Third, if the universe *is* purposive, then it must have been designed, and if a design, therefore a designer. In reinstating metaphysics Kant established the idea of God. Although Aquinas had argued similarly, for Kant these were not rational *arguments* proving the existence of God but deductions from transcendental, *a priori*, knowledge. A rational argument proving God's existence would make God a product of our reason. For Kant God is *a priori*.

So it seemed to Kant that to the questions about metaphysics—'Is genuine metaphysics possible? Is it defensible?'—the answer was 'Yes, it is possible to have knowledge which transcends the bounds of experience of the everyday world'.

Kant set out his argument in his *Critique of Pure Reason*, published in 1781. He then turned his attention to morality and asked himself upon what metaphysical assumptions morality rests. A study of what he called *practical* reason was required. For example, what does it mean to have values? On what do they rest? Do *a priori* rules tell us how to behave? Do they govern our will? Kant concluded that there was a 'categorical imperative' which is a given, *a priori*, setting or framework for our ethical judgments. Kant expressed this categorical imperative thus: 'In all that you do act only according to a principle that you would want to be a universal moral law'. For Kant, God was a necessary postulate, or fundamental condition, of practical reason.

Kant set out this argument in 1788 in his *Critique of Practical Reason*. This was followed in 1790 by the *Critique of Judgment* in which Kant attempted to find an *a priori* metaphysical principle for judgment, that is our capacity to reflect, to understand, to determine concepts and construct laws under which we can organise our experience of ourselves and nature. It is in this third critique that Kant addresses the question of our judgments about the beautiful and the sublime, both of which are 'aesthetic' because they are initially perceived (in Greek *aisthēsis*) by the imagination. This is clearly central to our theme and we must now give it some attention.

For Kant (though he had second thoughts about this between the first and second editions of his first *Critique*) reason alone does not initially bring order out of the random data presented to us through our senses. We rely upon *imagination* to do the first rough sorting. In his first *Critique* Kant speaks of the imagination—'this schematism of our understanding'—as 'art hidden in the depths of the soul'. His argument goes something like this: Reason is universal. I share reason with everybody. But only I experience the particular experiences that I am having at this moment. My experiences are unique to me. I connect the two, the universal reason I share with others and the particular experiences unique to me, through my imagination. My imagination, to use Kant's word, *synthesises* or builds into a whole or integrates the information I receive through my senses and from my reason.

We now hit a problem. In his second edition of the first *Critique* 'imagination' is replaced by 'understanding' as the synthesiser. For Kant imagination is now merely a function of understanding. Why the change? What Kant had created—or perhaps recognised—was an opposition between mind and nature. It is my natural capacity to imagine. I synthesise or integrate my experiences of the world behind the back of my mind, as it were. My imagination, as Kant uses the term, is primordial.

Now Kant recognises the 'abysmal power of the imagination', as Mark C. Taylor puts it.[4] My control over myself, my autonomy, is destroyed if my co-ordinating, integrating faculty, my imagination, works unconsciously (or, better, pre-consciously). In the second edition of the first *Critique,* as if fearful of the consequences of not so doing, Kant places the imagination under the control of autonomous reason. Synthesis is now achieved by the understanding.

Which of Kant's arguments are we to go with? For the moment let us run with the argument in Kant's first edition of the first *Critique*. A word first about what Kant calls 'synthesis'. Synthesis, says Kant, is 'the process of joining different representations to each other, and of comprehending their multiplicity in one act of knowledge. This synthesis is pure when the manifold is not given empirically but *a priori* (as that in space and time).'[5]

This synthesis, this bringing of the information from my senses to the bar of analytical reason, is achieved by imagination, that 'blind but indispensable function of the soul, without which we should have no knowledge whatever, but of the working of which we are seldom conscious'. Here is the abyss that Kant was soon to recognise. This synthesis, is, we might say, a result of preliminary sorting conducted by my primordial, pre-conscious imagination. To bring this synthesis to the point at which it can be spoken about, conceptualised, is 'a function of the understanding [what Kant calls "the faculty of thinking"] by which we can attain to knowledge, in the proper meaning of the term'.[6] But—the imagination is transcendental. It is an *a priori* given. It precedes conceptual thought. It is 'art concealed in the depths of the soul'.

Kant employs the words 'imagination' and 'understanding' in ways that are a little different to our use of these terms now. Part of the problem with philosophers is understanding the way they use familiar words! Now for other familiar words—the words 'beauty' and 'beautiful'—for at this point Kant comes to the heart of aesthetics, and to his third *Critique*, the *Critique of Judgment*. In this book Kant seeks to overcome the difficulties and stresses in this matter of the imagination and its role as he had sought to overcome the other tensions between theoretical reason (in the first

4. Mark C. Taylor, *Disfiguring: Art, Architecture, Religion* (Chicago: University of Chicago Press, 1992), p. 25. I am indebted to this work for much of what follows.

5. Kant, *Critique of Pure Reason*, p. 84.

6. Kant, *Critique of Pure Reason*, p. 84.

Critique) and practical reason (in the second). Here the key symbol, the reconciling concept, is the idea of the beautiful.

The beautiful, for Kant, is 'purposiveness without purpose', or, as John McIntyre helpfully puts it, 'purposiveness without design'. That apparently paradoxical definition is fairly easy to understand. Kant identifies two primary examples of purposeful purposelessness: the living organism in the natural world, and the work of art in the cultural world. The natural organism exemplifies purposiveness without purpose because its 'end' is itself. It has no other purpose than itself. It does not exist for any reason outside itself. Similarly a truly beautiful work of art is its own end. It exists for itself alone. In creating it the artist acts in freedom. She or he is free from the pressures to produce an artwork for any other purpose than to produce an artwork—or at least he should be if the artwork is to be truly beautiful. Beauty and freedom go together. Beauty, Kant says, is an expression of freedom.

Kant now moves a stage further. In his work the artist is at one with nature of which he is a part. If his work is alien to nature—to its hidden, inner unity—it cannot be beautiful. Insofar as it is beautiful an artwork reconciles nature and reason. This is so because artistic genius, Kant argues, is *of nature*. It is a natural talent. As it is of nature, artistic genius, embodied and expressed as it is in the artist, therefore reconciles nature and reason, imagination and understanding. What a truly beautiful work of art does is to demonstrate this primal unity. It overcomes the fragmentation and disunity of human experience by pointing to, indeed expressing, the primordial unity (or what Taylor calls the 'original accord'[7]) of which we all are heirs and which is the only source of our freedom. Thus art is absolutely fundamental to our freedom. In a truly beautiful work of art the artist's and the viewer's imagination secures that identity of nature and reason without which we cannot experience truth and become free.

Having taken us this far, Kant then places severe limitations on our imaginative capacity. The imagination, Kant says in his third *Critique*, is 'regulative' rather than 'constitutive'. That is, our imagination guides reason as reason organises our sense experiences, but it cannot offer us information. So aesthetic awareness is not a matter of knowledge (for this is a function of reason) but of *judgment*.

Kant argues that there are two kinds of aesthetic judgment: beauty and sublimity. Beauty, as we have seen, points to and gives form to the essential unity or harmony of our experiences. It is grasped by our imagination and presented to our understanding. But beyond beauty is the sublime. What we describe and experience as beautiful is that which exhibits inner harmony and gives us pleasure. But our imagination inevitably lets us down. When it does, we feel, Kant says, 'displeasure arising from the inadequacy

---

7. Taylor, *Disfiguring*, p. 27.

of the imagination'. We realise our failure fully to comprehend the significance of what we see. This experience, Kant says, is 'a negative pleasure'
because it prompts us to push beyond the limits of pleasure (or mere
'charm' as Kant puts it). What we yearn for but never experience is the
sublime beyond mere harmony of form. Kant puts it this way:

> The beautiful in nature is a question of the form of the object, and this
> consists in limitation, whereas the sublime is to be found in an object
> even devoid of form, so far as it immediately involves, or else by its
> presence provokes, a representation of unlimitedness, and yet its totality
> is also present to thought.[8]

So, as Taylor puts it, 'the sublime erupts at the *limits* of human consciousness'.[9] In fact the experience of the sublime *is the experience of the
boundary of limitation and limitlessness*. We only know limitation because
we know limitlessness. And this knowledge of limitlessness must be *a priori*.
It lies beyond experience. A work of art can provide us with this liminal
experience, and, so I would claim, can point us towards God.

However, in all this, Kant argues, the artist while belonging to nature is
secondary to nature. For Kant beauty is primarily the beauty of orderly,
causally determined, nature. Kant recognises the importance of art but 'art
can only be termed beautiful, where we are conscious of its being art, while
yet it has the appearance of nature'. For Kant the importance of the artist is
that he points us to nature and helps us to see nature as understandable—
as comprehensible—to our reason.

This is a rather low estimation of the importance of art and the artist. For
Kant, what the artist does is to point to the beautiful, and to see something
as beautiful is to see it as exhibiting an order that makes it comprehensible
to us. A contemporary critic of this approach to aesthetics would find this
emphasis on the orderliness of the beautiful as intellectual and emotionally
bleak. Objecting to it Ralph Walker says that

> Aesthetic appreciation is not a sort of failed cognition, nor is the enjoy-
> ment of beauty a side-effect in the process of finding things out. If what
> pleases us about a rose is its appropriateness for our cognitive faculties,
> a cockroach or a dead cow should please us as much; they are no less
> readily comprehensible. And an empty expanse of flat sand should be far
> more pleasing than a Sussex landscape, being much more regular and
> more easily reduced to rule by reason.[10]

After all that what would Kant's answer be to our question: Do art and religion reveal their origin in the same God? Although Kant would question the
question his answer would probably be 'Yes'. In the end, as art points us to
nature and nature displays an essential, and seemingly pre-established,

8. Kant, *Critique of Judgment* (Oxford: Oxford University Press, 1973), p. 90,
quoted in Taylor, *Disfiguring*, p. 30.
9. Taylor, *Disfiguring*, p. 30.
10. Ralph C.S. Walker, *Kant* (Routledge & Kegan Paul, 1978), p. 146.

harmony then this can only be convincingly understood in terms of a beneficent God who has a purpose for the universe he created. Is this the God of the Christian religion? Is this God a *saving* as well as a beneficent creator, and is art therefore salvific, at least potentially? On these questions Kant is inevitably silent.

The German philosophers who followed Kant made aesthetics a principal issue. For example J.C.F. von Schiller believed that art and beauty were central to human freedom. For Kant, beauty belonged to the ideal world. For Schiller beauty belonged to the real world. It is 'freedom in phenomenal [i.e. that which is seen] appearance' and 'it is through beauty that we arrive at freedom'. Freedom is made objective and observable in a work of art. As such beauty restores unity between man and nature and man with man. Aesthetics therefore has a role in teaching man the nature of the moral life. This comes close to acknowledging that true beauty is salvation and that art can be thus salvific. We come now to two philosophers who in opposition and agreement carried the debate forward.

Schelling and Hegel: Art, Intuition and the Absolute

We have seen that Kant argued that beauty and the beautiful evokes a 'disinterested' sense of pleasure in us. He held that this pleasure can be 'negative' when we realise that we have reached the limit of our under-standing and are confronted by the limitless sublime, but at least this confrontation convinces us that the experience of beauty is no *mere* sensuous or hedonistic and transient experience.

But if the experience of the sublime, the beautiful, is more than mere sensuousness then what is this 'more'? We might say that the experience of beauty is a visceral experience, that is, that when we are confronted with the truly beautiful we have what we crudely call a gut feeling that the beautiful or sublime has opened a door upon some intangible but utterly real truth beyond itself. It has opened a door on ultimate, unconditioned reality.

The German philosophers who followed Kant referred to this ultimate, unconditioned reality as *das Absolute*. F.W.J. Schelling (1775–1854) sought the fundamental unity behind what seem to be the divisions and opposi-tions which appear on all sides in our experience of ourselves and the world: nature and reason, theory and practice, subject and object, con-sciousness and unconsciousness, the real and the ideal, plurality and individuality, finitude and infinity. For Schelling the common basis for everything, the neutral 'identity' (as he called it) of everything, is the Absolute. He speaks of this Absolute variously as 'God' and 'the infinite'. In Schelling's earlier work the full revelation of the Absolute is to be found in a work of art. Art is the organ of the Absolute because art can reveal what conceptual analysis—philosophy—cannot reveal. In an illuminating phrase he said that the 'potence of art' lay in its ability to present the Absolute 'in a reflex or reflected image'. Very many people today feel this to be true. However, in the years after Schelling the development of modern empirical science, and the positivist philosophical movements to which the new science gave rise, seemed to call into question all claims to truth that were not based on hard facts. The views of philosophers such as Schelling were dismissed as mere romanticism and 'mystical hyperbole', as Andrew Bowie puts it. Indeed, David Hume (1711–76), the great Scottish philosopher, had maintained, a generation before Schelling, that judgments about beauty were based not on fact but on 'sentiment' and 'sentiment has a reference to nothing beyond itself'. Beauty, for Hume, is not an attribute that something possesses. It exists only in the mind of the person making a judgment about that thing—and judgments vary from person to person. A generation after Schelling F.W. Nietzsche (1844–1900) also rooted his aesthetics in the everyday world. For him good art is art which sustains or 'promotes' life. Bad art is art which denies or 'hinders' life. Both Hume and Nietzsche had complex, sophisticated, and not always consistent philosophies of art, but both grounded their arguments in the real world of the everyday. They had no time for mere metaphysical speculations—the search for the supposed ultimate truth behind the real world, the Real behind the real.

Yet the feeling, perhaps even the conviction, that art is an arbiter of truth, that it 'reflects the Absolute', has survived the criticisms of scientific materialism and philosophical positivism. Art, like God, has survived claims that it is dead, and it has done so because it seems to many of us to point us towards ultimate truth.

So why did Schelling choose art as the key to truth? Given that we are aware of contrasts, contradictions and divisions in our experience of ourselves and the world, and given too that we seek to make some sense of these contradictions and divisions, where can we look for that unity or, as Schelling put it, the 'identity' we crave? For Schelling this unity or identity is to be found in the Absolute. But the Absolute cannot be the product of our reason, because our reason lies on one side of any number of contrasts and divisions. Our reason, we may say, takes sides. So, if our knowledge of the Absolute does not come from our reason, from whence does it come? Schelling here prophetically anticipated Freud. Schelling believed that we can never understand what drives us unconsciously if we rely solely on our conscious thoughts, perceptions and reasoning. Our *self*-consciousness arises from our *un*-consciousness. But how do these unconscious motives and drives show themselves to our consciousness? They do so, said Schelling, in works of art. The artist works consciously. He plans and executes his work with precision and care. What distinguishes the work of the artist from the work of the (often equally skilled) craftsman or architect is that a work of art *possesses something more* than, say, a table or a building. This something more is that which unifies our experience, unites our conscious and our unconscious selves and reveals the Absolute. Now of course a table and a building may do the same thing. If they do then they are more than merely works of craftsmanship and design, they are works of art. A work of art can therefore be defined as that which reveals the common ground upon which every element of our experience stands, individual and corporate, conscious and ordered, unconscious and chaotic, subject and object.

Though Schelling later came to believe that knowledge of God is to be sought not in art but in the history of religions he remained convinced that the knowledge that the arts provide for us transcends in significance and depth the knowledge of analysis and reason. Philosophy, for Schelling, has to come to terms with art—and with religion too.

But what precisely is this Absolute which is the unifying ground which everything shares? It is one thing to assert that the Absolute exists (in some sense) but unless we can say what the Absolute is the assertion of its existence is meaningless. Hegel famously said of Schelling's Absolute that it is 'the night in which all cows are black'.

G.W.F. Hegel (1770–1831) is one of the most influential, and one of the most impenetrable, figures in Western philosophy. Though he stood in the same philosophical tradition as Kant in that he gave primacy to reason Hegel was a fierce critic of his great German predecessor. Hegel thought Kant too abstract. Kant's philosophy, especially his moral philosophy, was too remote from life, too empty of content.

We must restrict ourselves to Hegel's philosophy of art. He believed in God but, for Hegel, the Absolute is God from whom all mystical and theological and anthropomorphic assumptions have been removed. The Absolute is the God of the idealist philosophers. His response to Schelling went like this: We cannot claim that the Absolute exists unless it manifests itself in the everyday world *and* unless we also know what the relationship is between the Absolute and the everyday world. We can only claim that the Absolute exists if we realise that it is (a) what it is in itself, (b) what it is in its expression or manifestation, and (c) what the relationship is between the two. Put this way, the Absolute depends on its manifestations in the world just as much as they depend on it. The Absolute depends too on us understanding that the everyday world *is* its manifestation, for if we did not know this we would have no knowledge of the Absolute, and indeed would not know whether it exists or not! That, put very simplistically, is also Hegel's criticism of Kant. Kant's God is totally remote from the world. However transcendent such a God is the very notion of transcendence is a rational construct. So Hegel began not with the notion of transcendence but with the course of world history. That history shows clear evidence of development or progress. Because it does so, it follows that history has meaning, and if history has meaning and purpose so do we. The issue then becomes this: Are we to be controlled by the forces which shape history or can we control them? Are we free or are we not, and wherein does our freedom lie? To develop this further would take us away from art and aesthetics, but that discussion does indicate the major differences between Kant, Hegel and Schelling.

Against that background we come now to Hegel's philosophy of art and to his aesthetics. As we have just noted Hegel concludes, against Schelling (and Kant), that the Absolute does not lie outside the everyday (or phenomenal) world but is present in it as the system of thought which gives it purpose and by which it understands itself (or rather as we, as part of the natural world, understand it). Hegel frequently speaks of this Absolute as *Geist*, 'spirit'. *Geist* is that which is present in the natural world as its unifying principle of thought or rationality.

Having introduced *Geist* let us pause to take stock. As we have seen, Hegel's great predecessor, Kant, had taught that our confrontation with the beautiful promotes in us what he called 'disinterested pleasure'. It does so by engaging with our imagination. The beautiful is beyond rational analysis. It is 'purposeful purposelessness' in that it is not directed to a practical end. The artist is merely instrumental in a purposiveness which originates outside himself. He brings to our awareness a beauty which directs us to the sublime—a sublime transcendence beyond our experience of the world. The world is not beautiful in itself and we are bound to it as creatures of nature, yet although we are bound to the world we intuit a sublimity—a transcendent beauty—beyond the world of phenomena and appearance. For Schelling, beauty was a manifestation of God as the Absolute, and therefore the artist is a mediator between mind and nature. Thus Kant's German successors had begun to allow a much greater place for art in their philosophy than Kant had allowed. For Kant, the artist reflected nature. For Schelling the artist was effectively a mediator between God and man, because the beauty of nature was not to be compared to the beauty of art. Art pointed beyond nature in reconciling nature and reason.

Now Hegel held that the Absolute or *Geist* is embedded in nature. It is nature's understanding of itself. It is *Geist* which tells us what beauty is by compelling us to compare (unfavourably) the beauty of nature with the beauty of the manifestations of *Geist* or 'Absolute Spirit'. Art is a manifestation of *Geist*. So for Hegel art is instrumental in realising, and therefore revealing, the Absolute and the everyday world's relationship to it. Art's contribution is that it reveals this relationship in *sensuous* ways such that we intuit (his word) the whole from the parts. Art enables us to see things as a whole. Art, we might say now, helps us to see the big picture. Hegel was later to reject this notion of *immediate* intuition through our senses in favour of a more conceptual, considered, logical cognition. Yet he seems never entirely to have deserted the view that sensual, visceral experience is not fully reducible to conceptual analysis. Sensory intuition is the contribution of art and the artist to our awareness of the Absolute *Geist*. However, for Hegel art's sensuousness makes it inferior to the contributions of religion and philosophy. As Michael Inwood summarises it, philosophy can comprehend art, but art cannot comprehend philosophy.[11] Hegel does not therefore allow to art the place that Schelling allows. For Hegel, art's sensuous intuition is not the equal of worship, the unique contribution of religion, and neither can it match in importance conceptual analysis, the contribution of philosophy.

So how would Kant, Schelling and Hegel have answered our question: Do art and religion reveal their origin in the same God? Do they stand upon the same ground? Despite their profound differences each would probably have answered with a heavily qualified 'Yes'. But who or what is their God? Kant believed in God as the Highest Good, the guarantee of law and 'the postulate of pure practical reason'. Schelling's God is absolute reason, the 'indifference of nature and spirit, of object and subject', Hegel's God is Absolute Spirit, the purpose of the world and expressed in its history but requiring human reason to come to consciousness of itself. Through reason humanity is aware of God and, paradoxically, has become like God.

These Gods seem far from the God of the Bible. As Hegel's monumental philosophy was achieving its pre-eminent place, further north, in Denmark, his most bitter critic had already launched his onslaught. For this man God was either the God and Father of Jesus Christ or he did not exist. He is a God revealed by faith and not deduced by reason.

Søren Kierkegaard: The Seduction of Aesthetics

Søren Kierkegaard (1813–55) was a Danish philosopher, theologian and social critic whose sustained attack on the German idealist philosophical tradition represented in particular by Hegel had a profound influence on twentieth-century thought. His writing attacks not only Hegel's position but the whole edifice of rationalism. For Kierkegaard the philosophy of reason had negated the individual. While Hegel stressed the importance of historical development and of man's place within that development against Kant's transcendentalism, ordinary men and women with individual perceptions and feelings and with decisions to take about the course of their own existence had no place in Hegel's scheme at all. For Hegel personal choices were but a sharing in a general rational framework of understanding, but for Kierkegaard what is personally and existentially important for *me* is all that really matters. The fundamental truths, the life and death truths, that I grasp and in the light of which I make the decisions that shape my life are not truths that I arrive at by somehow sharing in a universal rational process. These individual decisions and these life-enhancing truths are beyond the reach of reason. They are outside its limits. They are truths grasped intuitively and by faith. For Kierkegaard reason has been crucified

---

11. Michael Inwood, *A Hegel Dictionary* (Oxford: Basil Blackwell, 1992), p. 43. I am indebted for much of the foregoing to Inwood's excellent summary.

in faith. However, it is not that they are grasped irrationally. Faith, for Kierkegaard, is not non-sense. Rather it is a journey through life, deliberately undertaken but undertaken in anxiety, towards an as yet undisclosed end. It is also a journey taken alone. It is a 'walk without meeting one single traveller', Kierkegaard wrote. For Kierkegaard Abraham is the great exemplar of faith. He is a 'knight of faith'. He sets out, in faith, not knowing what his journey will hold or where it will end. He is ready to sacrifice his son Isaac in defiance of all ethical norms but in obedience to God. Such an act is beyond reason yet Abraham's call is to suspend rational judgment, to rise above the cruel absurdity of what he was commanded to do in, as Kierkegaard puts it, 'a teleological suspension of the ethical'. Abraham is called to trust God and to obey.

In that very cursory and outline sketch we have encountered three key concepts in Kierkegaard's thought: existential decision and anxiety, subjective truth, and faith. Existential *decisions* are the crucial life-changing decisions that I must take for myself, alone and thus inevitably in anxiety. They are my decisions, subjective and personal decisions, decisions which raise me above the detached objectivity of Hegel's universal reason and the grey conformity of those who, as we would say, go with the crowd.

The fundamental *truths* that I come to are truths *for me*. They are subjective not in the sense that they are mere casual opinions, of no more value that the opinions of anyone else, but in the sense that they are truths in the light of which I lead *my* life and which determine its end. In the end I must be true to myself, no matter how much the conventional wisdom of the world or the dogmas and ethical criteria of the Church may deny that the truth for me is *the* truth.

Lived thus, life must be and can only be a life of *faith*. It must be a life lived in abandoned faith to God and without benefit of the supposed guarantees provided by reason or imposed by dogma. Does God exist objectively? If I say 'Yes' either because I have become convinced that he does on the ground of reason or because I rely upon the authority of the Church which tells me he exists then I do not have faith. As Kierkegaard said, precisely because I cannot grasp God objectively I must believe! Faith, he wrote, is 'holding fast to the objective uncertainty' of God's existence. It is, to use Kierkegaard's own metaphor, swimming out of sight of land with seventy thousand fathoms below!

Put very simply these are the three fundamental concepts for which Kierkegaard is most widely known. They underpin Kierkegaard's analysis of the three 'stages' (his word) or spheres of human life and experience. These are the *aesthetic stage,* the *ethical stage* and the *religious stage.* Kierkegaard employs the word 'stage' to imply that one can remain in one or other of the aesthetic and ethical stages all one's life, or can move from them to the higher religious stage.

The person living in the *aesthetic stage* is one who lives his life either in the enjoyment of intellectual ideas or in the pursuit of sensuous pleasure, that is, he directs his life to the achieving of temporal and transient ends. These goals may not by any means be purely hedonistic or frivolous. The pleasures a man seeks, even sensuous pleasures, may be bound up with very serious matters. Take Caravaggio's *The Supper at Emmaus.* The picture itself, its composition, its subtle tonal contrasts and its foreshortened perspective and the application of the paint delights my eye before I notice the scallop shell worn by one of the disciples and realise that it marks him out as a pilgrim or that the grapes in the foreground may have a eucharistic significance—and well before I learn from the catalogue that the composition of the painting may derive from Venetian precedents and that the beardless Christ appears in sixteenth-century Milanese painting. The painting *as a painting and quite independently of its subject* has, for me, a tremendous physical, sensuous, impact. I am drawn back to it time and again. Learning something of the place of Caravaggio's masterpiece in the history of art affords me intellectual pleasure, and knowing the picture deepens my theological (indeed religious) appreciation of Lk. 24.13-32. These sensuous and intellectual pleasures are very far from sinful. Yet, Kierkegaard warns us, they are pleasures nevertheless and as such they never last. They are inevitably transient and their failure truly to give a man life will lead him to *despair* (another key concept for Kierkegaard). So, Kierkegaard warns,

> To believe that art helps us to enter into reality is just as misguided as to believe that the more artistically perfect a sermon, the better it is able to transform life. Ah no: the more aesthetic is its effect, away from the existential.[12]

Nevertheless, and here Kierkegaard's thought is complex and often seems self-contradictory, the man living in the aesthetic stage is not necessarily pursuing pleasure for pleasure's sake, for this man may be seeking meaning for his life. However, he is seeking it in this temporal world and through the pursuit of temporal and transient goals, however worthy. The temporal and the transient are not real. Thus, under one of his many pseudonyms Kierkegaard wrote of works of the imagination—art, drama and poetry—that 'they provide only an imperfect reconciliation with life...when you fix your eye upon poetry and art you are not looking at actuality'.[13]

In the *ethical stage* a man commits himself not to the pursuit of intellectual or sensuous pleasure but to ethical goals. This man tries to live his life in terms of moral duty, of achieving conformity to ethical codes or

---

12. Søren Kierkegaard, *The Last Years: Journals 1853–1855* (London: Collins, 1968), p. 180.

13. Quoted in Ann Loades' note on Kierkegaard in David Cooper (ed.), *A Companion to Aesthetics* (Oxford: Basil Blackwell, 1995), p. 254.

expectations. Of course, as Kierkegaard points out powerfully, trying to meet these goals may merely mean that we live life conforming to the expectations of our neighbours or of the Church or of the State, but so to conform is not obedience to God. It may lead us to follow a morally upright life but it is a life lived in obedience to what Paul called 'the works of law', an ethical code imposed upon us by temporal authority and not freely chosen by us in obedience to God.

For Kierkegaard those who live their lives in either the aesthetic stage or the ethical stage come to despair, because they have tried to found their lives on a finite and crumbling foundation. Only when this point is reached, Kierkegaard says, does a man realise that he must found his life on God and on God alone. This involves, Kierkegaard says in a famous phrase, 'acting absolutely towards absolute ends and relatively towards relative ends'.

That, in broad outline, is the main thrust of Kierkegaard's thought. One would think from this that, since art belongs to the aesthetic sphere, Kierkegaard would have little time for art, or, for that matter, little time for the duties of the moral life. But Kierkegaard is a very complex and confusing writer. For one thing he was a master of irony and therefore of communicating indirectly. For another he wrote under a number of pseudonyms or adopted the role of a supposed editor working with recently discovered papers. This ruse enabled Kierkegaard to present to his readers a variety of points of view. The difficulty this causes in interpreting Kierkegaard is well illustrated by George Pattison in his introduction to *Kierkegaard on Art and Communication*. The essays in this volume were originally presented at a conference in 1990 the title of which was 'Kierkegaard: The Christian in Love with Aesthetics'. Pattison says

> 'The Christian'—but what kind of Christian was this man who attacked the whole edifice of Christian doctrine and Church practice as understood in his time and place? '...in Love'—but what kind of love was the love of this man who wrote so convincingly of love's solitudes and sufferings as he did of its duties and joys, for whom love (perhaps tragically) could in no way imply the necessary fulfilment of its own longing? '...with Aesthetics'—but what kind of aesthetic values and awareness are in play when the term 'aesthetic' itself can come to connote humanity's alienation from God?[14]

A brief sketch of Kierkegaard's thought would lead one to suppose that rigid boundaries separated the three stages of life, that God is utterly remote from the sensuously pleasurable or from mere codes of moral rectitude. But this is not the whole story. Although Kierkegaard, under one of his pseudonyms, can say that the arts are not 'actuality', he loved poetry and the theatre and wrote extensively about these works of the imagination as

---

14. George Pattison (ed.), *Kierkegaard on Art and Communication* (Basingstoke: Macmillan, 1992), p. xiii.

giving a genuine insight into the human condition before God. So, did Kierkegaard believe that art can direct us to God? Clearly not in one very important sense. If, in the aesthetic stage, a man is concerned only to pursue the finite goal of pleasure then he is not in pursuit of God. However, since for Kierkegaard, writing under one of his pseudonyms in *The Sickness unto Death*, can say that 'since everything is possible for God, then God is this—that everything is possible' then God can employ any means he chooses to communicate 'his passion to love and be loved' as Kierkegaard says. For the wholly other, absolutely different God everything is possible. Now, of course, this 'communication' through art or otherwise, is for Kierkegaard most decidedly not Hegel's *Geist* embedded in the world as its system of self-understanding, or Schelling's Absolute. This is the God and Father of our Lord Jesus Christ being, as Kierkegaard himself says in a remarkable passage 'acting like a poet'.[15] As a poet allows his created work, the poem, to express feelings or opinions that are not necessarily his own, so God relates to his creation similarly. Creation, for Kierkegaard, is a work of art by God. This at least implies that art provides some insight into the human condition and therefore of the ways of God with us. Could it be otherwise? The very language of religion, Kierkegaard acknowledges, even the language of scripture, is metaphorical. It is the language of poetry.[16] We know God, and can only know him in one profoundly important respect, through art! Does this mean that to be truly religious one must be aesthetic, and to be truly aesthetic one must be religious? Art seems here to be redefined in terms of incarnation.

Friedrich Schleiermacher: A Taste for the Infinite

This question, though not in these terms, engaged a remarkable group of young writers, poets, artists and philosophers who met in the University of Jena throughout the 1770s. It included J.W. Goethe, the poet, dramatist and novelist. This extraordinary man is widely regarded as the founder of modern German literature. He was deeply influenced by Shakespeare to whose works he had been introduced by his friend J.G. Herder, the poet, philosopher, critic and collector of folk songs and another member of the Jena group. Another member was Friedrich Schiller, dramatist, poet and historian whose *On the Aesthetic Education of Man* written in 1794–95 was to have a seminal influence, not least on Karl Barth. Another was August Schlegel, poet and critic and translator of Shakespeare, and his younger brother Friedrich, a pioneer of the comparative study of religion and who, with August and others in the group, was a founder of the Romantic

15. Quoted in Sylvia Walsh in 'Kierkegaard: Poet of the Religious', in Pattison (ed.), *Kierkegaard on Art*, pp. 1-22 (14-15).
16. See Brayton Polka, 'Aesthetics and Religion...', in Pattison (ed.), *Kierkegaard on Art*, pp. 23-54 (39-40).

movement in literature, music and the arts. Then there was Johann Tieck the poet and collector of folk stories, and Novalis (the pen name of Friedrich von Hardenburg) the Romantic[17] poet for whom 'poetry heals the wounds inflicted by reason', and J.G. Fichte the idealist philosopher who greatly influenced two of the group whom we have already met—F.W.J. Schelling, and the man destined to be the most important Western philosopher of the nineteenth century, G.W.F. Hegel. Another in the group was the lyric poet Friedrich Holderlin, and another was a young Protestant theologian who, profoundly influenced by his extraordinary friends, was to re-cast Christian theology to meet the challenges to it of a new age. His name was Friedrich Schleiermacher (1768–1834).

In 1799 Schleiermacher published his essay *On Religion: Speeches to the Cultured among its Despisers*. As the title suggests it is essentially a work of apologetics, that is its purpose is to offer, in defence of Christianity, an argument for it which would meet the criticisms of its contemporary opponents. Schleiermacher did this by re-casting Christianity by, so far as he could, avoiding the traditional style and language of orthodox Christian dogma. He argued that the way that religion apprehends truth is not the way of rational knowledge, which is the way of science, nor of the doing of good, the way of morality. Of course, knowing and doing have their rightful place in religion but they are not what Schleiermacher called 'the essence of religion'. This is 'the sensibility and taste for the infinite'. In contrast to reason's 'knowing' (represented by Hegel) and the morality's 'doing' (represented by J.G. Fichte who argued that religion consists in 'joyously doing right') the way that religion apprehends truth is by 'feeling' or, as he came later to define it, 'immediate self-consciousness'. Note that by 'feeling' Schleiermacher did not mean mere transient subjective emotions as the later definition makes clear.

In *The Christian Faith* in 1821 Schleiermacher set out a comprehensive re-structuring of Christian theology based upon his understanding of religion's true essence. He argued that our 'immediate self-consciousness' is our 'consciousness of being absolutely dependent'. Whereas in *On Religion* Schleiermacher had spoken of the essence of religion as 'the sensibility and taste for the infinite' he now identifies this as the 'sense' or 'feeling' that we are aware of God. The God of the Christian faith in which 'everything is related to the redemption accomplished by Jesus of Nazareth' in *The Christian Faith* and whom we know 'immediately' through 'feeling', is 'the infinite' in *On Religion* known through our 'sensibility' and 'taste'. In

17. Novalis is credited with inventing the words *Romantik and Romantiker* during these years, though the term 'romantic' had been in use since the seventeenth century. Originally the term was applied to mediaeval romances but it came to be used to refer to styles in contemporary literature, music and the visual arts that emphasised the personal feelings or emotions, imagination and creative originality of the individual artist. 'To thyself be true' was the watchword of the Romantics.

other words, as Mark C. Taylor says, Schleiermacher, in 'reflecting the interests and preoccupations of his day...rereads religious faith in terms of artistic awareness' he 'approaches religion in terms of art'.[18] It is worth noting that two years before publishing *The Christian Faith* Schleiermacher had lectured on aesthetics at the University of Berlin. His theology and his aesthetics go hand in hand.

What is this 'feeling' or 'immediate self-consciousness' that we are 'absolutely dependent' upon God and which makes this so unique a way of apprehending truth? It is a sensation of 'primal oneness' as Mark C. Taylor puts it.[19] In *On Religion* Schleiermacher describes this as 'the first mysterious moment that occurs in every sensory perception, before intuition and feeling have separated, where sense and its objects have, as it were, flowed into one another and become one'. For Schleiermacher this is *the* uniquely religious experience.[20] We are 'immediately conscious' of this fundamental unity of ourselves with the object of our contemplation. That is to say, it is a direct awareness (of God) which is not mediated through anything outside ourselves. To say that this sense of primal oneness is 'conscious' is a paradox as Schleiermacher seems himself to have realised, for once we *are* conscious of it we lose it as our reason and critical faculties take control. As Ehrenzweig was to point out (from a position well outside conventional religion) we fragment the original 'undifferentiated unfocused vision inherent in any creative search' and force a distinction between 'surface and depth sensibilities, between intellect and intuition'.[21]

If we follow Schleiermacher, this sense of oneness with, say, a work of art, and through it with all that is finite and thus with the infinite, is what religious awareness is. As soon as this sense of primal oneness is recognised and identified by reason it is lost. As Taylor says, interpreting Schleiermacher, 'since religious awareness slips away in the very effort to grasp it, the unity or identity it portends can only be "present" as "absent"'.[22]

In words reminiscent of the Zen masters Schleiermacher describes religious awareness in terms of seeing the world in the fragment and the fragment as representative and interpretative of the whole for 'to accept everything individual as a part of the whole and everything limited as a representation of the infinite is religion'. This *essential* wholeness is displayed in, he says, 'the harmony of the universe, the wondrous and great unity in its eternal work of art'.

18. Taylor, *Disfiguring*, p. 21.
19. I am indebted to Taylor's *Disfiguring* for what follows, including the quotations from Schleiermacher.
20. As we will see later this is the experience that Anton Ehrenzweig was to interpret psychologically 170 years later.
21. Anton Ehrenzweig, *The Hidden Order of Art: A Study in the Psychology of Artistic Imagination* (London: Weidenfeld, 1993 [1st edn Berkeley: University of California Press, 1967]), pp. 41, 64.
22. Taylor, *Disfiguring*, p. 22.

This 'feeling' of a primal unity in diversity is for Schleiermacher what for Schelling is the Absolute. For both, art and religion are therefore indivisible or certainly inseparable. For Schleiermacher the imagination in its consciousness of absolute dependence can and does know the infinite, the absolute, as, as it were, the gift of the infinite. For him this is the God and Father of Jesus Christ. Art, like everything else in the created order, is thus potentially salvific. In a religion which proclaims the incarnation of a God of redemptive love how can it be otherwise?

Friedrich Nietzsche: The Death of God and the Evening Twilight of Art

The romanticism that inspired the Jena group is long dead, or at the very least it fails to excite contemporary philosophers and theologians. In general the new science which emerged in the years following Schleiermacher, with its accompanying philosophies and psychologies, regarded metaphysical and romantic speculations as no more than sentimental non-sense. For Nietzsche (1844–1900), *par excellence* the philosopher of the new age, God was long dead. Under the influence of Schopenhauer he could, in his earlier work *The Birth of Tragedy* (1872), speak of art's (romantic) portrayal of the tragic as offering us 'metaphysical comfort' such that 'we are, for a brief moment, the primordial being itself ', but in *Human, All Too Human* (1876) he dismisses the idea of a metaphysical world of which the world of nature is a mere appearance. All we have is a material world. Following Schopenhauer this world, for Nietzsche, is a place of meaningless terror and suffering without hope of redemption. Traditional religion, conventional morality and metaphysical speculation have nothing to say to this world, and indeed have contributed to its miseries. The material and the actual is all that exists. Hope lies solely in managing and manipulating this material reality for the benefit of humankind. Art, like religion, is useless unless it serves this purpose and does not seduce us into attempting to escape this reality. As God is long dead, now even art, Nietzsche says, is in its 'evening twilight'. Yet even in this most uncompromisingly materialist of his books, Nietzsche cannot fully escape art's seductiveness:

> How strong the metaphysical need is, and how hard nature makes it to bid it a final farewell, can be seen from the fact that even when the free spirit has divested himself of everything metaphysical the highest effects of art can easily set the metaphysical strings, which have long been silent or indeed snapped apart, vibrating in sympathy... If he becomes aware of being in this condition he feels a profound stab in the heart and sighs for the man who will lead him back to his lost love, whether she be called religion or metaphysics. It is in such moments that his intellectual probity is put to the test.[23]

23. Friedrich Nietzsche, *Human, All Too Human* (Leipzig: E.W. Fritzsch, 2nd edn, 1886), p. 153, cited in Philip Novak, *The Vision of Nietzsche* (Shaftesbury: Element Books, 1996), p. 56.

In *The Gay Science* (1882) Nietzsche changes course again. Art has it place in helping us to stand back from the human situation so that we may the better bear it. Like the Greeks we should not try to understand too much of the awfulness of life but to 'stay courageously at the surface' and to be 'superficial—*out of profundity*'.[24]

This materialist view, though subsequently not always so powerfully and uncompromisingly expressed, marked a profound departure not only from idealism but even from the empiricism of David Hume and has had a profound influence on twentieth-century thought, not least in the arts. We live in a very different world from that in which Immanuel Kant lived. Yet art and religion survive and flourish in rich diversity. How they relate to each in a postmodern world is as exciting and perplexing as ever it was.

Having subjected the questions with which we began to the scrutiny of the fathers of modern philosophy and the influential theologians of the twentieth century no final and definitive answers have emerged. Do art and religion stand upon the same fundamental ground? If they do what must Christianity learn from the arts? But there is a prior consideration. The answers to those questions will depend on what kind of Christianity we profess. R.A.D. Grant ends a perceptive summary of the relationship of art and religion by asking whether 'we see religion primarily as a "world-open" receptivity to the transcendent, or as a "world-closed" claim finally to have captured it in doctrine. If the first, how is religion to be distinguished from art, or from its supposed effects.'[25] He might have added, 'If the second, then how is religion to be distinguished from superstition or its actual effects'.

There may be a third way. Some key concepts have featured in this account so far. They have to do with the infinite, with transcendence, with the nature of moral goodness, with embodiment of meaning and with primal unity or wholeness. I want now to introduce another. This is the idea of witness. What a faithful witness does is courageously and independently to assert a truth that has been observed. In this sense art witnesses to religion's sense of the *transcendent* and *the good.* In Christianity we might speak of this as the sense of the otherness of a righteous God for which worship is the response. For its part religion witnesses to art's genius in *embodying meaning,* and to its sense of the *unity* or *wholeness* of all things. In Christianity we might speak of this as incarnation and salvation. Christianity witnesses to the truly spiritual in art while art witnesses to the transcendent in religion.

Of course, in such a statement as that all depends upon what we regard as religion. We might speak, for example of 'true religion' as over against superstition or indoctrination, and of art as 'art proper', that is, art with no

24. Quotations from Julian Young's note on Nietzsche in Cooper (ed.), *A Companion to Aesthetics*, pp. 303-307.
25. Cooper (ed.), *A Companion to Aesthetics*, p. 364.

end or purpose beyond itself, as contrasted with 'magical art' or manipulation. But even that proviso begs a host of questions. By no means all men and women who take religion very seriously would agree on what 'true religion' is, and those with a genuine commitment to the arts would disagree fundamentally on what constitutes 'art proper'.

From a theological point of view there is another crucial factor to be taken into account. The relationship between art and religion is not only a matter of, say, recognising that art is incarnational or salvific. The principles or presuppositions which a Christian believer and a lover of art bring to a shared experience will determine the way each interprets that experience. In other words the *hermeneutical* question is prior to everything else.

There is no space here to develop these issues fully. What will be attempted in Part II is to follow some paths through Hugh Kenner's 'whispering forest of all traditional poetries' and see where they lead as theologian and lover of art explore together the border country between art and religion, that beautiful but dangerous no-man's land patrolled by the border police from both sides!

Part II

Chapter 5

As the Bird Sings

Theologians need to do theology impressionistically.[1]

An Eye on the World

In Paris, on 15 April 1874, a group of thirty-nine young artists calling themselves the 'Société anonyme des artistes, peintres, sculpteurs, graveurs
etc.' exhibited their work in the former shop of the photographer Nadar on
the corner of the Boulevard des Capucines and the Rue Dannou. The exhibition ran for four weeks. These young men (and at least one woman, Berthe
Morisot) had found no acceptance in the established Salon, controlled by
the Academie des Beaux-Arts and had rejected the prospect of showing
their work with the also-rans at the Salon des Refuses. So they arranged
their own exhibition. It was hung by one of their number, Auguste Renoir.
The exhibition was a critical and a financial failure, and the society dis-
banded, but it changed the way we look at the world.

Of the 165 paintings in the exhibition, number 98 was a revolutionary
work by Claude Monet (1840–1926), *Impression: Sunrise*, painted in 1872
and now in the Musee Marmottan. It is a small picture, just under 19 inches
by 24 inches.[2] In 1889 Maurice Guillemot recounted a conversation with
Monet in which the artist said that

> a landscape is only an impression, instantaneous, hence the label they've
> given us—all because of me for that matter: I'd submitted something
> done out of my window at Le Havre, sunlight in the mist with a few
> masts in the foreground jutting up from the ships below. They wanted a
> title for the catalogue; it couldn't really pass as a view of Le Havre, so I
> answered: 'Put down "Impression"'. Out of that they got impressionism,
> and the jokes proliferated.[3]

1. This chapter is based on my article 'As the Bird Sings', in *Modern Believing* NS
36.2 (1995), pp. 12-18.
2. The canvases of the *plein air* painters were invariably small. They worked in
the open air in sometimes windy locations where a large canvas would have acted like
a sail, or in small rooms (as Monet did when painting *Impression: Sunrise* and his
Rouen Cathedral series) where space was very limited.
3. Maurice Guillemot, 'Claude Monet', *La Revue Illustrée* (15 March 1898), reproduced in Charles F. Stuckey (ed.), *Monet: A Retrospective* (New York: Hugh Lauter
Levin Associates, 1985), pp. 195-201 (196).

It was the term applied, originally well intentioned but later somewhat derisively, to what was to be recognised as the most important movement in
nineteenth-century art. This picture is a representation of the play of light
on water. As we look at it we gaze straight into the sun as it rises in the
morning. Monet employed a rapid technique giving a flecked, dappled effect.
In so doing he attempted to render in paint on canvas what his eye saw.
Monet had to work quickly for the light changed rapidly as the sun rose. He
later carried with him several canvases on the same subject so that he
could switch from one to the other as the light changed.

So was Impressionism born. Although it was the first modern movement
in art, to speak of it as a movement is incorrect. Attempts to define Impressionism in terms of its aesthetic principles have largely failed. It has been
said that it was 'a form of sensualism' and that its practitioners attempted
'to achieve ever greater naturalism, by exact analysis of tone and colour'.[4]
The Impressionists were indeed united in this aim but this is far too superficial a definition. Although they were deeply interested in the science of
colour[5] they related to nature in an almost semi-religious sense, as Phoebe
Pool notes, sometimes implying, she says, that there was 'some link or
interplay between the outside world and the soul of man'.[6] Yet unlike many
of their predecessors and successors the Impressionists enunciated no
principles or aesthetic theories, propounded no dogmas and produced no
manifestos. Renoir, for one, rejected aesthetic theories. 'Don't ask me
whether painting ought to be subjective or objective', he said, 'I don't give
a damn', and, 'You construct a theory—and nature knocks it down'.[7] Renoir's
only aesthetic theory, Phoebe Pool says, 'was a mock defence of the irregular in art—a theory of no theory at all'.[8] In common with many thinkers of
their time in France the Impressionists distrusted general philosophical
speculations. Pool cites Flaubert, Sainte-Beuve and the Goncourts. She
could have added Mallarmé who, in an article in 1876 on the Impressionists
and Manet, wrote this on Manet's approach to painting:

> Manet, when he casts away the cares of art and chats with a friend
> between the lights in his studio, expresses himself with brilliancy. Then it
> is that he tells him what he means by Painting; what new destinies are
> yet in store for it; what it is, and how that it is from an irrepressible

4.   P. and L. Murray, *A Dictionary of Art and Artists* (London: Penguin Books,
1972), p. 216.
5.   There is clear evidence that the Impressionists, notably Monet and Pissarro
and later Seurat, knew of the researches, a generation earlier, of the French chemist
Michel-Eugène Chevreul into colour harmonies and that this led them, for example, to
render shadows in the colour complementary (i.e. opposite in the colour circle) to that
of the object casting the shadow (see Phoebe Pool, *Impressionism* [London: Thames
& Hudson, 1967], pp. 14-15, 243-44).
6.   Pool, *Impressionism*, p. 10.
7.   Pool, *Impressionism*, p. 52.
8.   Pool, *Impressionism*.

instinct that he paints, and that he paints as he does. Each time he begins a picture, says he, he plunges headlong into it, and feels like a man who knows that his surest plan to learn to swim safely, is, dangerous as it may seem, to throw himself into the water. One of his habitual aphorisms then is that no one should paint a landscape and a figure by the same process, with the same knowledge, or in the same fashion; nor, what is more, even two landscapes or two figures. Each work should be a new creation of the mind. The hand, it is true, will conserve some of its acquired secrets of manipulation, but the eye should forget all else that it has seen, and learn anew from the lesson before it. It should abstract itself from memory, seeing only that which it looks upon, and then for the first time; and the hand should become an impersonal abstraction guided only by the will, oblivious of all previous cunning.[9]

Manet denied that he was an Impressionist, but he was certainly the father of Impressionism. His conviction was that no painter should be controlled by a preconceived aesthetic theory. If the Impressionists had a principle, perhaps that was it, reacting as they did against the classicist, romanticist and realist ideals that preceded them in the development of European art in the nineteenth century. They also shared a conviction that they should work in the actual presence of the subject be it in the open air or not.

Perhaps because they had no overarching, determining aesthetic the major exponents of Impressionism, with the exception of Alfred Sisley, developed their style throughout their lives. By the mid-1880s, as George Heard Hamilton notes, 'a movement that had once appeared so coherent no longer expressed the intentions of those responsible for its first presentation in 1874'.[10] So it was that by 1880 Monet was to express his misgivings about impressionism as a movement. Artists who were nowhere near his stature had succumbed to the temptation, as Robert Hughes observes, 'to work up a bag of Impressionist tricks'. By then, Monet, Hughes says, wanted 'to show the deeper transactions between eye and mind'.[11] About 1885 Renoir too was to express profound misgivings about his own ability or desire to sustain the Impressionism of which he had been thus far the simplest and most direct exponent. He told his dealer Ambrose Vollard that at that time 'a break occurred in my work. I had reached the end of Impressionism and had come to the conclusion that I knew neither how to paint or how to draw. In a word I was in a blind alley.'[12] He looked for something more and turned to the old masters for inspiration.

We will come to this subsequent development later. For the moment let us stay with *Impression: Sunrise*. In this painting Monet certainly attempted to convey the impression of light striking the surface of things, but more

---

9. Stéphane Mallarmé, 'The Impressionists and Édouard Manet', *The Art Monthly Review* (London, 30 September 1876), reproduced in full in James H. Rubin, *Manet's Silence and the Poetics of Bouquets* (London: Reaktion Books, 1994), p. 232.

10. Hamilton, *Painting and Sculpture*, p. 21.

11. Robert Hughes, *The Shock of the New* (New York: McGraw–Hill, 1980), p. 118.

12. Quoted in Hamilton, *Painting and Sculpture*, p. 21.

than this he was concerned to bring into the consciousness of the viewer of his painting the emotional power created by what he saw.[13] He was trying to render, he said earlier, in 1868, and was to say again in the 1890s, 'ce que j'eprouve'. Paul Hayes Tucker notes that

> the verb *eprouver* has no real equivalent in English; 'to experience' or 'to feel' is about as close as we can come. However, neither of these conveys the many implications of the French, for *éprouver* suggests experience of a complex kind. It refers not only to participation in or perception of an event and the feelings directly associated with it, but also to a broad range of sensations, *with things revealing themselves slowly so that they become known in their fullest dimension. Thus it refers to a heightened awareness of knowledge and emotion that is stored in the depths of one's unconscious as well as to what one sees and feels in the present.*[14]

Tucker is worth quoting in full for what is to follow. But whatever Monet meant by *éprouver* he succeeded in producing in the sympathetic beholder the impact which he was to have on my youngest daughter on seeing for the first time one of Monet's *Grainstacks* series painted in 1890–91: 'Dad, Dad, you can feel the heat of the sun!' For her it was a revelation of this-worldly transcendence that reached to the depths of her being. It is not surprising that, as we have noted, the greatest artist of this period, Paul Cézanne, was to say of a painting that it was a coloured state of grace,[15] and to ask in exasperation whether art is not a priesthood that 'demands the pure in heart who must belong to it entirely'.[16] In saying this, Cézanne hinted that true religion, that is religion which is not driven by the logic and dogmas of metaphysics and which is free to use myth and image, story and poetry for the art that they are, has the same simple ability to recreate, to embody or incarnate, the essence of truth-filled experience. True religion (or rather, perhaps, a true spirituality), as does true art, brings these things to our true *anamnēsis*—our true re-calling, re-creating, re-living, re-membering. The relationship of religion and art thus understood is intimate. Indeed, who, relying on this experience, dares claim that they are *in essence* distinct? What must be re-discovered in Christian faith and practice is that 'heightened awareness of knowledge that is stored in the depths of one's unconscious as well as to what one sees and feels at the present'.

13. This is the *content* which the *form* of the painting, that is the relation of its masses and the ways in which paint is applied, conveys. The relation of *content* and *form* to the *subject* (ostensible or not) of a painting or sculpture is the key to its 'meaning'.

14. Paul Hayes Tucker, *Monet in the 90s: The Series Paintings* (Boston: Museum of Fine Arts, Boston, in association with Yale University Press, 1989), p. 95 (my italics).

15. Quoted in Milner, *On Not Being Able to Paint*, p. 25.

16. Letter to Ambrose Vollard, 9 January 1903, in Rewald (ed.), *Paul Cézanne*, p. 293.

It would be difficult to find a more comprehensive definition of the meaning of incarnate revelation than that. Revelation is being confronted with what we already know but has been hidden. If we did not know it, how could we know what is being revealed? A religion as profoundly concerned with this world as is Christianity cannot afford to ignore so powerful a statement of its true nature expressed in so non-theological a way. A religion which, as so many of its believers claim, asserts that its substantive claims are 'literally' (that is objectively) true has nothing to offer. Such a religion has at its heart a God who is no more than an object in a universe of objects. Its so-called literal objectivity, its false facticity, destroys the ability of religious discourse so understood to interpret the world and the experiences of men and women through myth, image and symbol—that is *through the art which is the very essence of what it is as a religion and which is the fundamental way in which it communicates its truths.*

But to return to that first Impressionist exhibition in 1874. The majority of the critics, with the whole art establishment of the time in Paris, did not see its paintings as connecting eye and mind in revolutionary ways. The critics were strikingly at odds. Most of them reacted abusively. Among the first was Louis Leroy writing in the satirical magazine *Le Charivari* within four days of the exhibition's opening. Leroy recorded the imaginary reaction of an imaginary painter, Monsieur Vincent, trained in the accepted, realist, Salon style of landscape painting. Faced with Monet's *Boulevard des Capucines* the old man 'laughed diabolically... "Here's an impression if I don't say so myself... Hell and damnation! Are you trying to make a fool of me?"' Confronted with n. 98 in the exhibition, Monet's *Impression: Sunrise,* old 'Papa Vincent' cried '*Impression*—I knew it. I was just saying to myself, if I am impressed, there must be an impression in there...'

Other critics were far more accepting of the radically new approach of these young painters. Jules Castagnary writing in *Le Siècle* on 29 April invented the term which was thereafter to identify the group—a group, he said, united by a consensus 'that...makes them a collective force in our disintegrated age'. He continued:

> If we are to characterize them with one explanatory word, we would have to coin a new term: *impressionists.* They are impressionists in that they render not the landscape but the sensation evoked by the landscape. The very word has entered their language: not *landscape* but *impression*, in the title given in the catalogue for M. Monet's *Sunrise.* From this point of view, they have left reality behind for a realm of *pure idealism.*

A week later Ernest Chesneau in *Paris-Journal* wrote that Monet had sounded 'a clarion call for those with ears to hear, and how it echoes into the future'.[17]

---

17. These quotations are taken from Stuckey (ed.), *Monet: A Retrospective,* pp. 57-59.

Yet as we have seen, even in 1874 Monet was attempting much more than merely to render a superficial and fleeting effect. Art has always been far more than merely a way of recording. He wanted, he said later, 'to paint as the bird sings'. Monet may have been, as he was for Cézanne, no more than an eye on the world, but, as Cézanne remarked of him, 'my God, *what* an eye!'

Leroy was of course not alone in his bitter reaction to these mere 'impressionists'. We have noted already Tolstoy's bitter reaction to the art of his day. He endorsed, and quoted at length, the opinion of 'an amateur of art' written in 1894 recalling a visit the Paris exhibition twenty years earlier. He condemned out of hand the paintings of Camille Pissarro. While acknowledging that Pissarro was 'comparatively the most comprehensible' of the Impressionists, he was 'out of drawing', he was lacking in subject matter, and he painted in improbable colours. Indeed 'the drawing was so indefinite that you were sometimes unable to make out which way an arm or a head was turned'. And then comes the principal criticism: 'The subject was generally, *"effets"—Effet de brouillard, Effet du soir, Soleil couchant.* There were some pictures with figures, but without subjects.'[18] In his scathing attack Tolstoy admits that the reason why he cannot understand and cannot like what he calls 'the new productions of art' may be 'merely that I am still insufficiently developed to understand them'. He does not denounce the new art because it was bad art, for he did not feel qualified to judge whether it was or was not bad,[19] but rather because it is incomprehensible to the masses. If it is intelligible 'only to the very smallest number of the elect, and, eventually, to two, or to one, of our nearest friends, or to oneself alone' then can it be said to be art at all? And this, Tolstoy argued, was what was effectively being said by the modern artists of his day, namely: 'I create and understand myself, and if anyone does not understand me, so much the worse for him'.[20] In saying this Tolstoy had correctly perceived a significant development in modern art expressed most notably by Gustave Moreau (1826–98) when he said that he believed neither in what he saw or touched but rather, 'I believe only in what I do not see and solely in what I feel'.[21] However, Tolstoy was incorrect in supposing that art thus conceived and executed had no significance for anyone other than the artist.

I have chosen the judgment of a contemporary artist of genius, albeit an artist in a different medium, because his opinion is so significant for what is to follow. The new art, he says, appealed only to 'the elect', significantly

18. Tolstoy, *What is Art?*, p. 95.

19. Tolstoy says that 'Because I am accustomed to a certain exclusive art, and can understand it, but am unable to understand another still more exclusive art, I have no right to conclude that my art is the real true art, and that the other one, which I do not understand, is an unreal, a bad art' (*What is Art?*, p. 99).

20. Tolstoy, *What is Art?*, p. 100.

21. Quoted in Hamilton, *Painting and Sculpture*, p. 79.

but perhaps unconsciously employing a religious and biblical word. In our day it is dogmatic religion which appeals only to 'the elect' and is regarded by so many as a matter of personal and esoteric preference alone, while 'the masses' flock to exhibitions of Impressionist art as if they are on pilgrimage!

Subject and Object in Art and Religion

Tolstoy's recognition of the essential subjectivism of the Impressionists, and their contemporaries the Neo-Impressionists and the Symbolists, has been well rehearsed since. Indeed their affirmation of the subjective has been held to be their principal artistic virtue. Herbert Read reflected the general view of the Impressionists of the critics of his day when he wrote that these painters

> had seen the world *subjectively*—that is to say, as it presented itself to their senses in various lights, or from various points of view. Each occasion made a different and distinct impression on their senses, and for each occasion there must necessarily be a separate work of art.[22]

It would be unfair to Read to see this comment as being dismissive of the Impressionists. Far from it, for he was too knowledgeable and sympathetic a critic for that. Rather, Read makes his comment principally to introduce his readers to the founding genius of the modern movement in art, Paul Cézanne,[23] who strove, Read says, to see the world *objectively*, that is, '*as an object*, without any intervention either of the tidy mind or the untidy emotions'.[24] But were the Impressionists, on the one hand, even in the early period, merely concerned with subjective impressions, and was Cézanne, on the other, concerned solely with the objective quality of the natural world? To take Cézanne first. He did indeed speak of wishing to 're-do Poussin over again, according to nature', and Maurice Denis called him 'the Poussin of Impressionism'. Both Poussin and Cézanne were concerned with what one might call the architectonic qualities of the natural world. Yet Cézanne himself was rarely specific as to this supposed objectivity. His famous letter to Émile Bernard,[25] written in what has been called his 'baroque old age' and in which he urges his young friend to 'treat nature by means of the cylinder, the sphere, the cone, everything brought into proper perspective so that each side of an object or a plane is directed towards a central point' is concerned entirely with the intrinsic structure of the landscape and not at all with an aesthetic philosophy. He writes on another occasion that 'there is a logic of colours, and it is with this alone, *and not*

22. Herbert Read, *A Concise History of Modern Painting* (London: Thames & Hudson, rev. edn, 1968), p. 13.
23. For Picasso 'my only master'!
24. Read, *A Concise History*, p. 13.
25. 15 April 1904, in Rewald (ed.), *Paul Cézanne*, p. 301.

with the logic of the brain, that the painter should conform'.[26] He speaks of depth but primarily in terms of aerial perspective. A few weeks later he writes to Bernard that

> the man of letters expresses himself in abstractions whereas the painter, by means of drawing and colour, gives concrete form to his sensations and perceptions. One is neither too scrupulous nor too sincere nor too submissive to nature; but one is more or less master of one's model, and above all, of the means of expression. Get to the heart of what is before you and continue to express yourself as logically as possible.[27]

Now 'getting to the heart of what is before you', this interest in 'logical' expression, this concern that 'in order to make progress, there is only nature, and the eye is trained through contact with her',[28] is certainly opposed to any mere superficiality. Towards the end of his life Cézanne continually laments that he makes progress only with great difficulty and with many painful disappointments. He says that 'perception of the model and its realization are sometimes very long in coming'.[29] He was profoundly concerned with the permanence of things. Even before his Impressionist period Cézanne was committed, as Frank Elgar says, to purging a seascape of detail and to pare it down to a sequence of masses and planes,[30] but he was motivated by no externally imposed, *a priori*, assumptions about the nature of the natural world. What Elgar somewhat unfortunately calls Cézanne's 'intellectual speculations' about the material of nature arise from his true vision of the world before him as he painted. His 'speculations' arose from his observations and were always subservient to them. His vision of the geometric construction of the landscape was derived from his *personal perception that it was so*. References in his correspondence to a pre-conceived overarching philosophy asserting objectivity in art are altogether missing. When he writes to Charles Camion that 'everything, especially in art, is theory developed and applied in contact with nature' it is principally to relationships of tone and colour and what they tell him about structure and not to a philosophical or aesthetic theory that he refers.

Cézanne therefore may not have been as impervious to 'impression' and certainly to sensation as he is sometimes made out to be by his commentators. Light and shade and colour sensations have to be handled such that what he calls the 'concentric' quality of nature is revealed through the artist's 'looking and working', but this comment has less to do with contemplating the world *as an object per se* and more with having, he says, 'a sense of art', for, in a very revealing remark, he says that 'with a small

---

26. Quoted in Malraux, *Voices of Silence*, p. 346 (my italics).
27. 26 May 1904, Rewald (ed.), *Paul Cézanne*, pp. 303-304.
28. 25 July 1904, Rewald (ed.), *Paul Cézanne*, p. 306.
29. Undated, but c. November–December 1896, Rewald (ed.), *Paul Cézanne*, p. 255.
30. Frank Elgar, *Cézanne* (London: Thames & Hudson, 1969), p. 98.

temperament one can be very much of a painter'.[31] It is true, as André Malraux so perceptively notes, that what M. Cézanne wrote and what Paul Cézanne painted were two very different things, for 'when Paul Cézanne wants to speak he imposes silence on M. Cézanne whose fatuous remarks get on his nerves, and he says with his picture what words could only falsify'.[32] Yet how M. Cézanne feels profoundly influences how Paul Cézanne paints. Interiority and exteriority, subjectivity and objectivity, feeling and expression, are fused in the eyes and hands of a painter who, supremely among his contemporaries, brought a powerful organising mind to the aid of sensation in the realization of a work of art.[33]

And is the contrary criticism fair that implies that the Impressionists were concerned only with so-called surface impressions, with mere 'subjectivity'? Manet wrote that 'sincerity gives works of art a quality which makes them seem like a challenge or a protest, though actually all the artist wanted was to paint his impression'.[34] That may possibly be true of his *Rue Mosnier Decorated with Flags* (1878) painted two years later or of his last flower paintings, though this is questionable, but can it be said of *Luncheon on the Grass* or *Olympia* painted thirteen years earlier? We must leave aside the extraordinarily important philosophical question of what the words 'objectivity' and 'subjectivity' signify. Von Hügel, certainly no sentimentalist, was to say in 1908, in an extraordinary phrase, that 'the truly real is a thing that has an inside',[35] that is, that what is real is necessarily both objective and subjective. Henri Matisse said of Edouard Manet that 'he was the first to work by reflexes and thus simplify the painter's task...expressing only what affected his senses and feelings immediately'. But it would be very wrong to imply that there is nothing else to his painting. What *is* true, and it is true of all authentic art and of all authentic religion, is that artists are not primarily concerned with what Malraux calls abstractions and ideologies, or even with 'values'. For the painter painting is no more and no less than painting. Artists are never primarily concerned with theories and dogmas. Their 'impressions' or significations may have an 'inside' but painters do not begin with a notion of what that interiority is or even, in philosophical terms, what it is that they perceive as the 'meaning' of the natural world which gives rise to their 'impressions'. It is very important to note that this is true of so-called realist painters also. A landscape by Corot is no more 'true to life' (as a photographic image might be said to be) than one by Morisot. The theory-led, dogma-bound painter is no artist. Yet it is precisely because artists attend so carefully (including, and perhaps

---

31. Letter to Emile Bernard, 25 July 1904, Rewald (ed.), *Paul Cézanne*, p. 306.
32. Malraux, *The Voices of Silence*, p. 347.
33. As Cézanne said, quoted by his son (Elgar, *Cézanne*, p. 123).
34. Quoted in Malraux, *The Voices of Silence*, p. 346.
35. Friedrich von Hügel, *The Mystical Element of Religion* (2 vols.; London: Dent, 1923), II, p. 264.

especially, the abstract artists) that they see *through* what they see per-haps not to 'meaning', philosophically expressed, but rather to the macro-cosm both within and yet beyond the microcosm. They express their emotional response to the universe in which they are set and of which they are part, and enable us to make our emotional response also. It may be proper to say that they glimpse the transcendent in the immanent. Thus it is that the Impressionists delighted to paint the ordinary and everyday—a street on a festive occasion[36] or figures sitting in a garden.[37] It would be a bold critic who would say of Monet or van Gogh that they do nothing more for us than merely render *effets*! If this was so then why did so many flock to, say, the van Gogh centenary exhibition in Amsterdam, as, Marina Vaisey wrote, people used to go on pilgrimage? Why was Burlington House so packed during the *Monet in the '90s* exhibition in 1990 that one was almost taken round the show by the crush of people? It was because the work of these masters is now familiar to the masses in a way that it was not to those in Tolstoy's day, that we now see as these masters have taught us to see. They have enabled us *to see in the everyday and the familiar the source from which all life springs.* What was supposedly (though was it really so?) incomprehensible to the masses in Tolstoy's Paris is now an eye on the universe in today's London or Amsterdam or New York. As these men and women sought and found the 'deeper transactions between eye and mind' for themselves *then*, so they have enabled us *now* to make those deep transactions for ourselves.

This is so with all true art. André Breton hailed Marc Chagall's work as 'the triumphal appearance...of the metaphor in modern painting... No work was ever so resolutely magical.' Commenting on this, Sidney Alexander writes that '*all* art is metaphor; *all* art results from the transformation of the real'. He goes on to say of Chagall's dream paintings that 'an art so very "physical" expresses the spiritual; the "thinginess" is at the service of mysticism; tangibly incarnating the intangible'.[38] So it is with true religion. A Christianity which denies its metaphors their radical extravagance in the cause of coding its truths in objective propositions *loses its art and destroys its magic* and becomes a Christianity which, for vast numbers of people, thereby loses its capacity to engage them at the very depth of their being in and through the everyday experiences of life. A supposedly subjective art engages people profoundly. A supposedly objective, propositional, religion alienates them. From a very different perspective the Marxist Ernst Fischer, noting that art, religion and science were undifferentiated in the early

36. A favourite subject for Claude Monet, see also his *Rue Montorgueil Decked Out With Flags* (Musée d'Orsay, Paris).

37. See, for example, Berthe Morisot's beautiful and moving *Woman and Child in the Garden at Bougival* in the National Museum of Wales.

38. Sidney Alexander, *Marc Chagall: An Intimate Biography* (St Paul, MN: Paragon House, 1989), p. 291.

history of humankind, says that 'Art is necessary in order that man should be able to recognize and change the world. But art is also necessary by virtue of the magic inherent in it.'[39]

Seeing and Believing

In a postmodern world which rejects the totalitarianism of all dogma we need to be free to believe impressionistically, that is, we need to free ourselves to believe the truth in what we truly see in the Christian story and not in what we are told that we must or should or ought to see. We need to restore image, story, picture and metaphor as the central focus of our believing and reject out of hand and at once those dogma-ground lenses through which, for so very long, Christian believers have been compelled to see the truth of whatever it may be that 'God' is and have inevitably failed to see it. And here it is that we must allow the Impressionists—and indeed all authentic artists—to be prophets. Bound by no interpretative dogma they can reveal the everyday world as a window on the truly real. They paid such careful attention to the everyday that they saw in it its abiding significance, a significance far beyond the material benefit that it offers. John Whale wisely wrote that great art 'teaches us how real things can be looked at and loved without being seized and used, without being appropriated into the greedy organism of the self'.[40]

Immanent Transcendence

In so doing these painters stood in a very long tradition. Monet never visited Japan, but he acknowledged his debt to Japanese art. Responding to a journalist's question he said that

> If you absolutely must find an affiliation for me, select the Japanese of olden times: their rarefied taste has always appealed to me; and I sanction the implications of their aesthetic that evokes a presence by means of a shadow and the whole by means of a fragment.[41]

Here, perhaps without realising it, Monet penetrated to the heart of Zen. The Zen masters taught that 'One speck of plum blossom and the three thousand worlds are fragrant' and 'One speck of dust contains everything in

---

39. Ernst Fischer, *The Necessity of Art* (London: Penguin Books, 1963), p. 14.
40. *Church Times* (8 March 2002).
41. Quoted in an article by Derek Fell, *The Times* (London, 21 May 1994). The Catalan artist Antoni Tapies likes the notion, which he links with St Francis, that 'in the most banal objects can be the most important things of the universe'. 'A sock can contain the whole universe', he says. 'I once made a painting of an armpit. It is not in itself an attractive subject, but it was valuable because it was an embodiment of reality. It bore out the saying of St Teresa: one can find God in kitchen pots' (quoted by Peter Strafford, *The Times* [London, 27 May 1994]).

the universe' and 'When a single flower blooms, it's spring everywhere'.[42] The impressionism of the Chinese artists of the Sung period similarly, as Malraux puts it, 'aimed at suggesting by a subtle use of the ephemeral that eternity in which man is swallowed up, as his gaze loses itself in the mist that blurs the landscape'.[43] This is all surely very biblical. The writers of the Bible tell of the sin of the one man Adam bringing about the death of all and of the cross of the one man Jesus bringing about the resurrection of all—the whole by means of a fragment—in language which is not that of dogma but supremely that of poetry. As the Jesuit theologian Kakichi Kadowaki says, the Bible 'teaches us that the dynamic dialectical relation-ship between the part and the whole cannot be grasped by rational specu-lation. Instead we must abandon our egos and unite with God who is the Source of all creation.'[44] When Julian of Norwich (c. 1342) wrote of the 'small thing the size of a hazelnut' she was telling the same truth, as did Federico Garcia Lorca when a snail was brought to him and he found within it 'an ocean of maps'.[45] That abandonment and that union is the goal not of reason but of a true imagination. Further than this the biblical writers, from the psalmists and the prophets to the Evangelists, insist that the ordinary and the everyday, the microcosm, is a window on whatever eternity is for us. The 'kingdom' surrounds us if we can only become as little children and truly see that not one sparrow falls to the ground without our father know-ing, or that in a strong wind blowing a judgment is immanent, that is, that incarnate in the everyday is its true significance. Now of course those who struggle with Christian believing should know this, but they rarely have the courage to escape the prisons of rational dogma and authoritative inter-pretation and live as though it is true, and believe and pray accordingly.

Moments of Vision

We may approach the same truth in a different though intimately related way. In his Romanes Lecture in 1954 Kenneth Clark wrote of the 'moments of vision' which the true artist has. He speaks not of visions in the meta-phorical sense, the sense in which, he says, preachers, public speakers and far-sighted men of action use the word, but of 'moments of intensified physical perception'[46] such that enabled W.B. Yeats to see, in 'a moment of magical perception' in the bleached collar-bone of a hare, or Wordsworth in 'a tree, a stone, a withered leaf' or Coleridge in 'yonder moon dim glimmer-ing through the dewy window pane' what Clark calls self-discovery and

42. Quoted in J.K. Kadowaki, *Zen and the Bible* (Routledge & Kegan Paul, 1982), p. 68.

43. Malraux, *The Voices of Silence*, p. 333.

44. Kadowaki, *Zen and the Bible*, p. 69.

45. Federico Garcia Lorca, 'Snail', in *idem*, *Songs and Ballads* (Montreal: Guernica Editions Inc., 1997), p. 15.

46. Kenneth Clark, *Moments of Vision* (London: John Murray, 1981), p. 1.

self-identification, or, as Coleridge puts it, a 'dim awakening of a forgotten or hidden truth of my inner nature'.[47] Here is what one struggling with religious believing might call the transcendent in the immanent—a perception that the Kingdom surrounds us. So it was too for D.H. Lawrence. For him the blackbird's song, whatever its narrowly biological cause, is demonstrative of life taking hold of the blackbird and tossing him, *and Lawrence and each of us if we will allow it to happen*, 'into the ether of a new firmament, where he bursts into song as if he were combustible. What is the past, those others, now he is tossed clean into the new, across the untranslatable difference?'[48] Can we do our theology, and live out the life of faith, with that extraordinary and visionary abandon? Can we dare to believe 'as the bird sings' and thereby ourselves, with the blackbird, be 'tossed clean into the new, across the untranslatable difference'?

47. Quoted in Clark, *Moments of Vision*, p. 11.
48. D.H. Lawrence, 'Whistling of Birds', in *idem*, *Selected Essays* (London: Penguin Books, 1950), p. 112.

Chapter 6

Tossed Clean into the New

Theologians need to do theology poetically.[1]

Words and Dogmas

The first chapter, and the best, of John W. Dixon's *Art and the Theological Imagination*[2] is a fascinating treatment of a significant element in the relationship between art and theology. In Dixon's opinion the most serious question facing theology in our day is whether or not it has a right to exist. For centuries that right was taken for granted as was its assumed right, in consequence, to exercise authority in religious affairs. Theology, by definition, is verbal. Dogma, which is theology at its most authoritative, is propositional in essence. Dogma *is* its verbal statement. Thus, as Dixon points out, 'the whole principle of heresy and persecutions is built on the assumption that a verbal statement so exactly sets forth the sacred that denial of the statement is an offense against the Holy One himself'.[3] However, other than for a comparative few, that grant of authority has by now largely been withdrawn. For some theologians the resulting trauma has meant that God, as subdued to theology, is now effectively dead. Without the essential, canonical, authoritative proposition, God is essentially no more for *God is no more than what he is authoritatively stated to be.*

How is theology's problem to be resolved? Certainly not by attempting to reassert its old authority. We must either abandon theology completely (as very many have done) or we must accept the possibility that the question about theology has been wrongly put. Dixon argues for the latter position. May it not be that 'the true problem [is] not the existence of theology nor even its authority, but its *nature*'? Given the death of dogma we are now free to ask the exciting questions: 'What does theology do that cannot be done better another way?' and 'What language is the appropriate one for

---

1. This chapter is based on my article 'Art and Religion as Metaphor', in *The British Journal of Aesthetics* 35.2 (1995), pp. 145-53.
2. John W. Dixon, *Art and the Theological Imagination* (New York: Seabury Press, 1978). The chapter is entitled 'Form and Faith'.
3. Dixon, *Art and the Theological*, p. 1.

theology?'[4] Now these are startling questions for church theologians, for the history of theology is largely the history of its authoritative definition of truth, and, consequentially, of theological language. Words have been thought to be, not simply the most appropriate language for theology, but the only language in which theology is possible. However, all who think seriously about religion know very well that sensible *propositional* speech about a God who is *by those same propositions* supposedly omnipotent, omniscient and omnipresent is impossible. Such speech about such a God is non-sense, not least for theologians for they know full well that a God who can be so described is a God kept in bondage to propositions. As Pastor says to Jesus in Jose Saramago's remarkable novel *The Gospel according to Jesus Christ*, 'your God is the only warder of a prison where the only captive is your God'.[5] We find very sophisticated and knowledgeable theologians falling into this self-created trap. Even when his existence is not asserted or defended propositionally, it is still assumed. Thus the symbol 'God' is supposedly validated by God. God stands behind 'God'. And if such an attempt to describe God or to assert his objective existence in propositional terms is now seen to be at best restrictive and in fact positively idolatrous with respect to God, supposedly defined by the propositions, it is also being increasingly seen to be at best unhelpful by those for whose enlightenment these propositions were framed and for whom they are interpreted—religious believers themselves.

Words and Spaces

The truth is that we do not live by propositions. Indeed we live without words at all for much of our life. Now this is not to say that we do not live *with* words, or, as Dixon prefers to put it, *in* words or *according to* our language, for 'we experience the world according to the picture we have built up in our words'. Thus, 'poetry is not an entertainment; it provides us with the shapes of our emotional life'.[6] Nevertheless when the question is put 'how much of our life do we live outside words, according to forces other than words?', Dixon is ready to say, 'all of it', for

> all our life, all our corporate lives are lived outside words. Words insert themselves into the vast reverberating web of our common life, disturbing and shaping the interacting relations of our somatic life. In turn, words are seized by the forces of our life and shaped to the expression required of them. Words are an indispensable instrument of being human as they undoubtedly serve to our becoming human. But our life is not in words.[7]

4.   Dixon, *Art and the Theological*, pp. 1-2.
5.   Jose Saramago, *The Gospel according to Jesus Christ* (London: Harvill, 1993), p. 177.
6.   Dixon, *Art and the Theological*, p. 3.
7.   Dixon, *Art and the Theological*.

And this is true not merely in a metaphysical sense, but in the circum-stances of ordinary everyday living. That myriad of occasions when we experience the 'indecipherable and indescribable web of interaction between sensation, memory, emotion, purpose' comprise the very nature of hum-drum daily life. We live, Dixon says, in a world not of words but of sights and sounds and weight and surface, and of lines and colours, of tones and textures, of forms and of space. And this world—this kingdom—of sensa-tions cannot possibly be described in words, not even in the words of a genius with words.

Dixon is here speaking not of 'life' in its cosmic or metaphysical sense, but of what we would normally speak of as everyday life. He points to the obvious truth that our life is lived out physically in an intensely physical world. We live in a series of spaces: the intimate spaces of our homes and the open spaces of the world in which we work and play. We clothe our-selves in costumes appropriate to those purposes and spaces.[8] The words we use in these spaces and when dressed in these costumes are appropri-ate to these spaces and costumes. But the spaces and costumes determine the words, the non-verbal determines the verbal, and not vice versa.

This everyday life we lead is thus 'quite beyond description'. And we are largely unaware that this is so, so confident are we that we live by words and by our mastery of them. Thus,

> we forget who we are. We forget that the lunch we ate indifferently while we argued metaphysics or policy is now being dissolved and transformed into flesh, bone, blood and faeces. We void our waste in a straining indignity of posture, never believing other than that we are lords of the universe![9]

This wilful forgetfulness of our true nature as physical beings came about because of our overweening admiration for our minds, which man has come to regard as the source of knowledge and will:

> Being human became defined as mind, which was identified with knowl-edge and will. The awareness of the flesh, the acts and the being of the flesh in the earth, fell away, became part of the other. The flesh, the body, as the other, could be seen, observed, described, explained, by the know-ing will.[10]

But in allowing our minds and wills to be considered morally, and certainly intellectually, superior to our bodies, allegedly civilised men and women have cut themselves off from the natural order to which they belong. Our conviction that, as cerebral entities, we are morally superior to the non-cerebral world has led us to control and exploit nature sometimes to a dis-astrous extent. Perhaps even worse than this, Dixon argues, we have cut

8.   Dixon, *Art and the Theological*, p. 5.
9.   Dixon, *Art and the Theological*, p. 6.
10. Dixon, *Art and the Theological*.

ourselves off from our true selves—from our very being. Because we have convinced ourselves that we constitute humanity corporately possessed of an all-knowing intellect, we have lost all sense of our fallibility as men and women.

Such a definition of what we are, framed solely in terms of our mind and will, is thus destructive of our true being. Admittedly it is a less destructive definition than that which sees human beings (or for that matter other animals) as no more than collections of genetically pre-programmed neurons, but it is destructive enough. It is also a wrong, or at least an incomplete, definition, because we are not humanity but men, women and children—we are *persons*. There is much more to life than knowledge, narrowly defined. There is more to being human than mere mind.

What a true religion should do (and could do, were it not so verbal, for, at least within Christianity, we have spent two millennia re-wording the flesh into propositional dogma) and what art most certainly can do, is to enable us to redefine ourselves in terms of the totality of our beings in the time and space of what Christianity speaks of as eternity. We need to toss ourselves into the new, into the ether of a new firmament as D.H. Lawrence tells of it so beautifully.

This point is crucial. At the very least we live in a spatial, and not a cerebral or mental, environment. It is in space that we live our physical and our emotional lives. Our relationships with each other and with the world at large are primarily *spatial* and *dramatic* relationships, Dixon argues—that is to say that our relationships are 'enacted in a space and the space imposes its shape on the relation'.[11] And together with the dramatic and the spatial co-ordinates of our being-in-relationship, there is a third. It is *purpose*. Our lives have purpose, even if it is only to participate in the 'vast reverberating web of relations that is the life of nature'.[12] So far as we can tell the rest of the animal world does not know that it is essentially purposive. *Homo sapiens* does know this (or believes that it knows this), and this places humankind in a paradox, for 'as humans, we are a part of nature' but 'by nature we are apart from nature'.[13] This is the fatality, but also the eternal life, of the human. Are we at one with our world, or are we separate from it? Do we obey our bodies and seek to reconcile ourselves with the physicality of our world, or do we obey our heads and affirm the separation and the otherness of all that is not ourselves? This paradox 'generates a sense of enmity (the other is false, an evil to be fought) or another sense of unity (the other is a subject to be subdued)'.[14]

Now the categories of the arts—space and drama—help us to come to terms with this potentially fatal paradox. Thus art is 'not an ornament to an

11. Dixon, *Art and the Theological*, p. 9.
12. Dixon, *Art and the Theological*, pp. 9-10.
13. Dixon, *Art and the Theological*, p. 9.
14. Dixon, *Art and the Theological*, p. 10.

existing world [but] the primary means of forming that world'.[15] Space and drama are also the forming categories of theology in that religion too is a way in which we seek to make sense of our world: its myths and narratives interpret it, and its rites enact those myths in ways which form or shape our relationship to the world.

Art-Works and Religion-Works

To put this another way: religion—and supremely the prophetic religions, Judaism and Christianity and Islam—create what Eliot Deutsch calls 'religion-works' which parallel art-works and through which, collectively and through rite, ritual, dance and hymn we bring ourselves (or are brought) into a relationship with the sacred. Incidentally, as Deutsch points out, this is the difference between an art-work and a religion-work:

> In contrast to the artist's exciting sense of *discovery*...the creative partici-
> pant [the worshipper] in the religion-work has an awesome sense of
> *recovery*. The (modern) artist feels that one is bringing something new
> into being; the participant in the religion-work that one is re-enacting a
> timeless possibility.[16]

The role of religion-works—myths and rites—in creating and shaping our understanding of the world has formed the life work of Joseph Campbell and Mircea Eliade and has been of the greatest importance in beginning to release Christianity from its captivity to propositional dogma. In what we might call *true* religion we are not confronted primarily by dogmas; rather we are embraced by the poetry of true myth. Of course, as Carl Gustav Jung noted, modern man has done much to destroy the myths and rites with which so-called primitive man made sense of the upsurgings of a cha-otic unconscious into the world of his consciousness. Modern man is in search of a soul which he has himself destroyed.

Yet it is only by means of what Kenner calls 'the whispering forest of all traditional poetries', that is by the means and processes and mysterious interconnections and correspondences of art and religion, that we can articulate or otherwise express the meaning of life. As Dixon says: '...human life is too intricate, too varied and complex, to be dealt with by any formula [and note here that a dogma is a formula], far too complex to receive its definitive statement in any one language'.[17] What true religion does, and what art does, is to give *form* to life. The fact is that our lives are lived in space and in purposive, dramatic, relationship with others. We live in a sen-sory order in which we find all the elements of art—shape, texture, colour, sound, rhythm, line, edge, weight, movement and much else besides. And

15. Dixon, *Art and the Theological*, p. 12.
16. Deutsch, *Essays*, pp. 91-92.
17. Deutsch, *Essays*, p. 11.

in the midst of this sensory order we each find sacred places—places where we come to the very centre of ourselves as persons. These sacred places may well be actual spatial areas, but they are at least as often places occupied, perhaps very temporarily, by sacred objects or sacred persons—darkness, light, storm, water, bread, the breast; or the king, or the innocent victim, or the suffering servant or the child or the mother.[18] It is upon such poetical truths that a truly incarnational religion is founded.

Here Dixon observes that it is theoretically possible to catalogue these separate elements. What is not possible is to catalogue their manifold interconnections or the myriad forms in which, separately and in combination, they appear. They constantly interchange and interlock. This is metaphor, which Dixon defines as 'the linking of apparently different things by some profoundly felt connection between them'. Thus, 'metaphor is the basic act of thought'[19] as it is certainly the basic means of articulation in religion for it is the work of the imagination functioning intuitively. Thus the making of a work of art is a metaphorical activity— 'the penetration into the secret life of things to find the bonds between them'.

Form, Meaning and Metaphor

At this point we leave Dixon's thesis for a moment in order to define what the word 'form' means, while remembering the warning attributed to Picasso that 'from the point of view of art, there are no abstract or concrete forms, there are only forms, and they are all lies that are more or less convincing'. The word is used by artists and art theorists in several linked ways. Rudolf Arnheim describes the elements of 'simple form' thus:

> A straight line is simple because it uses one unchanged direction. Parallel lines are simpler than lines meeting at an angle because their relation is defined by one constant distance. A right angle is simpler than other angles because it produces a sub-division of one and the same angle. An additional simplifying factor is conformity to the spatial framework of vertical and horizontal orientation.

Symmetry is another attribute of simple form. And 'true simplicity' also involves a 'correspondence in structure between meaning and tangible pattern'.[20] How simple form, thus defined, conveys meaning to us is described by Erwin Panofsky:

> Primary or natural subject matter is apprehended by identifying pure forms, that is: certain configurations of line and colour, or certain peculiarly shaped lumps of bronze or stone, or representations of natural

18. On this and much else, see Joseph Campbell, *The Power of Myth* (New York: Doubleday, 1989), and especially his *Myths to Live By* (London: Souvenir Press, 1973).

19. Dixon, *Art and the Theological*, p. 12.

20. R. Arnheim, *Art and Visual Perception* (Berkeley: University of California Press, 1974), pp. 57, 63, quoted in Chave, *Mark Rothko*, p. 156.

objects such as human beings, animals, plants, houses, tools, and so forth, by identifying their mutual relations as events... The world of pure forms thus recognised as *carriers of primary or natural meanings* may be called the world of artistic motifs.[21]

The italics are mine. Form carries meaning. Yet form in this basic, simple or pure sense of line and colour is a metaphor. Line and perspective have no existence in the real world. They are visual convention or codes. Similarly the two-dimensional flat plane of, say, a Turner landscape is not a landscape. Yet it is more than a mere representation or even portrayal of a landscape. In the hands of such a master as J.M.W. Turner or Paul Cézanne or Vincent van Gogh it is a metaphor—a 'penetration into the secret life' of nature such as to reveal 'some profoundly felt connection' between the natural order and the heart, mind and hand of the artist and the medium he uses *such as* not merely to reveal these connections to the viewer of the picture in some detached, cerebral, way (or, least of all, in such a way as to call attention to the brilliance of the artist), but above all to enable, even to compel, the viewer actively and personally to participate in that 'secret life' to which he belongs by virtue of being human but from which he has become alienated.

This use of form as metaphor thus, as Gombrich puts it, embodies, or *incarnates* meaning. But the form is not itself the meaning. It is the vehicle for the meaning. In fact form can obscure meaning as can all vehicles of meaning. To convey meaning artistic forms must be conventional or coded such that the viewer can interpret them. Art is thus a language. But the conventions and codes can become too familiar. As Anna Chave says,

> viewers tend to respond to received codes and accustomed forms in an habitual or reflexive, and thus often unthinking and unfeeling, way. Unfamiliar forms may help to engage and prolong the viewer's attention and so revivify the experience of perception itself or 'make the stone stony' in Shklovsky's terms.[22]

Thus Mark Rothko decided in 1945 that he could no longer present his understanding of the human condition using familiar forms or codes, not least because, as he wrote, he wanted to find 'a pictorial equivalent for man's new knowledge and consciousness of his more complex inner self'.[23] And there were few received conventions by which this could be accomplished. A new form had to be found, an image-sign or metaphor, to portray the inner self.

It is remarkable how often, in writers as diverse as the two quoted in this chapter, John Dixon and Anna Chave, the notion of 'metaphor' becomes a key concept in the understanding of art. Art is, for Dixon, 'basically a

---

21. Erwin Panofsky, *Meaning in the Visual Arts* (Garden City, NY: Doubleday, 1955), p. 28, quoted in Chave, *Mark Rothko*, p. 31.

22. Chave, *Mark Rothko*, pp. 123-24.

23. Letter dated 8 July 1945, cited in Chave, *Mark Rothko*, p. 124.

metaphorical activity, the penetration into the secret life of things to find the bonds between them'. For Chave what Rothko sought in his painting was a 'pictorial metaphor or equivalent'. Like all metaphors the metaphors which comprise much art convey essential meaning which can be conveyed in no other way. Chave says that 'the placement of forms in a pictorial space carries symbolic inflections, however ambiguous or indeterminate those inflections might be in the case of an abstract image'.[24]

So metaphor is form and form metaphor in art. So too in theology. How do men and women speak of whatever or whoever is 'God' for them other than by a process of 'forming' or metaphor? Our words about God can no more define and encompass, least of all describe, what it is that we signify by the word 'God' than is a painted landscape capable of defining and encompassing the natural world in front of the painter, yet both the words and the painting are essential vehicles for conveying the meaning that the theologian and the painter perceive and wish to convey.

This chapter can be no more than a very brief and extremely superficial investigation of a complex subject, yet what cannot be omitted is a testing of the observation that *as metaphors* theology and art are intimately linked because their verbal or pictorial codes both derive, classically, from the interaction of humans and their environment and of forms in space and in time. Both tell stories or enact dramas which seek to interpret these inter- actions. To return to Dixon. He distinguishes between story and narrative. By 'story' he means those things we ordinarily think of when the word is used—the recital of events as they develop in time. By 'narrative' he means

> the deeper structures of our experience which emerge into story but also emerge into other aspects of experience also. Thus the formal quality of experience through time *is* inherently narrative, but story is not the only way to get at narrative.[25]

What interests Dixon is the extraordinary way in which the narratives of the Greek and Hebrew peoples, exemplified and illustrated in the stories which convey their religion, are rooted in the natural and human environment of these peoples. Christianity, indeed Western history generally, is both Greek and Hebrew in origin. This duality of origin has created tensions within Christianity which have led to the virtual irreconcilability of these two great historical and cultural forces. Dixon says that 'our imaginative structures have not succeeded in carrying those forces past an uneasy tension into fruitful union'. As an example of this tension he cites contemporary biblical interpretation. Hebrew is a language of poetry and story. It is not even a language through which, as such, mere history is recorded. Through it, by poetry and story, the history of the Hebrew people is interpreted *as it is recorded* such that one can rarely, if ever, tell where 'history' as event can be distinguished from its essentially theological and moral interpretation.

24. Chave, *Mark Rothko*, p. 159.
25. Chave, *Mark Rothko*, p. 23.

Indeed, the history *is* its interpretation. Christian theology, both Protestant and Catholic, has been profoundly influenced by biblical hermeneutics in recent centuries. But the intelligence which has sought an understanding of what Dixon calls 'the Hebraic side of Christianity' has been Greek and philosophical. The rational intellect has been brought to bear upon the artistic imagination: 'The intelligence brought to the work is decidedly Hellenic but the concerns are the working out of the moral will in time—which is the definition of story'.[26] He explains the tension that this double-faceted hermeneutics illustrates by interpreting the relation of space and time to story and thus to theology by arguing that the land of the Hebrews —the spaces in which they worked out their destiny—is a nearly featureless desert across which the people travelled not knowing where they were going immediately but upheld by the conviction that they would arrive eventually in the Promised Land. The principal historical symbol of the Hebrew Bible is therefore the journey—the way. But Greece is very different. Greece 'is great clear masses in the light'. Greece has clear edges such that there is, Dixon observes, always and everywhere a harmonious balance of clearly defined forms. Thus it is that 'Greece is a meditation on forms in space as Judea is a meditation on events in time'.[27]

Religion as Art

With that quotation we will leave Dixon's analysis of one example of the relationship between art and religion. Both are creators of forming metaphors. There are many other intimate connections between the two but this is the most significant. Another American writer, Thomas R. Martland, in his *Religion as Art* (1981), argues along much the same line. Both art and religion provide directions on how to see and indirectly on what to do. 'More specifically...art and religion present collectively created frames of perception and meaning by which men interpret their experiences and order their lives'.[28] Martland's 'frame of perception and meaning' is what Dixon speaks of as a forming metaphor. Martland emphasises the notion of art and religion as metaphor, although he does not himself employ the term. This is to say that for him neither art nor religion provide *illustrations* which describe the world. Rather they both 'contribute the fabric of new worlds which men now come to see and understand as their world',[29] or as Dixon says of a work of art, it is a metaphorical activity which penetrates into the secret life of things and is thus critical in shaping the human world. Through the poetries of true religion and true art we can be tossed clean into the new, into the ether of a new firmament.

26. Chave, *Mark Rothko*, p. 26.

27. Chave, *Mark Rothko*, pp. 26-27, citing Rhys Carpenter, *The Esthetic Basis of Greek Art* (Bloomington: Indiana University Press, 1959), p. 11.

28. Martland, *Religion as Art*, p. 1.

29. Martland, *Religion as Art*.

Chapter 7

Did I Love a Dream?

Theologians must do theology touched by the mystical.

Marc Chagall said that

> Some people wrongly fear the word 'mystical' and give it too orthodox,
> religious a colour. One must tear off the term's outlived, musty exterior
> and take it in its pure, lofty, sound form. Mysticism! How often this word
> has been hurled at my head... But without mysticism would there be a
> single great social movement in the world? Every organism—be it individ-
> ual or social—if it is deprived of the force of mysticism...will it not die?[1]

Was the encounter with the splendour of the creator God that I believed
that I had when I stood transfixed before Cézanne's *Large Pine and Red
Earth* no such thing but only a moment of aesthetic pleasure? Was my
profound spiritual experience on seeing Michelangelo's *Palestrina Pieta* for
the first, and perhaps the last, time *merely* an emotional reaction to a portrayal of human suffering? Was my experience in each case *no more than*
one of emotional arousal the effect of which my galvanic skin response can
measure? Did these consummate artists connect me with the divine, or 'did
I love a dream'.[2]

This chapter considers a few of the connections between art and mysticism. First, it will outline very briefly the contributions of two writers on
mysticism who, writing in the early years of the twentieth century, did much
to develop a Christian understanding of mystical experience which drew
upon psychological insights which were currently being developed.[3] These
writers were Friedrich von Hügel, the first edition of whose *The Mystical
Element of Religion*[4] was published in 1908, and Evelyn Underhill, whose

---

1.   Quoted in Susan Crompton, *Chagall: Love and the Stage 1914–1922* (London:
Royal Academy of Arts/Merrell Holberton, 1998), p. 19.
2.   From the fifth line of Mallarmé's *The Afternoon of a Faun*.
3.   Freud had developed his theory of the unconscious in Paris in the 1880s and
1890s and had published his definitive work on dreams in 1901. However, neither
author cites him.
4.   The full title is *The Mystical Element of Religion as studied in Saint Catherine
of Genoa and her Friends* (London: Dent, 1908).

Mysticism was published in 1911.[5] Secondly, it will draw on artists (principally painters) who were contemporary with or slightly pre-dated von Hügel and Underhill, namely the Impressionists and those who immediately succeeded them. This restriction is, as elsewhere in this book, for the sake of brevity, though the period in Western art from the 1860s to the 1920s saw the beginning of the modern movement in art and is particularly rich in providing insights from art into the nature of transcendence. It is with transcendence that, supremely, mystical religion has to do.

Friedrich von Hügel and the Three Elements of Religion

Drawing on William James,[6] von Hügel[7] argued that there are three 'modalities' or 'modes of apprehension' or 'forms of appeal and outlook' which shape the religious life of an individual. These are, first, 'Sense and Memory, the Child's means of apprehending Religion'; secondly, 'Question and Argument, the Youth's mode of approaching Religion'; and thirdly, 'Intuition, Feeling, and Volitional requirements and evidences, the Mature Man's special approaches to Faith'. In the first, religion is above all 'a Fact and Thing',[8] imposed by the authority of parents, teachers and the church. Religion here works quasi-automatically. In this stage of religious development 'the External, Authoritative, Historical, Traditional, Institutional side and function of Religion are everywhere evident'. In the second stage 'the reasoning, argumentative, abstractive side' of human nature comes into play. Direct experience of the world 'brings home to the child that...sense-informations are not always trustworthy, or identical in its own case and in that of others'. Thus 'Religion here becomes Thought, System, a Philosophy'.[9] In the third and final stage of religious development (as of all human development) sense-impression followed by critical reflection are succeeded by what von Hügel calls 'the discharge of will and of action' in which a person 'grows and gradually comes to his real self, and gains certain experiences as to the existence and nature and growth of this his own deeper personality'. In this process of growth to emotional and volitional maturity an individual is fed by 'the third side of religion, the Experimental [we would say now the experiential] and Mystical. Here religion is *rather felt than seen or reasoned about, is loved and lived rather than analyzed, is action and power, rather than either external fact or intellectual verification*'.[10] Von Hügel notes that in the mature adult no one of these elements

5. Evelyn Underhill, *Mysticism: A Study in the Nature and Development of Man's Spiritual Consciousness* (London: Methuen, 1911).

6. William James, 'Reflex Action and Theism', in his *The Will to Believe* (London: Longmans Green, 1897), pp. 111-14.

7. Von Hügel, *The Mystical Element*, I, pp. 50-82.

8. Von Hügel, *The Mystical Element*, I, p. 51.

9. Von Hügel, *The Mystical Element*, I, p. 52.

10. Von Hügel, *The Mystical Element*, I, p. 53 (my italics).

is ever separated from the other two. There is constant tension between them 'of a fruitful and dangerous kind'. With great perception, von Hügel writes of 'the two crises of the soul, when it adds Speculation to Institutionalism, and Mysticism to both'.[11]

He notes that there are parallels to this triad of religious elements. First, they are paralleled by what he calls 'the three constituents of Knowledge... the sensational, the rational, [and] the ethico-mystical'.[12] It is the last of these, von Hügel notes, which gives real value to the two previous ones,

> For only on the condition that I am willing to trust these intimations of necessity, to believe that these necessities of my subjective thought are objective as well, and correspond to the necessities of Being, can I reach the trans-subjective, can I have any real knowledge and experience of anything whatsoever, either within me or without. The most elementary experience, the humblest something to be granted as really existing and as to be reasoned from, is thus invariably and inevitably composed for me of three elements, of which only the first two are directly experienced by me at all... Thus...at the very source of all our certainty, of the worth attributable to the least or greatest of our thoughts and feelings and acts, we already find the three elements: indubitable sensation, clear thought, warm faith in and through action.[13]

Similarly, these three religious elements have psychological parallels: sense-impression, mental abstraction and reflection (the contribution of mind), and 'the discharge of will and of action'.[14] Wherever we look in human experience we find these three elements, which, in their multiplicity in unity, 'alone bear with them all the meaning, all the richness, all the reality of life'.[15] It is clear from this that, as J.P. Whelan notes, von Hügel sought to locate mysticism well within what he considered to be centrally human for 'the mystical is *what man is*, what he may expect to do and to have happen, *because God is*. It is man's "deepest requirement and characteristic".'[16] Thus von Hügel locates the mystical sense, the sense of true religion, at the very heart of the human psyche. He argues that it is inevitably profoundly connected to ethical awareness or conscience, and is the great motivation for all constructive human activity.

11. Von Hügel, *The Mystical Element*, I, p. 54.
12. Von Hügel, *The Mystical Element*, I, p. 55-56.
13. Von Hügel, *The Mystical Element*, I, p. 57.
14. Von Hügel, *The Mystical Element*, I, pp. 57-58.
15. Von Hügel, *The Mystical Element*.
16. J.P. Whelan, *The Spirituality of Friedrich von Hügel* (London: Collins, 1971), p. 82. J.N. Findlay has said that '[the] mystical way of looking at things enters the experience of most men many times' and 'mysticism enters into almost everyone's attitudes, and it is as much a universal background to experience as the open sky is to vision: to ignore it is to be drearily myopic, and to take the splendour and depth out of everything' (*Ascent to the Absolute* [London: Allen & Unwin, 1970], p. 164). Findlay justifies this view by comparisons drawn from art, music and mathematics. See also G. Parrinder, *Mysticism in the World's Religions* (Oxford: Oxford University Press, 1976), p. 189, from which this quotation is taken.

Evelyn Underhill and the Characteristics of Mysticism

Evelyn Underhill corresponded with von Hügel, and a note to the third edition of her *Mysticism* warmly acknowledges von Hügel's friendly criticism. We may assume that he endorsed Underhill's analysis of the of mysticism of which, in her view, there were four. True mysticism is, first, 'active and practical, not passive and theoretical. It is an organic life-process, a something which the whole self does; not something as to which its intellect holds an opinion.' However, secondly, the aims of mysticism are 'wholly transcendental and spiritual. It is in no way concerned with adding to, exploring, rearranging, or improving anything in the visible universe'. While the mystic never neglects his duty to the many, 'his heart is always set upon the changeless One'. Thirdly, 'this One is, for the mystic, not merely the Reality of all that is, but also a living and personal Object of Love; never an object of exploration'. Fourthly, 'living union with this One—which is the term of his adventure—is a definite state or form of enhanced life'.[17] Thus mysticism entails, for Underhill, a definite psychological experience. The mystic needs a temperament (or what Underhill calls 'a nature') 'capable of extraordinary concentration, an exalted moral emotion' and, and here we touch on the very limited topic of this chapter, 'a nervous organization of the artistic type'.[18] In developing these characteristics Underhill makes mystical experience a much more positive matter than does William James whose four marks of mysticism she says 'fail to satisfy us'.[19]

Von Hügel on Mystical and Aesthetic Experience

At first sight there seems to be no connection between religious mysticism, so defined and characterised, and art.

Von Hügel explicitly denied any direct connection when he wrote that

> Never, as truly as creation will never be absorbed in the Creator, nor man, even the God-man, become...simply and purely God, will or can science and art, morals and politics be without each their own inside, their own true law of growth and existence *other than, in no wise a department or simple dependency of, religion.* The creature is not the Creator..., it is not a little god... Even so are science and all the other departments of life not religion.[20]

17. Underhill, *Mysticism*, p. 96.
18. Underhill, *Mysticism*, p. 108.
19. Underhill, *Mysticism*, pp. 96, 396. See William James, *The Varieties of Religious Experience* (London: Longmans Green, 1902), p. 380. James's four marks are ineffability and noetic quality (which Underhill acknowledges are 'well observed' characteristics of contemplative experience), transiency and passivity.
20. Quoted in Whelan, *The Spirituality of Friedrich von Hügel*, p. 69 (von Hügel's italics). Whelan notes a later statement by von Hügel in which he speaks of the necessity 'for all fruitful human life, and especially for all powerful religious life...of friction, tension, rivalry...between this religious life and other men's...tasks; and...the

Nevertheless von Hügel readily acknowledged that religion is not the only significant constituent of social life. It is not the only value which shapes human existence but is 'a factor in life'.[21] Whelan summarises von Hügel's position well: 'man is essentially constituted by the interconnections and the interactions which is his sociality. And still further—this man is a being in a world which makes the journey with him.'[22] In fact von Hügel explicitly repudiated the existence in humankind of a distinct faculty of mystical apprehension, which, as Whelan correctly says, is, 'a conception violently at odds with incarnationalism and the whole press of Christ as God-with-us in and through the history of human becoming'.[23]

Given this broadly humanistic approach we might have expected von Hügel to speak at some length of these other social constituents, and especially art, as they influence the spiritual life. But he does not, perhaps because, while they are what he acknowledges as 'God-given' they are necessarily 'non-religious activities, duties [and] ideals in man'.[24] However important they may be, however ideal, even God-given, they are not religious. Yet, and this is most significant, von Hügel readily acknowledges that the same 'psycho-physical organisation' is shared by mystics, philosophers, musicians and poets.[25] He argues, for example, that if we are to classify mystics as psychologically abnormal we would need to add Kant and Beethoven to the list. By this criterion alone both would be regarded as 'hopeless and useless hypochondriacs'. He could have said the same of many great painters and sculptors. Artists and mystics alike share a 'larger amount of psycho-physical impressionableness and reaction utilized by the mind' just as 'the mathematician, the tactician and the constructive statesman'[26] share with the mystic a high degree of 'mono-ideism and auto-suggestion', that is they are alike dominated by some great central idea which they have interiorised before it is expressed in action.[27]

---

persistent danger...of working religion in such a way as to remove from its path, as far as possible, any and all of these frictions which in reality are essentially necessary to its own force and fruitfulness' (Whelan, *The Spirituality of Friedrich von Hügel*, p. 255). Elsewhere von Hügel approvingly cites C.P. Tiele who, in his *Elements of the Science of Religion* in 1897, argued that whereas art, ethics, science and philosophy exercise an influence on religion they are by no means identical with it (*The Mystical Element*, II, p. 262).

21. Quoted in Whelan, *The Spirituality of Friedrich von Hügel*, p. 76 (von Hügel's italics).

22. Whelan, *The Spirituality of Friedrich von Hügel*.

23. Whelan, *The Spirituality of Friedrich von Hügel*, p. 96.

24. Quoted in Whelan, *The Spirituality of Friedrich von Hügel*, p. 89.

25. Von Hügel, *The Mystical Element*, II, p. 42.

26. Von Hügel cites Newton, Napoleon and Richelieu (*The Mystical Element*, II, p. 41).

27. Von Hügel here draws heavily on William James's *Varieties of Religious Experience*. Given von Hügel's understanding of human psychology it is extraordinary that

This shared psychology is one very significant link between the mystic and the artist in von Hügel's thought. However, the primary link is to be found in his third element of religion, where 'intuition, feeling, and volitional requirements and evidences' predominate in the full flowering of religion where 'it is rather felt than seen or reasoned about, is loved and lived rather than analyzed, is action and power, rather than either external fact or intellectual verification'.[28] Von Hügel quotes Kant, who, following Leibniz, wrote that 'we are mediately conscious of an apprehension as to which we have no direct consciousness'. The sphere of human intuitive response is the place of both mystical and aesthetic experience. Von Hügel says that

> when engrossed in a great landscape of Turner, the Parthenon sculptures, a sonata of Beethoven, Dante's *Paradiso*; or when lost in the contemplation of the seemingly endless spaces of the heavens, or of the apparently boundless times of geology; or when absorbed in the mysterious greatness of Mind so incommensurable with matter, and of Personality, so truly presupposed in all these appreciations yet so transcendent of even their collectivity—we are as little occupied with the facts of our engrossment, our self-oblivion, our absorption, or with the aim and use of such immensely beneficial self-oblivion, as we are in our ordinary, loosely-knit states, occupied with the impression...produced on our senses and mind by some small insect or slight ray of light to which we are not giving our attention...[29]

It would be hard to find a better example of profane mysticism that this. The power of these 'under-impressions' as with those 'over-impressions' can only be felt from the 'peculiar cogency' of their after-effects. Of course, given his view of the separation of art and religion, von Hügel is not here arguing that such 'dim apprehensions' followed by 'clear perceptions' is religious mysticism. God is real, to be apprehended with, and contrasted to, other realities. Central to von Hügel's theology is the reality of God. The purpose of religion and therefore of mysticism is to adore the God who reveals himself in Christ. Art is for the enjoyment and enrichment of men and women. Mysticism is for the adoration of God. Perhaps this is why the passage quoted above is the only major reference in von Hügel's writings to the extraordinary power of great art. He grants that 'we can...see that beauty and the sense of beauty come from God by noticing how narrow and hard, or vague and empty, remains the specifically religious sense in souls greatly lacking in the aesthetic capacity',[30] but there is little else on the subject of art. While apparently missing the previously quoted passage Whelan notes that nothing in von Hügel's writing amounts to

Whelan can find no record that he had ever heard of Freud, and seems to have been very disparaging of Jung (Whelan, *The Spirituality of Friedrich von Hügel*, p. 265).

28. Von Hügel, *The Mystical Element*, I, pp. 52-53.
29. Von Hügel, *The Mystical Element*, II, p. 266.
30. Quoted in Whelan, *The Spirituality of Friedrich von Hügel*, p. 254.

a considered appreciation of the purely aesthetic, the playful, and even the wasting of time which would significantly estimate the role of these activities in the humanization process and see them, not just as means whereby to recover from and prepare for the serious business of life, but also as ends in themselves which, when pursued *for* themselves, are values to become man by.[31]

Yet what we have from von Hügel about art is the more important almost because of this omission brought about by his confident but nevertheless subtle concept of the reality of God and the nature and purpose of religious mysticism. Indeed, he would probably deny that a non-religious, profane, mysticism exists. He grants that mystical and aesthetic experience belong to the same area of intuitive apprehension and impression. A contemporary radical theologian for whom the notion of an objectively existing 'realist' God is by definition nonsense if not even idolatrous, and agreeing with von Hügel that human beings do not possess a specifically religious faculty, would want to take the small step of affirming that mystical experience and aesthetic experience while perhaps different in subject and form scarcely differ in content.

Here we should introduce a distinction which is crucial to the argument. In the context of sculpture and painting the *subject* is the 'topic' (if any) of the artwork; its *form* is the relationship of the masses—its inherent structure and composition; and its *content* is the experience which it communicates. The question of whether content comes before form or form before content was hotly debated in the early years of the twentieth century. The issue was whether a work of art had to be seen as a system of formal relationships before it could be recognised as a kind of communication or whether the significance of an artwork was primarily formal—whether it was, before all else, a perceptual experience.[32]

Underhill on Mysticism, Art and the Intuition of the Real

Whereas von Hügel makes little mention of art, Evelyn Underhill discusses the relationship between mysticism and art quite fully. She begins by acknowledging that unlike the practice of magic and of science, mysticism, like art, cannot exist in the absence of 'passionate emotion' for 'we must feel, and feel acutely, before we want to act on [the] hard and heroic scale'[33] demanded of both mystic and artist. More importantly for our present purposes she argues that both artist and mystic share an 'intuition of the Real lying at the root of the visible world and sustaining its life', though, for the artist, this intuition is present 'in a modified form'. Perhaps, Underhill says, it would be better to say *must* be present if the arts

31. Whelan, *The Spirituality of Friedrich von Hügel*, pp. 220-21.
32. I am dependent here on Hamilton, *Painting and Sculpture*, pp. 180-81, see also pp. 209-10.
33. Underhill, *Mysticism*, p. 85.

are to justify themselves as heightened forms of experience. [For] it is this which gives to them that peculiar vitality, that strange power of communicating a poignant emotion, half torment and half joy, which baffle their more rational interpreters.[34]

It is this exercising of 'that strange power' that distinguishes the true artist from those who produce pictures which are 'like photographs', or who construct buildings 'that are at once handsome and commodious' or who write novels which are 'a perfect transcript of life'. These all fail to satisfy us, Underhill says, because

> these things have neglected their true business; which is not to reproduce the illusions of ordinary men but to catch and translate for us something of that 'secret plan', that reality which the artistic conscious-ness is able, in a measure, to perceive.[35]

She quotes William Blake: 'painting as well as music and poetry exists and exults in immortal thoughts'. Underhill says that artists have 'in a measure' this sense of reality. As Blake wrote this painters in France were seeking to express what they called *au dela*, the beyond. As does von Hügel, Underhill reserves for mystical religion a far richer perception—richer, for it is the perception of God. She is aware of, but does not name, what R.C. Zaehner was to call profane mysticism. Blake has no such reservation. For him, 'immortal thoughts' know no distinction between sacred and profane mysticism. Underhill herself immediately acknowledges the life-enhancing power of great painting which 'has its origin in this contact of the artistic mind with the archetypal—or, if you like, the transcendental—world; the underlying verity of things'.[36] Despite Underhill's caveats 'in a measure' and 'in a modified form' this brings the mystic and the artist, sacred and profane mysticism, very close together indeed for each has 'an intuition of the Real lying at the root of the visible world and sustaining its life'. She cites Laurence Binyon on the ideals which governed early Chinese painting (a most illuminating choice given the influence of Chinese and Japanese painting on the Impressionists, and especially on Monet) when he writes, first, of every work of Chinese art being thought of as an 'incarnation of the genius of rhythm' (we will return to this key notion later), and, secondly, of a picture being conceived of as '*a sort of apparition from a more real world of essential life*'.[37]

What distinguishes the artist from the mystic in Underhill's view is that though both inhabit this 'more real world of essential life', the artist does so only in his brief moments of creation, whereas the mystic may stay, indeed *must* stay, in that world. The artist is indeed called upon to 'interpret his free vision, his glimpse of the burning bush; to other men he is the mediator

34. Underhill, *Mysticism*, p. 88.
35. Underhill, *Mysticism*.
36. Underhill, *Mysticism*.
37. Binyon's italics, quoted in Underhill, *Mysticism*, pp. 88-89.

between his brethren and the divine, for art is the link between appearance and reality'. Yet, Underhill says, we may no more call an artist a mystic than we may describe as a musician everyone who has learnt the piano, for

> the true mystic is the person in whom such powers transcend the merely artistic and visionary stage, and are exalted to the point of genius: in whom the transcendental consciousness can dominate the moral consciousness, and who has definitely surrendered himself to the embrace of Reality.[38]

Of course this and the preceding statement raise critical questions. Can it safely be claimed that religious mystics *always* inhabit the 'more real world of essential life'? And is it not true that a person who has learnt to play the piano *is* a musician, whatever may be his or her level of musicianship? Underhill meets these points by saying that she is here speaking of *great* mystics, those who 'hover like the six-winged seraph before the face of the Absolute'. Yet both von Hügel and Underhill acknowledge that 'no deeply religious man is without a touch of mysticism'[39] for it is humanity's 'deepest requirement and characteristic' to be mystical.[40] The mystical *is what humankind is*.[41] Mysticism is, says von Hügel,

> the intuitive and emotional apprehension of the most specifically religious of all truths, viz., the already full operative existence of eternal beauty, truth, goodness, of infinite Personality and Spirit, independently of our action.[42]

Thus, while great mystics may alone permanently inhabit the real world of essential life, mystical awareness, the intuition or sense of *au dela*, 'the beyond' is an intuition natural to humankind. Now while artists will not necessarily recognise 'the already full operative existence of eternal beauty, truth [and] goodness', very many acknowledge the absolute importance of the intuition in the creation of an authentic artwork which links appearance and reality.

Despite her caveats, Underhill finds, as we have seen, close parallels between the artist and the mystic. As artists receive rhythms and discover truths and beauties in the phenomenal world which are hidden from (or at least not observed by) the rest of us, so the true mystic stands in the same relation to the transcendental world. Yet Underhill also acknowledges that William Blake, for one, laid claim to the 'fourfold vision' because, as he said, he has 'put off the rotten rags of sense and memory' and 'put on Imagination uncorrupt'.[43] Was Blake a mystic who was a painter or a painter who,

38. Underhill, *Mysticism*, p. 89.
39. Underhill, *Mysticism*, p. 84.
40. Von Hügel, quoted in Whelan, *The Spirituality of Friedrich von Hügel*, p. 82.
41. Whelan, *The Spirituality of Friedrich von Hügel*, p. 82.
42. Von Hügel, 'Gospel of St. John', in *Encyclopedia Britannica* (11th edn), XV, p. 455, quoted in Whelan, *Spirituality of Friedrich von Hügel*, p. 82.
43. Quoted in Underhill, *Mysticism*, p. 310.

in and through his art, was a mystic? Again, Underhill recognises that the artist gives us in sound, colour and words 'a hint of his ecstasy, his glimpse of truth'. Both artist and mystic find it difficult to convey these hints and glimpses to the rest of us.

Further, both the artist and the mystic obey 'the laws of rhythm'. The artist obeys unconsciously 'the rule by which all arts tend to approach the condition of music'. Similarly with mysticism, 'the most romantic thing in the universe...the art of arts...finds naturally enough its closest correspondences in the purely artistic and most deeply significant of all forms of expression'.[44] Recognising the enormous importance of imagery and symbolism in the writings of the mystics Underhill notes that 'the close connection between rhythm and heightened states of consciousness is as yet little understood'.[45] Underhill recognises that 'of all the arts music alone shares with great mystical literature the power of waking us to response to the life-movement of the universe... Beethoven heard the very voice of Reality, and little of it escaped when he translated it for our ears.'[46] Underhill was not alone at the time in noting what she calls 'the analogy between mystical and musical emotion' for 'mystical, no less than musical and poetic perception, tends naturally—we know not why—to present itself in rhythmical periods...'[47] Underhill's parenthesis is interesting. May it not be because the intuitions and means of expression of the artist and the mystic are dissimilar only in form and not in substance? As we find metaphor and magic, rhythm and revelation in both art and religion, are they not one *at root*?

The place of rhythm in art and mysticism is a matter to which Underhill returns several times. The business of poets is to 'translate Reality into terms of rhythm and speech'.[48] The rhythms of the mantras of the Indian mystics alike with those of Catholic liturgies create an untranslatable 'true magic "word" or spell...addressed to the subliminal mind' and which have a 'strange power...over the human will'.[49] The most lyrical passages in mystical literature are such because 'only by the use of aesthetic suggestion and musical rhythm' can the mystical vision be expressed. Indeed, when 'essential goodness, truth, beauty—Light, Life, and Love—are apprehended by the heart, whether the heart be that of lover, painter, saint, that apprehension can only be adequately communicated in a living, that is to say, an artistic form'.[50] Given rhythm, then dance. Underhill quotes at length Jacob Boehme who speaks of the soul dancing with the divine

44. Underhill, *Mysticism*, pp. 90-91.
45. Underhill, *Mysticism*, p. 94.
46. Underhill, *Mysticism*, p. 91.
47. Underhill, *Mysticism*, pp. 94-95
48. Underhill, *Mysticism*, p. 150.
49. Underhill, *Mysticism*, pp. 189-90, 197.
50. Underhill, *Mysticism*, pp. 287-88.

wisdom,[51] and from Plotinus's *Ennead* vi.9 where a similar sentiment is expressed, as it is also in very early Christian gnostic writings. Underhill notes that genuine mystical expression (which often has the character of so-called 'automatic writing') once 'it is divorced from the critical action of the surface intelligence, always tends to assume a dithyrambic form... Life, which eludes language, can yet—we know not how—be communicated by rhythm.'[52] This last observation raises interesting questions as to the psychology of mystical states, questions which interested von Hügel and Underhill at a time when modern psychology was in its infancy, as it does of the trance-like states, induced by rhythmic music and Christian mantras, in much contemporary charismatic worship. Once again the fundamental questions are raised about the nature of mystical and related states, and of aesthetic awareness and experience. Are these conditions or states related? Are they but different intuitions and manifestations of what we identify as transcendence? And what is this transcendence of which men and women claim to have a vision? Is it a revelation of God or (without the religious coding) an awareness of 'the beyond' or is it nothing more than a heightened state of physical perception, as Kenneth Clark argued[53] and some contemporary neuroscientists are suggesting? Whatever it is and however they speak of it artists seem to possess this sense of 'the beyond' and to this artistic sensibility we now turn, restricting ourselves to artists working approximately at the time that Friedrich von Hügel and Evelyn Underhill were writing.

Art, Adoration and the Sense of 'The Beyond'

For von Hügel, religious experience, like all given experiences 'from the givenness of the pebble and the star...on to the immensely greater givenness of the human spirit, and the primary, absolute givenness and reality of God' provides 'une affirmation ontologique'.[54] This fundamental affirmation is given in and with the finite yet it is beyond philosophy and dogma, indeed it is beyond religion as such. Von Hügel repudiates the notion of a separate and distinct religious faculty in humankind. It is not exclusive or pure. Rather, religious experience is a 'metaphysic of life'—it is an ontology —and it finds its expression in adoration in the face of this givenness and not at all in theology and dogma. Expressing von Hügel's conviction Whelan says that 'adoration is an immediate datum and demand of man's experience of the real'.[55] The questions arise: Do artists and those who are moved by art

---

51. Underhill, *Mysticism*, pp. 277-78, quoting Boehme's *The Way of Christ* (1612). The latest edition of this work in English (P.C. Erb and W. Zeller) has 'plays with Sophia' for 'danceth with Sophia'. The passage is erotic.

52. Underhill, *Mysticism*, pp. 333-34.

53. Clark, *Moments of Vision*, p. 1.

54. Quoted in Whelan, *The Spirituality of Friedrich von Hügel*, p. 90.

55. Whelan, *The Spirituality of Friedrich von Hügel*, p. 80.

find in it *une affirmation ontologique*? Is their response akin to adoration? If religion at its heart is adoration,[56] can the same be said, however differently expressed, of art? And even if it cannot, is there any sense of the transcendent in art, any sense of *au dela*, the beyond, such that we may suppose that artists and mystics are perceiving the same fundamental reality?

Evidence of how the artists of the time understood the creative process in which they were engaged is inevitably anecdotal. We have to work with necessarily imprecise articulations of feelings, apprehensions, perceptions and intuitions. No theories can be propounded from such sources as these. Indeed, the Impressionists and those who succeeded them distrusted theories and published no manifestos. Renoir's only aesthetic theory, as we have noted, 'was a mock defence of the irregular in art—a theory of no theory at all'.[57] As Phoebe Pool notes, in this rejection of philosophical speculation the Impressionists were at one with Flaubert, Sainte-Beuve and the Goncourts. She could have added Stéphane Mallarmé to the list. In this rejection of binding aesthetic theories these painters not only turned their backs on *salon* orthodoxy but reflected the general sense of *fin-de-siècle* disillusion with any notion of scientific and material progress. There was a related sense of disillusion with, even of alienation from, conventional religion too, which may explain what George Heard Hamilton has aptly called the 'pantheistic languors'[58] of the end of the century which attracted not a few European artists of the period. Piet Mondrian (1872–1944), for example, having been brought up in a strict Calvinist environment in his native Holland, rejected its rigidities and became a theosophist in 1909 in a religious conversion which was to influence his art profoundly. Emil Nolde (1867–1953), a deeply religious man, who was, Hamilton says, 'like many in his time frequently racked by doubt', sought inspiration in primitive art, perhaps there unconsciously to discover the roots of his mystical perceptions and intuitions. Ernst Barlach (1870–1938) was another deeply mystical artist whose work 'from the very first communicated his mystical interpretation of life as man's lonely search for himself, for others, and for his lost God, a search beset by invisible forms, from an "unknown darkness" within the artist's consciousness'.[59] Georges Rouault (1871–1958), though deeply Christian, was to produce paintings which expressed his friend Leon Bloy's desire

> at this dreadful close of the century, when everything seems lost, to thrust at God the insistent cry of dereliction and anxiety for the orphaned multitude which the Father in his celestial heights seems to be abandoning and which no longer has the strength even to die bravely.[60]

56. Von Hügel, quoted in Whelan, *The Spirituality of Friedrich von Hügel*, p. 85.
57. Pool, *Impressionism*, p. 52.
58. Hamilton, *Painting and Sculpture*, p. 130.
59. Hamilton, *Painting and Sculpture*, p. 188.
60. From a letter, 30 May 1886, quoted Hamilton, *Painting and Sculpture*, p. 176.

Rouault never deserted Christianity, though he interpreted Bloy's cry from the heart in ways which the Church rejected. He wrote thus to Abbé Mugnier in 1904:

> I love my art passionately, and there is a growing conflict between my art and my religion... It is at the very moment when I have the greatest need for religion to sustain me in life and in art, that the advice and counsel of very religious and very respectable Catholics have filled me with some confusion... You can well understand what it is to be an artist ...so dedicated to his work that it fills him with sadness to see that the conflict might end deplorably in letting go of religion.[61]

Other artists responded to the spiritual malaise in Europe at the close of the century by seeking a spiritual reality within themselves. The Fauves, the 'wild beasts' (1900–1910), principally Matisse, Derain and Vlaminck, who were painting their intensely subjective pictures as von Hügel and Underhill were writing about so intensely subjective an experience as religious mysticism, and were thereby creating the first truly modern movement in art in the twentieth century, placed unremitting emphasis on the subjective self and its experience. One of the first of the Fauves, Raoul Dufy (1877–1953), looking at his colours and brushes, exclaimed: 'How, with these, can I render, not what I see, but what is, what exists for me, my reality'.[62] Another artist who rejected religious orthodoxy at this time to express his highly subjective, intuitive, mystical awareness through his art was Ferdinand Hodler (1853–1918) who was attracted to the pantheistic theosophy of the Rosicrucians. In 1888 a group of artists, including Sérusier, Denis, Vuillard and Bonnard were greatly attracted to Rosicrucian rituals and later called themselves Nabis, a title which they employed to indicate their interest in Eastern religions and theosophy. At the same time the deeply depressive Edvard Munch (1863–1944) was expressing his state of mind and his reaction to the obsessive religion in which he was raised in such paintings as his naked self-portrait *In Hell* in 1904–1905 and *The Scream* in 1893. There were many other artists searching for a truth about themselves and a reality within themselves and in the world about them at a time when orthodox Christianity seemed to offer them little. So Wassily Kandinsky, in his classic statement in 1913 *Concerning the Spiritual in Art*, could say that 'the working of the inner need and the development of art is an ever-advancing expression of the eternal and objective in terms of the periodic and subjective'.[63] For Kandinsky 'the *Stimmung* of nature can be imparted by every art, not, however, by imitation, but by the artistic divination of its inner spirit'.[64] The spiritual was not the preserve of religion.

---

61. Quoted in Waldemar George and Genevieve Nouaille-Rouault, *Rouault* (London: Pall Mall Press, 1971), p. 65.
62. Hamilton, *Painting and Sculpture*, p. 158.
63. Kandinsky, *Concerning the Spiritual in Art*, p. 34.
64. Kandinsky, *Concerning the Spiritual in Art*, p. 20 n. 2.

Nearly a century earlier Samuel Palmer made a distinction between what he called 'general nature' which 'is wisely and beneficently adapted to refresh the senses and soothe the spirits of general observers' and nature as it is perceived by the visionary painter, as 'divine Art piles mountains upon [Nature's] hills'.[65]

A Strongly Transcendental Tinge

The attraction of pantheism and theosophy to many artists at this time is of great interest and should not be dismissed. Von Hügel noted that mysticism is greatly served by pantheism, for pantheism, unlike the Hebraic under-standing of God as Wholly Other, lays emphasis on the apprehension of God as the Infinite including all finite existences. It was this that attracted artists of the time. It gave them a quasi-religious framework within which to search for the Real within the real. What von Hügel calls a 'Pantheistic-seeming Mysticism' also enabled them to discover 'the truly spiritual function and fruitfulness of Deterministic Science'. Von Hügel devotes a long chapter to mysticism, pantheism and personality and concludes that although 'complete Pantheism is non-religious' and 'Christianity excludes complete and final Pantheism' nevertheless we should 'guard against...any exclusion of a seeking or finding of God in Nature and in Conscience'.[66]

But what was the pantheism to which these artists were attracted? What they appear to have sought was a sense of unity with the natural order and with the rest of humankind. As R.H. Zaehner showed, this is not panthe-ism—'all-is-God-ism' which necessarily involves belief in a divine being—but pan-en-henism or 'all-in-one-ism'. This is profane merely because no sacred power is implied. It may be that artists and critics of the time employed the word 'pantheism' indiscriminately. In his ground-breaking work *Abstraction and Empathy* published in 1908 Wilhelm Worringer (1881–1965) presup-posed that 'a work of art, as an autonomous organism, stands beside nature on equal terms'. He thus gave expression to the great step taken by the pioneers of modern art and we will return to it later. This assumption involved Worringer in himself taking 'a decisive step from aesthetic objec-tivity to aesthetic subjectivity': that is, the starting-point of investigation for modern aesthetics was to be not nature but the contemplating subject. This in turn culminated in a theory of empathy. Worringer argued that 'the urge to empathy is a pre-assumption of aesthetic experience', and this means that aesthetic enjoyment is in fact 'objectified self-enjoyment' for 'to enjoy aesthetically means to enjoy myself in a sensuous object diverse from myself, to empathize myself into it' and 'What I empathize into it is quite generally life'. In the development of what was to become a very influential

65. In a letter to John Linnell in 1828, quoted in Colin Harrison, *Samuel Palmer* (Oxford: Ashmolean Museum, 1997), p. 28.
66. Von Hügel, *The Mystical Element*, II, pp. 329-30.

contribution to Modernist thought, Worringer concludes that 'the precondition for the urge to empathy is a happy pantheistic relationship of confidence between man and the phenomena of the external world; in a religious respect it corresponds to a strongly transcendental tinge to all notions'.[67]

The Symbolist theorists made the quest for ultimate meaning in the natural world a manifesto item. Teodor de Wyzewa (1862–1914), working in Paris and writing in 1897, proclaimed that it was the function of artists to recreate a 'Life' which had been destroyed in 'this world of defiled, habitual appearances' and to build

> the holy world of a better life: better, because we make it intentionally and know that we make it. This is the very business of Art. But from where will the artist take the elements of this higher life? He can find it nowhere unless in our normal life, in what we call Reality... And so, this explains the necessity of realism in art; not a realism which transcribes the vain appearances that we think real, with no other end, but an artistic realism, which tears these appearances from the false reality of interest where we perceive them, in order to transport them into the *higher reality of a disinterested life*. We see around us trees, animals, men, and we assume they are living; but, seen in this way, they are only vain shadows which drape the shifting decor of our vision. They will only live when the artist, in whose special soul they have a more intense reality, inspires them with this higher life—*recreates* them before us.[68]

This is more than a late example of nineteenth-century Platonic idealism (though, as Underhill was to point out, 'Platonism is the reaction of the born intellectualist upon mystical truth'[69]). There is passion here. The call to the artist to 'tear' the truth of things from 'the false reality of interest' and recreate it in 'the higher reality of a disinterested life' has a genuinely mystical ring to it.

A seeking after the transcendent, this 'higher reality', is the mark of the true mystic. Evelyn Underhill says of mysticism that

> it is essentially a movement of the heart, seeking to transcend the limitations of the individual standpoint and to surrender itself to ultimate Reality; for no personal gain, to satisfy no transcendental curiosity, to obtain no other-worldly joys, but purely from an instinct of love.[70]

On this analysis, mysticism, like art, is intensely subjective and personal but equally intensely non-individualistic. This is a profoundly important distinction. However, the terms 'subjective' and 'individualistic' are easily confused. Von Hügel pleaded for

---

67. Reprinted in C. Harrison and P. Wood, *Art in Theory 1900–1990* (Oxford: Basil Blackwell, 1993), pp. 68-70.

68. From the English translation of 'L'Art wagnérien: la peinture', in *Nos Maitres* 11 (Paris, 1897), reprinted in Harrison and Wood, *Art in Theory*, pp. 17-18 (my italics).

69. Underhill, *Mysticism*, p. 99.

70. Underhill, *Mysticism*, p. 85.

a profound de-subjectivizing, a great shifting of the centre of [man's] interest away from the petty, claimful, animal self, with its 'I against all the world' to a great kingdom of souls, in which Man gains his larger, spiritual, unique personality, with its 'I as part of, and for all the world'.[71]

He rightly rejected what he called 'all empty, sentimental Subjectivism', yet he acknowledges that the search for exclusive objectivity is a 'will-o-the-wisp quest'. We must, he says, not be 'haunted by the bogey-fear of the subjective resonance within us...for the truly real...is a thing that has an inside'.[72] He goes on to assert that mysticism is predominantly individualistic in that mystics are not concerned with 'the great social spirituality which finds God in our neighbour and in the great human organizations, through which and in which...man in great part becomes and is truly man'.[73] The distinction here is therefore between the social and the individual, between what von Hügel calls 'the Corporate and the Lonely'. Underhill on the other hand draws a distinction between the limitations of 'the individual standpoint' interpreted in terms of 'personal gain' and that 'ultimate Reality' which can only be pursued for its own sake. True mystics, while seeking always to avoid sentimental subjectivism on the one hand and, on the other, the belief that exclusive objectivity can be obtained in the expressing of their vision, acknowledge that 'a coming and a going, a movement inwards and outwards, checks and counter-checks, friction, contrast, battle and storm are necessary ingredients of the soul's growth'.[74] Significant artists of the period would have agreed. Many were concerned with the world, with 'trees, animals, men', but solely in order, as Underhill says of mystics, to move 'from the life of sense to the life of the spirit'.[75] In an article published in 1909, Maurice Denis (1870–1943) quoted Albert Aurier in 1890 writing that

everywhere the right to dream is demanded, the right to fields of Azure, the right to fly to the stars of absolute truth. The myopic copying of anecdotes from society, the stupid imitation of nature's blemishes, dull observation, trompe-l'oeil, the glory of being as true, as banally exact, as the photograph no longer satisfies any painter, any sculptor worthy of this name.[76]

As we have seen, Underhill was later to compare the artist and the mystic in a very similar vein. Gauguin had said that 'working from vision, we search for the mysterious centre of thought'. Art, wrote Denis, is 'a creation of our spirit which nature provokes',[77] and

71. Von Hügel, *The Mystical Element*, II, pp. 330-31.
72. Von Hügel, *The Mystical Element*, II, p. 264.
73. Von Hügel, *The Mystical Element*, II, p. 365.
74. Von Hügel, *The Mystical Element*, II, p. 330.
75. Underhill, *Mysticism*, p. 99.
76. Maurice Denis, 'From Gauguin and van Gogh to Neo-Classicism', in *L'Occident* (Paris, May 1909), reprinted in Harrison and Wood, *Art in Theory*, pp. 47-53 (48).
77. Quoted in Harrison and Wood, *Art in Theory*, p. 50.

art does not have superior value unless it corresponds to the noblest and most mysterious characteristics of the human soul... The most painterly of painters, Rembrandt, Rubens or Corot, were never content with being superb technicians: the works which immortalized them are, properly speaking, religious, no matter what their literary content may be.[78]

Art finds it basis in 'the most subjective and the most subtle aspect of the human soul, the most mysterious spirit of our inner life'.[79] Here Denis was reasserting the importance of the Symbolist[80] agenda of the 1890s. The Symbolists placed great emphasis on artistic intuition and on 'vision' and on the 'inner life' of the artist, and this at a time when Freud was working in Paris in the 1880s in his new field of psychoanalysis.

Manet: Sight and Insight

So it was that as Freud was investigating the human psyche, and von Hügel and Evelyn Underhill were writing analytically about mysticism, European artists were expressing subjectively in their art what Munch, in 1918, was to call 'modern psychic life' in all its distress and trauma. The fact is that in the last years of the nineteenth century and the early years of the twenti-eth-century human consciousness (and thereby human *un*consciousness) became for the first time the object of its own study, not least by the paint-ers of the period. In art this concentration on the subjective was to lead inevitably to non-representational art and to abstraction, where a painting or sculpture is self-evidently *an object in its own right* and not a repre-sentation of some other object. But this process of deliberately making an artwork as an independent object had begin much earlier. Twentieth-century art seems far removed from the then much derided and so-called 'naturalist' pictures of the Impressionists which preceded it. Yet it was with the Impressionists, and supremely with a painter who was their leader (but who laid no claim to be an Impressionist), Edouard Manet, that this modern movement in art began. Manet's vision, more obviously so than that of his predecessors since the early Middle Ages, was highly personal, natural and subjective,[81] *and just because of this was so accessible to others.*[82] Manet began a movement which effected a paradigm shift. Modernism, says James Rubin,

78. Harrison and Wood, *Art in Theory*, p. 52.
79. Harrison and Wood, *Art in Theory*, p. 53.
80. Symbolism was the avant-garde movement of the 1880s and 1890s. It was concerned with art as a system of symbols, marrying that to the claim for the auton-omy of the aesthetic experience and insight of the artist.
81. But is not the work of every artist essentially personal and subjective however ostensibly objective it may appear to be in terms of its subject? A Corot landscape is no more literally 'true to life' than one by Morisot. Every true artist has sought to express spiritual values, however defined, in his or her work.
82. See Rubin, *Manet's Silence*, p. 12. Much of what follows immediately is depend-ent on Rubin's brilliant analysis.

recognized the futility of Realism and...dedicated itself to exploring and recording the space and function of subjectivity, variously defined as imagination, creativity or perception, in visual representation... By stressing the concept of subjectivity, the story of modern art can be recast as that of the self's self-discovery and of the mind's recognition of the role of the visual in its self-knowledge and definition.[83]

This introduces an important question which has dominated aesthetics since Aristotle—the relationship between subjective and objective in an artwork. But how do we define either? As James Rubin points out so well current deconstruction analyses show how what we take for granted, including and above all the distinction between subjective and objective, is actually an element of the ideology which makes the distinction 'and hence part of a system to which there might therefore be alternatives, rather than being an objective fact or a transcendent truth'.[84] This is clearly true—as true of religious dogma and the notion of the existence of God as of any aesthetic theory or any other epistemological or ontological theory. Is not an uncritically accepted religious dogma effectively what Derrida, following Kant, has called the 'absent condition', a *paregon*, effectively 'framing' belief and disallowing what lies outside the frame? This supremely important question cannot be discussed here and may seem to lead us away from our limited theme, yet Rubin has shown how Manet forced the viewer to recognise himself in his art and have life within it (I say 'himself' for the finest example of this is *A Bar at the Folies-Bergere,* painted in 1881–82, in which a male viewer of the painting is compelled to see himself in the lecherous man reflected in the mirror behind Suzon, the bar-maid, and Suzon's distainful expression as directed at him).

What is subject and object, sight and insight in art? As Rubin says: 'vision...always implies inseparable objective and subjective activities: it refers to sight and insight simultaneously'. Writing of Manet, Rubin goes on to say that 'artists have never settled for mere "reproductions" of the visible... They have always believed artistic vision to have original and personal dimensions that differentiate its product from mechanical representations and justify its spiritual value.'[85] However, Rubin does not include in his definition of 'vision' a specifically religious notion of the revelation of the Divine. Yet Underhill does include in her definition 'a radiant consciousness of the "otherness" of natural things. It is 'the simplest and commonest form of illumination [and] most people, under the spell of emotion or of beauty have known flashes of rudimentary vision of this kind'.[86] Kenneth Clark's 'moments of vision' find parallels here.

83. Rubin, *Manet's Silence*, p. 14.
84. Rubin, *Manet's Silence*, p. 16.
85. Rubin, *Manet's Silence*, p. 15.
86. Underhill, *Mysticism*, p. 282.

Art, Mysticism and Rhythm

A further connection between art and sacred and profane mysticism in the early years of this century is to be found in the idea of rhythm. As we have seen already, Underhill makes much of this. The artist obeys 'the laws of rhythm: obeying the rule by which all arts "tend to approach the condition of music".' So too the mystic, for 'of all the arts music alone shares with great mystical literature the power of waking us to response to the life-movement of the universe: brings us—we know not how—news of its exultant passions and its incomparable peace'. Underhill notes that the mediaeval mind, 'more naturally mystical than ours', was 'therefore more sharply aware of the part which rhythmic harmony plays in the worlds of nature and of grace'. She notes that the writing of mystics tends to present itself in rhythmical periods, and quotes von Hügel observing that 'rhythm... [was] ever present in all of Catherine's [of Genoa] authentic sayings'. Underhill acknowledges that 'it is only by the oblique methods of the artist, only by the use of aesthetic suggestion and musical rhythm that the wonder of [mystical] vision can be expressed'. What she calls 'essential goodness' can be adequately communicated only 'in a living, that is to say, an artistic form'.[87] To record parallels in writing about art from this period would be tedious. Rhythm in painting is the harmonious relationship between forms and is a fundamental concept. It was important in the construction of so-called realist painting, but with van Gogh and Gauguin, and, to a lesser extent Cézanne, descriptive realism gave way to a very different kind of art. Now, feelings and intuitions were symbolized and conveyed *primarily* through the rhythms of colour relationships and design.[88] Gauguin, in a letter to André Fontainas in March 1899, called attention to the musical elements in modern paintings, and wrote: 'Colour, which is vibration just as music is, reaches what is most general and therefore vaguest in nature: its interior force'. He spoke of the sources of his own art:

> Here in my hut, in complete silence, I dream of violent harmonies in the natural scents which intoxicate me. A delight distilled from some indescribably sacred horror which I glimpse of far-off things. The fragrance of an antique joy which I am breathing in the present. Animal shapes of a statuesque rigidity: indescribably antique, august, and religious in the rhythm of their gesture, in their singular immobility. In the dreaming eyes is the overcast surface of an unfathomable enigma. And comes the night when all things are at rest. My eyes close in order to see without comprehending the dream of an infinite space stretching before me, and I have the sensation of the melancholy progress of my hopes.[89]

---

87. Underhill, *Mysticism*, pp. 91, 94, 189, 197, 287, 333-34. See also pp. 90, 150, 281 etc.
88. See Hamilton, *Painting and Sculpture*, p. 100.
89. Quoted in Hamilton, *Painting and Sculpture*, p. 92.

This is a classic Symbolist statement and it has a metaphysical and a mystical content which link art and sacred and profane mysticism, notably through its recognition of the indispensability of harmony and rhythm. It is a recognition, from within this period, which serves to help dissolve the notional distinction not only between sacred and profane mysticism, but between mysticism and art. Only mysticism conceived as von Hügel and Underhill conceived it in narrowly Christian terms would repudiate this dissolution. Listening to the artists of the period one is reminded that fundamental to the idea of mysticism is union. What artists from Manet onwards sought was not to *represent* the natural world, nor did they even attempt to *represent their vision* in the materiality of their painting; rather, as Rubin says of Manet's art, his painting *actualized the act of artistic vision*. The painting *was* the vision, for

> it signals the spectacle of consciousness contemplating itself—a corporeal sense that is defined, it seems, by the paradox of discovering its own absence and by the uncertainty produced by suspicion *that its reality is inseparable from representation*.[90]

The painter's self is objectified in his art. By actualizing his vision, incarnating his vision, he becomes part of, at one with, the external world from which he has become alienated.

This insight from the history of art has important implications for the Christian believer. If the experience holds true that, in a truly incarnational relationship with God's world and by his grace, we are what we create ourselves to be as we actualise our vision of the essential unity of all things, then implications for rational notions of the objective reality of God, and for the nature of religion as a distinct human (and minority) activity, are raised yet again. We explore this further in the next chapter.

---

90. Rubin, *Manet's Silence*, p. 90 (my italics).

Chapter 8

The Reality of the Really New

Theologians must do theology imaginatively, recognising
that the Bible is art.

In attempting this they must break free from traditional theological categories, take the religion of the incarnation utterly seriously and learn from
the artist. To illustrate some imaginative connections between art and
theology we will explore just one theme in this chapter, that of chaos and
ordering. It is a powerful theme in both art and religion—not least in the art
and religion of the Bible, and that is where we will begin.

Chaos and Order

In 1806 J.M.W. Turner exhibited his unfinished painting *The Battle of
Trafalgar, as seen from the Mizzen Starboard Shrouds of the Victory*. Writing of this picture James Hamilton notes that in depicting Nelson slumped
on the foredeck as the shot that killed him rings out Turner took poetic
licence 'or at least the licence to shrink time and to depict both the act and
its immediate aftermath'. Turner's showing the disorder and noise of war is,
Hamilton says, 'to a late twentieth-century eye, oddly familiar. Now, given
the presence of the video camera in conflict, we know that chaos disjoints
clarity. Events cannot wait for classic composition to unfurl, a fact fully
appreciated by Turner.'[1]

The Jewish and Christian religions are founded on the experience of
salvation. The principal Hebrew word (*yeshūah*) rendered by the metaphor
'salvation' in the English versions has a root meaning of 'to be spacious', 'to
develop without hindrance' and consequently by extension 'to be victori-
ous'. It therefore carries the idea of completeness, wholeness, of being as
one has been created to be. In both the Old Testament and the New the
words we translate as 'to save' carry the primary meaning of 'to make

1. James Hamilton, *Turner: A Life* (London: Hodder & Stoughton, 1997), p. 94.

whole' and thus to save from danger, injury or suffering or to heal and restore to health. 'To save' and 'to make whole' are one and the same as modern English versions of the New Testament make clear.

Yet, as with most biblical metaphors, the notion of spaciousness or wholeness resonates always with its opposite, namely, in this case, fragmentation or brokenness or defeat, and this in turn with a foundational experience and image—chaos. There is only one Hebrew word, *tohu*, which can adequately be rendered 'chaos' in the biblical languages[2] but its nature and significance is conveyed through a number of images, notably those of deep or outer darkness (as in *tōhu wabōhu*, 'waste and void' in Gen. 1.2 and Jer. 4.23-26), perpetual desolation (e.g. *tōhu* in Isa. 34.11 and *shimamah* in Ezek. 35.9) and the apocalyptic 'time of troubles' in which 'no living thing could survive' were it not for God's salvation (Mk 13.20 in the Revised English Bible [REB]).

It is important to emphasise at the outset that in the Bible chaos is not itself evil, though it can be the consequence of evil. It is regarded as God's final judgment on sin and evil. Perhaps it is because chaotic primaeval matter is both the stuff of creation and also God's threatened final judgment that the Bible does not open with the cosmic abolition of chaos. It is not that (evil) chaos is purged in favour of a redeemed and therefore ordered universe. The chaotic primaeval matter (the 'vast waste' in Gen. 1.2 REB), or at least a proportion of it, is subjected to *order*. God separates disordered matter from ordered matter. Chaos, that is disordered matter, always exists and threatens. In the Myth of the New Creation (in the Revelation of John) the Sea of Glass is the ocean, the 'vast waste', of the Genesis creation myth. It remains in heaven as a symbol of a universe still not wholly subjected to God's ordering.[3] In the first of the two creation myths in the book of Genesis God is god and creator of both order and chaos. That which is without form is given form. The power of the void is restrained. Yet formlessness and the awfulness of the void are never done away with. The God of Genesis 1 saves from chaos but he does not abolish it. He 'separates' (the biblical word) the chaos above from the ordered universe beneath. In the myth God retains to himself the power, in his awful judgment, to dissolve the separation and allow chaos to overwhelm.

---

2.   The Revised English Bible (REB) uses the word 'chaos' at Jer. 4.23. Here the author employs the actual phrase *tōhu wabōhu* from Gen. 1.2, the only other place where it occurs. Isa. 34.11 has 'wasteness' (Heb. *tōhu*) which the older English versions render as 'confusion'. Here the Septuagint (LXX) has 'the measuring line of desolation' *geōmetrias eremou* which the REB and New Jerusalem Bible (NJB) render as 'the measuring line of chaos' ('...and the plumb-line of emptiness' NJB). It is significant that here chaos is God's 'measuring line' or judgment. Edom's boundaries will be reduced to 'a jumble of stones' (REB)—another image for chaos. The RSV employs the word 'chaos' at 2 Esd. 5.8. However, the REB has 'chasms' here.

3.   G.B. Caird, *The Revelation of St John the Divine* (London: A. & C. Black, 1984), p. 292.

The God of Ordering

Whatever else it is Genesis 1 is a foundational, cross-cultural, Myth of Ordering. This ordering of physical chaos is at once also, as many biblical writers maintain, the ordering of emotional, psychic, chaos. Sin and guilt result in chaos, evil results in chaos, mental disorder and physical disease are chaotic. All is redeemable by a God of ordering—an ordering which is at once healing and wholeness. To make whole is to restore to soundness and unity, to restore freedom, integrity, safety, peace, forgiveness and health from the chaos of captivity, brokenness, peril, conflict, sin and disease.

As the Creation Myth in Genesis 1 *is* a myth an important question has to do with its fundamental function. G.B. Caird argued that a biblical myth is a metaphor system for the theological interpretation of an historical event.[4] That the universe *is*, and that it had an origin, is, for the biblical writers, an historical event. Yet never far away from the consciousness of those men is an awareness that the physical universe has its parallel in the human condition. All is one. The question arises: Is the Creation Myth a myth which tells of the ordering of cosmic chaos or is it primarily a myth which tells of the equally historical 'event' of the human fear not only of physical disintegration on a universal scale but also of inner, psychic, disintegration? Almost wherever one looks in the Bible inner chaos is given a cosmic scale. For example what we would describe as mentally disturbed people are regarded as possessed by 'demoniacs' or 'unclean spirits', that is, as under the control of chaotic forces quite outside human control. Again, for the psalmist to have his 'soul...cast down' is to experience 'deep calling to deep at the thunder of thy cataracts; all thy waves and billows are gone over me' (Ps. 42.5-7). Similarly the psalmist is threatened with the 'torrents of perdition' which are 'the cords of death' (Ps. 18.4-5) and 'the floods' which 'lift up their roaring' (Ps. 93.3). These references to 'waters', 'waves', 'cataracts', 'billows' and 'torrents' are all clear allusions to the Ocean of Chaos in Genesis 1 but they all have to do here with personal, psychic chaos.

Now the psalmist knows that God is greater that the threats of uncontrollable chaos ('mightier than the waves of the sea, the Lord on high is mighty' [Ps. 93.4] for 'the Lord commands his steadfast love' [Ps. 42.8]). Nevertheless just because God *is* mightier than the power of chaos, he can unleash chaos. There is in the Bible the always implicit fear (occasionally made explicit as it is, principally, in the story of the Flood) that God can at any time withdraw the dam or roof[5] which separates unordered matter from ordered matter, a dam which separates 'the [ordered] waters which are under the firmament from the [disordered] waters which are above the

---

4. As is eschatology, G.B. Caird, *The Language and Imagery of the Bible* (London: Gerald Duckworth, 1980), p. 219.
5. Interestingly, in English translation, the 'firmament' (Heb. *ragia*, 'expanse'; LXX *stereōma*, 'a solid body', thus 'a support').

firmament'. The great disordered ocean can, at the command of God, pour down upon and extinguish all life. Chaos can ensue as God's judgment on a sinful people. Despite the promise at the conclusion of the classic biblical Myth of Disorder, the story of the Flood, that God will never again 'destroy every living creature that I have made', the threat of overwhelming disaster remains. The myths of the Flood and of the Exodus and the warnings of Job, the psalmists and the prophets that God can, if he so wills, initiate overwhelming disaster (Job 15.22-23; 27.20-23; 38.34-38; Pss. 33.6; 93.3-4; Isa. 34.11; Jer. 4.23-26; Nah. 1.8 etc.) provide confirmation of the notion that disordered chaos can at any time engulf the ordered universe.

It is significant that water is often seen as *the* stuff of chaos as it is portrayed in biblical myth, poetry and symbolic narrative. The sea can be an ordered calm but it can also be a chaotic, disordered storm (note the Exodus myth, probably influenced, as is the first Creation Myth, by Ugaritic imagery). The poetic narratives of the Stilling of the Storm in the New Testament Gospels, each of them deeply influenced in turn by Old Testament imagery (notably in the language and structure of Ps. 107.23-32), convey the same message. The Sea of Galilee becomes a glassy sea. Yet the storms or floods can come at the behest of a God who can will to 'blot out...everything that I have made...from the face of the ground' (Gen. 7.4). In another biblical genre, apocalyptic, the theme of chaos imposed at God's command is also very evident.

The fear of chaos and fragmentation and the instinctive need to bring about order is clearly cut deep into human psychology. It is found in the Bible itself. As we will see, it is found also in the post-biblical processes of rationalisation and simplification which ordered the Bible's imagery and resulted in early Christian doctrinal formulations.

This fear (or at least uneasiness and insecurity) in the face of the (apparently) chaotic, and the processes of its rationalisation and resolution are to be seen also in our response to art. What follows is a very brief and superficial note on the phenomenon of order and disorder in art and religion. It considers two issues in broadest outline: apocalyptic and the early development of doctrine in Christianity, and 'the undifferentiated fabric' of art and the subsequent process of 'secondary revision' or 'verticalisation' to which this 'hidden order' is subjected. The first is discussed by David Tracy in his *The Analogical Imagination* published in 1981. The second in Anton Ehrenzweig's *The Hidden Order of Art: A Study in the Psychology of Artistic Imagination* first published in 1967. They tell of the role of the imagination in the production and interpretation of the Christian 'classic' text (Tracy) and of the artwork (Ehrenzweig), the first from a Christian orthodox perspective and the second from a Freudian psychological viewpoint. Both books were regarded as either 'most important' (*The Analogical Imagination*) or 'groundbreaking' (*The Hidden Order of Art*) when they were first published though the insights of neither book have been adequately followed up in the intervening years. What we will try to do here will be to set

Tracy and Ehrenzweig side-by-side and to see whether any correlations become evident suggesting a relationship *of kind* rather than mere similarity between the ordering processes of religion and art. We begin with Ehrenzweig.

Anton Ehrenzweig and the Psychology of Artistic Imagination

Ehrenzweig's principal theme is founded on the notion that, while reason is always at hand, the processes of the creation of an artwork are largely well outside the conscious control of the artist. They are basically, but only apparently, chaotic:

> Modern art displays this attack of unreason on reason quite openly. Yet owing to the powers of the creative mind real disaster is averted. Reason may seem to be cast aside for a moment. Modern art seems truly chaotic. But as time passes the 'hidden order' in art's substructure (the world of unconscious form creation) rises to the surface. The modern artist may attack his own reason and single-track thought; but a new order is already in the making.[6]

Ehrenzweig's key theme is that from the standpoint of both the artist and the viewer or listener of a work of art the process of coming to terms with it begins with what he calls elsewhere variously 'unconscious scanning' or 'low-level vision' (that is, significantly for my argument, 'imagination') or 'undifferentiated perception'. He employs these terms to describe what he calls the 'superior efficiency' with which we *first* scan the total visual (or audible) field of a work of art. We take it in at a glance. The artwork makes an immediate impact upon us in its totality however fragmented or chaotic or immediately unintelligible (as we say revealingly) it is. Its 'hidden order' imposes itself upon us though we almost certainly do not notice this. This unconscious scanning is conjunctive and serial, Ehrenzweig says. That is to say, we do not, at this early stage, ask questions about the logical (or otherwise) connections between the various elements of the artwork. We do not dissect and analyse. Ehrenzweig says that, at this first stage and almost instantaneously, we grasp, subliminally, 'in a single undivided act of comprehension data that to conscious perception would be incompatible'.[7] As we say, we 'take it all in'. This 'taking it in' is supremely the work of the imagination and is quite independent of any subsequent stage as a result of which we may say whether or not we understand or like or dislike the artwork. He cites the example of serialisation in the music of Schoenberg and Boulez in which the various elements are scrambled up in many possible sequences such that their relationship is incomprehensible to conscious perception. What the (admittedly sympathetic) 'naive listener' or

---

6.   Ehrenzweig, *The Hidden Order*, pp. xii-xiii.
7.   Ehrenzweig, *The Hidden Order*, p. 32.

viewer does it unconsciously and imaginatively to integrate supposedly disparate elements and to 'see' the essential inner unity of the artwork—a unity or order which he or she does not consciously comprehend.

Ehrenzweig could have cited a first reading of highly imaginative passages in the Bible as other examples of unconscious scanning. At first reading (that is 'at first sight' as we say) much of this material appears fantastic and incomprehensible. It is 'undifferentiated'. It is often impossible to 'make sense' of it. Take, for example, the vision of the Chariot of the Lord in Ezek. 1.4-28. It is impossible to create in one's mind's eye a coherent visual picture of what Ezekiel 'saw'. Of course that is not the point. This is a 'vision' to which only language is capable of giving expression. As we read Ezek. 1.4-28 we are compelled very early on to suspend our rational faculties, as the author clearly intended, and allow our imagination to see the truth that the vision conveys. Ezekiel himself builds in what G.B. Caird calls 'a triple guard against literality' (we might say rationality) when he tells of the figure at the heart of the vision having 'the appearance of the likeness of the glory of the Lord'. This is an artwork to be grasped and seen whole by the imagination and not dissected by reason.

Note here a point to which we will return. We wish always to 'make sense' of something unusual—to remove its uncertainties *and therefore our insecurities* and to bring about some kind of (usually imposed) order. What Ehrenzweig calls 'modern art', by which he seems to mean mainly Cubist, Expressionist and abstract art, rejoices in surface chaos—in the attack of unreason on reason, in the victory of chaos. Yet what appears to our consciousness *and to the consciousness of the artist* as chaos and fragmentation betrays a deeper unity which is revealed not by the exercise of our rational faculties but through our unconscious, imaginative, scanning of an artwork. An example of this for me was the first performance of Harrison Birtwhistle's extraordinary work *Panic* during the BBC's *Proms* concert series in 1995. I might not have watched and listened had I not known the parents of the solo percussionist, Paul Clarvis, for forty years. Rather than try to make 'sense' of it I allowed this (for me) strange and apparently 'chaotic' but clearly extremely disciplined work slowly to display its unity—though I could not then and cannot now articulate of what that unity comprises.

Thus Ehrenzweig would subscribe to the idea that the initial, sudden, impact of a new (to us) artwork reveals a reality, that is a coherence or unity, grasped by our 'low level' apprehension. This is what David Tracy in another context calls the reality of the really new. The artwork may have a fragmented appearance or be subject to rational inconsistencies (say, the lack of aerial, single-point, perspective in some Impressionist landscapes or the gross lack of proportion or multiple angles of vision in Cézanne's still-lifes) but at first sight we do not notice this fragmentation or these inconsistencies. These become apparent almost immediately at the second stage of the apprehension of an artwork.

This second stage is the first of two intellectual stages. At this stage we become consciously aware of the logical fragmentation or impossibility of what we are looking at or listening to. We realise, for example, that if we were directly facing Suzon at the bar of the Folies-Bergere in Manet's master-work we could not see her back, or our own face (for surely it is), reflected well to the right in the mirror behind her, as Manet has depicted. This is one of at least nine different linear perspectives[8] that Manet has deliberately employed in his great picture but which become apparent only at a second (at least) glance. What is true? Do we grasp the reality or 'truth' of the picture at first glance? Do we reject it as untrue when, at second glance, we notice its 'untrue' inconsistencies? It is this second stage which Ehrenzweig calls the stage of 'verticalisation' or 'secondary revision'. To an extent, he says, this second stage must be resisted because during this stage of intellectual, conscious, awareness we destroy the essential and hidden order of the artwork of which we became unconsciously aware when we first encountered it. At first glance we recognised the essential unity of, say, Kandinsky's *Untitled (First Abstract Watercolour)*. At second glance we perceive a fragmented or logically inconsistent surface. Because we cannot live easily with chaos we 'solidify' or 'verticalise' the surface. In fact what we actually do now is to fragment it—through secondary, or second glance, revision. Because we cannot easily live with the fragmentations and inconsistencies of which we have now become aware we impose (or try to impose) a new unity, a new gestalt, upon the artwork. This is the third stage of the apprehension of an artwork. It is a complex, conscious, systematic and quite deliberate process by which we bring order to what Kenneth Clark called 'lawless and intuitive' modern art. Let us take a very simple example of *unconscious* re-patterning. It is not used by Ehrenzweig and does not properly belong to his thesis. In fact it belongs to another field of enquiry in the psychology of artistic creativity but it serves to illustrate a closely related way in which, imaginatively, we bring order out of chaos.

Seeing Faces

We say, for example, that we can see faces in an abstract action painting by Jackson Pollock. We smile as we say it because we know that Pollock does not intend us (does he not?) to see faces in his work—yet the fact that we indeed *do* see faces shows that, psychologically, we *must* see faces, we must bring familiar, recognisable, order out of apparent chaos. Ernst Gombrich, referring not to our psychological need to bring order out of chaos but rather to our biological need to relate to our environment (but may they not be the same thing?) argues that we extend our basic reading

8.   See Mary Mathews Gedo, *Looking at Art from the Inside Out: The Psychoicono-graphic Approach to Modern Art* (Cambridge: Cambridge University Press, 1994), p. 391.

of a person's face into our visual interrogation of the world around us.[9] In his seminal book *Art and Illusion* he maintains that 'our reaction to faces and physiognomic expression may not be wholly due to learning, and...the mental set which makes us read faces into blots, rocks, or wallpapers may be biologically conditioned',[10] that is, we probably have an inborn disposition 'to respond to certain configurations of biological significance for our survival... Whenever anything remotely facelike enters our field of vision, we are alerted and respond.'[11] This propensity is very well known to, and utilised by, designers and advertisers.

A very good example of seeing faces in the apparently chaotic surface of an artwork are those supposedly seen by Mary Mathews Gedo (and therefore supposedly subliminally concealed therein by the artist) in the backs of the bonnets of the Breton women in the foreground of Gauguin's *The Vision after the Sermon (Jacob Wrestling with the Angel)*.[12] Mary Mathews Gedo, an art historian and a clinical psychologist, may conceivably be right when she says that Gauguin unconsciously places faces in the bonnets—faces which, she says, recall those found in Peruvian effigy pots that Gauguin knew from childhood—but she produces no evidence that there *are* specific faces painted, however unconsciously, in the bonnets. It is at least as likely that Gedo is imposing her own gestalt on random marks in Gauguin's painted surface, a gestalt, moreover, itself the result of the psychological theories she brings to her viewing of Gauguin's painting. On the other hand are there such things as random, chaotic marks? If not, then a first glance will reveal their hidden order. However, Gedo's supposed discovery of a pattern is very much at second glance and may be sponsored by a predetermined psychological theory that she is propounding and which she (unconsciously?) imposes on the painting. Of course, we 'see' far more complex patterns in everyday objects also. Leonardo da Vinci, in his *Treatise on Painting*, advised young painters thus:

> you should look at certain walls stained with damp or at stones of uneven colour. If you have to invent some setting you will be able to see in these the likeness of divine landscapes, adorned with mountains, ruins, rocks, woods, great plains, hills and valleys in great variety; and then again you will see there battles and strange figures in violent action, expressions of faces and clothes and an infinity of things which you will be able to reduce to their complete and proper forms. In such walls the same thing happens as in the sound of bells, in whose strokes you may find every named word which you can imagine.

For this consummate Renaissance master what he describes as this 'trivial and almost laughable' process 'is none the less of great value in quickening the spirit of invention' and we have all experienced it.

9. See his essay 'On Physiognomic Perception' for a developed argument.
10. E.H. Gombrich, *Art and Illusion* (Oxford: Phaidon Press, 1977), pp. 288-89.
11. Gombrich, *Art and Illusion*, pp. 88-89.
12. Gedo, *Looking at Art*, pp. 77, 79.

But we have moved somewhat away from Ehrenzweig's theory to another (though I think closely related) field. To recapitulate: Stage 1: we 'take in' the total painted surface and are unconsciously aware of its hidden order beneath its apparent chaotic fragmentation and inconsistency. We, say, notice the marks on the bonnets of the Breton women in Gauguin's painting but do not pay them particular attention. Stage 2: we notice detail and inconsistencies. We 'fragment' the pictorial space and 'solidify' and separate the fragments. For example, we now notice that Gauguin has painted his picture with what Gedo claims is a 'wilful disregard of the laws of perspective'.[13] Stage 3: we impose a pattern or new gestalt or unity on the painting. We, in this case, see faces in the bonnets, or we criticise Gauguin's lack of perspective by pointing to the out-of-scale cow in the picture. But we do so in the light, *not* of the painting's intrinsic, hidden order which once we 'saw' though we were not consciously aware of it, but now in terms of an imposed, essentially alien, external, historical knowledge and psychological or aesthetic theory (or even, as with perspective, a so-called 'law'): that is, we resort to a secure tradition in the face of artworks that provoke in us experiences which range from inconsistency to lawlessness, revolution, disruption and chaos.

The Fragmentation of Modern Art

For Ehrenzweig this third stage is well illustrated by the reaction of critics to Impressionist landscapes and of the art schools in the 1920s and 1930s to Cézanne and to the Cubists. The Impressionists ('wilfully'?) disregarded the conventions of perspective which had controlled painting since the Renaissance and which had stabilised and ordered the visual field. The fiction of perspective, as Robert Hughes notes, solved a problem. Somehow, 'the chaos of the "view" must be made to reflect order, structure, and system'.[14] The convention of perspective achieved this. It brought order out of chaos. The Impressionists rejected the fiction of aerial perspective. They were concerned only with the picture plane—the pictorial space. However, within ten years critics convinced Impressionist painters that they had constructed a new kind of atmospheric space that was 'in no way less precise or stable than the space constructed according to the rules of Renaissance perspective'![15] By diktat of the critics Impressionist chaos had been tamed by a new theory of illusionistic space which could be seen as a development of, and no less precise than, the first. Every painter now got into the Impressionist act. It is little wonder that, with perhaps the sole exception of Claude Monet, Impressionist painters became disillusioned. Their jumbled, chaotic, scattered, brush-strokes now, after a decade and more of rejection and

13. Gedo, *Looking at Art*, p. 58.
14. Hughes, *The Shock of the New*, p. 114.
15. Ehrenzweig, *The Hidden Order*, p. 68.

ridicule, 'revealed' to critics stable patterns of solid surfaces and outlines. Their landscapes had been said by early critics to 'grimace' or 'convulse'. We have already noted that in 1898 Leo Tolstoy quoted with approval the opinion of an 'amateur of art' who had visited the 1894 Impressionist and Symbolist exhibitions in Paris that the work exhibited was not merely 'wretchedly executed' but, crucially, 'beyond human comprehension'.[16] Even Cézanne had said to van Gogh (with more frankness than tact as Phoebe Pool notes): 'In all sincerity you paint like a madman'![17] But in general well before the end of the century the novelty had worn off, the unfamiliar had become familiar, the Impressionists had become accepted and famous—and the spring of their art ran dry when it was channelled by far lesser artists into acceptable paths. This happened generally with the modern movement. What Kenneth Clark described as the 'lawless and intuitive character' of modern art[18] became acceptable and widely copied. What had been new and unacceptable had now become old and acceptable. The Impressionists' contemporary, Jules Laforgue, correctly noted that, for them, 'the only criterion was newness. In short, that which the instinct of the ages had always exalted when it proclaimed as geniuses, according to the etymology of the word, those and only those who revealed something new'.[19] But now the reality of the really new had been killed and had been replaced by a prosaic explanatory theory. The same fate befell Cézanne, and the Cubists.[20] By the 1920s many art students were being taught to see the human figure and the natural landscape in terms of spheres and cylinders. What had been 'fragmentation and eye-wandering effects' in 'the attack on our conscious sensibilities'[21] by artists of the early modern movement now became both a new orthodoxy and a programme which could easily be followed by all!

Now, the doubt is always there as to whether the third stage gestalt is not the now consciously recognised first stage hidden order! We have to live with that doubt. If we come to the conclusion that it is, then at the very least we must continually identify and monitor our motives for so believing and consciously search for correctives. This process requires considerable courage, honesty and self-awareness. Not least is this so when we consider the fundamental classics—the foundation artworks—of Judaism and Christianity. I will take just one example, the genre of the apocalyptic literature, to make the simple point that rational dogma brings order to imaginative scripture.

16. Tolstoy, *What is Art?*, p. 96.
17. Pool, *Impressionism*, pp. 219-20.
18. Clark, *Moments of Vision*, p. 23.
19. Clark, *Moments of Vision*, p. 216.
20. 'Cubism' was a term which, like 'Impressionism' and 'Expressionism', brought some kind of notional order to a radically innovative art.
21. Ehrenzweig, *The Hidden Order*, p. 68.

David Tracy and the Reality of the Really New

Whereas the explication of Ehrenzweig's theory (crudely simplified in this chapter) is the main purpose for writing his book, David Tracy's discussion of the relationship of the highly imaginative biblical apocalyptic writing to the doctrines of early Catholicism is an element in his discussion of what he calls the 'Christian classic'.

A candidate for status as a 'classic' is *experienced*, Tracy says, in 'a text, a gesture, an image, an event, a person with the force of the recognition: "This is important! This does and will make a difference!".' He continues: 'If one's own experience has been verified by other readers, especially by the community of capable readers over the centuries, the reflective judgment should prove to be that much more secure'.[22] Tracy is here latterly speaking of the classics of literature, though his first words in this quotation speak of the classics of any, or no, art form. What classics do, he says earlier, is

> to endure as provocations awaiting the task of reading [or, as we would also say, of attentive and sympathetic listening and viewing]: to challenge our complacency, to break our conventions, to compel and concentrate our attention, to lure us out of a privacy masked as autonomy into a public realm where what is important and essential is no longer denied. Whenever we experience even one classic work of art we are liberated from privateness into the genuine publicness of a disclosure of truth.[23]

This is, for our purposes, an extremely important definition. Among the Jewish and Christian classics are works within the genre called 'apocalyptic'. This word is employed as an adjective and as a noun. In both cases its essential meaning has been determined by the opening two verses of the New Testament book, the Revelation of John. There the 'revelation' (*apokalupsis*, an uncovering, a laying bare)

> is the revelation of Jesus Christ which God gave him so that he might show his servants what must soon take place. He made it known by sending his angel to his servant John, who in telling all that he saw has borne witness to the word of God and to the testimony of Jesus Christ. (Rev. 1.2-2 REB)

The salient features of apocalyptic (though not all examples of the genre have every one of these elements) are that (1) it is *visionary* (the author 'saw' what he now describes); (2) it is *urgent* (the events so described will soon take place); (3) it is both *prophetic* and *eschatological* (it bears witness to the End); (4) it is *revelatory* or disclosive ('...to *show* to his servants...'); (5) it claims to offer disclosures of *divine mysteries*; (6) it is *extra-ordinary* or *fantastic* in the sense that it contains information about the heavenly realms, angels, wonderful beasts and so on; and (7) it is produced in times

---

22. David Tracy, *The Analogical Imagination* (London: SCM Press, 1981), pp. 115-16.

23. Tracy, *The Analogical Imagination*, p. 115.

of grave *crisis*. Finally it is very important to note that apocalyptic, as we will see, is *literary* and can only be appreciated as literature. The ability of, say, realist painters to render the content of apocalyptic in their media is extremely limited. It is readily seen that only art possesses these features and can fulfil these functions. Whatever else apocalyptic is (and, for that matter, myth, symbol, poetry, poetic narrative and all other biblical genres) it *is* art. As G.B. Caird said of the Revelation of John: 'it is a great work of art [the ideas of which] are expressed in symbols almost as old as the mind of man'.[24]

David Tracy describes apocalyptic as a *corrective* genre in the Bible.[25] It is, he says, marked by principles of intensification and negation. As it is a genre evoked in times of crisis (say, the destruction facing Jerusalem or the captivity of the people or, as with the Revelation of John, the persecution of the Church), it is marked by hope for the oppressed and destruction for the oppressors, both expressed in intense, even extreme, terms. Above all, apocalyptic, especially Christian apocalyptic in the New Testament challenges assumptions very radically. In particular, Tracy says, apocalyptic challenges

> any purely 'private' understanding of the Christian event by forcing a recognition of the genuinely public, the political and historical character of all Christian self-understanding; as a challenge to all the privileged to remember the privileged status of the oppressed, the poor, the suffering in the scriptures; as a challenge to all the living not to forget the true hope disclosed in these texts of a future from God for all the dead; as a challenge to all wisdom and all principles of order to remember the reality of the pathos of active suffering untransformable by all thought ordering cosmos and ethos; as a challenge to each to remember all; as a challenge to face the reality of the really new, the *novum*, and the future breaking in and confronting every present, exploding every complacency; as a challenge of the sheer intensity of the 'pain of the negative' in the cross needed as an intrinsic moment in any adequate theology of incarnation or any present-oriented theology of resurrection; as a challenge to remember the eschatological 'not-yet' in every incarnational 'always-ready' and even every 'but-even-now' resurrectional transformation; in sum, apocalyptic may be viewed as a major context and signal key to the intensification principle itself in all New Testament expressions.[26]

That is beautifully and strikingly put. Intensification and negation marks all great art. This is why great art is so radically challenging. Because it intensifies and negates, Tracy argues, apocalyptic pervades the New Testament as a profoundly important corrective to all Christian claims to adequacy and to the lapse into complacency which follows acceptance of these claims—and must be allowed so to do for the post-New Testament Church also.

24. Caird, *The Revelation of St John the Divine*, p. 289.
25. For what follows, see Tracy, *The Analogical Imagination*, pp. 265-68.
26. Tracy, *The Analogical Imagination*, p. 266.

Compared to apocalyptic, early Catholicism and its major genre of doctrinal confessions 'discloses an entirely different world'. Here Tracy observes,

> the tension seems relaxed, though not spent; the sects, the charismatic communities, have become an ordered institution of the 'great church'; the act of proclamation and its disclosure of the sheer 'that it happens now' has largely yielded to the content of its confession; the tensions of the narratives of the passion–resurrection, the shock of the proverbs, parables and eschatological sayings of Jesus, the tensive character of the symbols resurrection–cross–incarnation are transformed not into steno-symbols,[27] but into the specificity, explicitness and measured clarity of the genre 'doctrine'.[28]

However, Tracy seems to be unwilling fully to accept the implication of his own analysis. This is that the superabundance of biblical art is effectively replaced by the narrow philosophical logic of Christian credal doctrine. Strictly orthodox Christians claim that this is not so, yet, for all practical purposes, they give credence to dogma rather than live in the light of the subversive extravagance of scripture's art. The fires of the art of the Bible are easily extinguished by cool philosophy. Tracy argues that what doctrine does is to bring us down from the heights of apocalyptic and makes Christian faith accessible in the ordinary, everyday world. But too often, the force of the biblical literature *as art rather than merely as a supposed authority for doctrine* is lost. Doctrine, Tracy says, discloses the extraordinariness of the ordinary. He is right to remind us of this truth. But he goes further. What doctrine does, he says, is to remind us that God's self-disclosure is an event that happens in 'the everyday, the stable, the measured, the ordered, the nontensive, nonchaotic world of the ordinary'.[29] Notice his words. The world to which doctrine speaks is stable, measured, ordered and non-chaotic. But what if it is the very desire for such a world which *itself produces cool, measured, nontensive doctrine.* On that argument doctrine is the result of our second glance at the art of the Bible. It is the way we attempt to tame its chaos and superabundance. We, as it were, make the Bible submit to our rational understanding. We attempt to make it conform to us rather than allow it radically to challenge and bewilder us. The truth is that our social world is not stable, measured and non-chaotic. Far from it. Perhaps the fact that it is not is one reason why the cool, measured tones of Christian doctrine do not chime with the cries of humankind.

27. *Stenosis*, 'narrowing', from *stenoō*, 'to make narrow'. Thus a stenosymbol is a symbol with a sharply attenuated, narrowed focus. For example, the cross (and therefore redemption) is regarded by many Christians as a purely Christian symbol with no universal relevance and power in the sense that to benefit from the cross one must become a Christian. However, a stenosymbol is a symbol nevertheless.
28. Tracy, *The Analogical Imagination*, p. 266.
29. Tracy, *The Analogical Imagination*, p. 267.

David Tracy speaks much of art.[30] Art can shock, surprise and challenge us. We can be caught up in its world, and challenged by

> its startling beauty and its recognizable truth, its instinct for the essential. In the actual experience of art we do not experience the artist *behind* the work of art. Rather we recognize the truth of the work's disclosure of a world of reality transforming, if only for a moment, ourselves: our lives, our sense for possibilities and actuality, our destiny.[31]

And, he might have added, the principles of order and stability which we impose on our world and in terms of which, often complacently, we interpret it. Tracy's language at this point is remarkably similar to that which he later employs to describe the experience of apocalyptic. Apocalyptic, and of course the Bible as a whole, is art, and must be allowed to challenge the stabilities of dogma. In his discussion of the experience of art Tracy laments the loss of 'the actual experience of art' when we impose upon it what he rightly calls 'alien, aesthetic theories of taste'. When we do this, he says, 'we are tempted to misinterpret the experience as a purely, indeed, merely "aesthetic" one'. Now what an aesthetic theory (or, worse, a notion of taste) does is to tame an artwork, to fit it into an understandable frame of reference, to remove from it its ambiguity, to make it no longer alien. Yet it does this by alienating art from itself. Aesthetic theories tend to domesticate art. As such they are, of course, very useful vehicles for the processes of secondary revision by which art is ostensibly rendered understandable. A work of art becomes more comfortable once it can be interpreted by a theory, or set within a supposed developmental process. Chaos gives way to order, discomfort to comfort. The expert is in control. All is well with the world of art. Of course, as we have seen, the essential and hidden order of the artwork, its reality, may be lost for ever in favour of a new, understandable, consciously recognised gestalt. The artwork has been brought down to earth. It is now replete with ordinary everyday meanings. The artist is no longer a strange figure who cuts off his ear, he no longer inhabits the world of the extraordinary or the mad but is now one of us. He is a prophet with honour in his own country. We hang his work in great galleries. So it is too with the authoritative canons by which Christianity is defined and circumscribed. The alien philosophy of Middle Platonic metaphysics brought clarity and order to the mystery and essential strangeness of the Bible's poetry. It is the Church's secondary revision, its re-ordering, of its foundation classic.

Doctrine as Secondary Revision and Re-Patterning

Just as so-called canons of criticism embody aesthetic theories which are themselves the results of secondary revisions of the initial low-level

30. See, for example, *The Analogical Imagination*, pp. 109-15.
31. Tracy, *The Analogical Imagination*, p. 110.

experience of art, so Christian canonical dogma was the solidified, ordered, result of the long process of secondary revisions of the initial Christ-event. Tracy rightly notes that 'the development of the genre doctrine, leading to such expressions as Nicaea and Chalcedon, has the ability to specify, clarify and order what the beliefs, the "doctrines" *implied by this basic belief* in the event of God's self-manifestation in Jesus Christ are'.[32] The emphasis is mine. Who or what determines what these 'implications' are, and by what process are they determined? For Christian orthodoxy it is the trans-histori- cal Church, and the process is the divinely inspired process of doctrinal development and formulation. Examples of the readiness with which the specificities of later philosophical doctrine can subvert, contain and control the extravagance and openness of biblical art are legion. We will take just one example from the work of two leading biblical theologians: Raymond E. Brown and Ernst Kasemann. John 17.3, in Brown's own translation, reads:

> And eternal life consists in this: that they know you,
> the one true God, and Jesus Christ, the one whom you sent.

Brown comments: 'Kasemann rightly stresses that the idea of faith as the acceptance of orthodox doctrine is already present inchoatively in John. To receive eternal life one must accept as a creedal doctrine that Jesus is the Son of God' calling 1 Jn 2.22-23 in support.[33] Convinced of the divine inspiration of the later Nicene formulation, orthodox theologians read back the revisionary processes that led to catholic orthodoxy into what they claim is the 'inchoativity' of John's art, and thus deprive John's thought of its extravagance, mystery and radical openness. Again, the only reason for arguing that John's thought *is* 'inchoate', that is, that it is at the very beginning of a process of development, is the belief that later Nicene orthodoxy was the culmination of that development. The later doctrinal position is held, *as an article of faith*, to be implied in the earlier biblical text. Many years ago Willi Marxsen pointed out that

> in Christology one can show development from an 'implicit' to an 'explicit'
> Christology, from a Christology that is indirect to one that is direct, from
> a 'Christology in action' to a considered Christology.[34]

This is a process much considered since.[35] Tolstoy in his *What is Art?* com- pared 'Church Christianity' unfavourably with 'true Christianity' and argued that it had made 'blind faith in the Church and its ordinances the essential

---

32. Tracy, *The Analogical Imagination*, p. 306 (my italics).
33. Raymond E. Brown, *The Gospel according to John* (London: Geoffrey Chap- man, 1971), pp. ii, 752.
34. Willi Marxsen, *The Beginnings of Christology* (Philadelphia: Fortress Press, 1979), p. 88.
35. For a radical analysis of the development of christology in the New Testament see Maurice Casey, *From Jewish Prophet to Gentile God* (Cambridge: James Clarke, 1991).

point of its teaching'.[36] Orthodoxy tames. Little wonder that Pope Innocent III, in Eliot Deutsch's *Francis*, asks 'how can we condone a brotherhood of those who, although loyal to the Church, follow only the Gospel?'![37]

By what developmental, revisionary, process does the inchoate become choate, the implicit explicit? It seems clear that it results primarily from the human need to bring order out of seeming chaos. The world of art provides numerous examples. 'It was', writes Belinda Thomson, 'in large part, the eagerness of certain critics to *locate, define, almost conjure* the long-anticipated new art out of the range of existing tendencies that gave such immediate potency to the name Impressionism'.[38]

Similarly, by what process does the historian move from the study of an event in the past to a declaration of causes and then, successively, to the offering of interpretations, the formation of theories and the provision of explanations?

But in theology God is involved. What if the process of definition and codification is not divinely inspired but arises from a human desire for order and explanation? Tracy acknowledges that doctrinal developments are only 'relatively adequate' and that we must ever keep in mind 'the "corrective truth" of the demand for the intensification of negations'. Indeed, he says: 'Apocalyptic serves its corrective function as a minefield in store for all christologies, waiting to explode any attempt at complacency'. But the minefield has long been swept by the Church. For this reason Tracy holds the two corrective tensions, apocalyptic and doctrine, in uneasy harmony. He seems not fully to appreciate the process by which the second imposes itself upon and controls the first. His doctrine of the Church and of its authority seems to prevent him seeing that what happens in art in this regard happens in religion also. Tracy himself notes that doctrines lack the intensity—the tensive character—of the Christian symbols resurrection–cross–incarnation. So, he freely acknowledges, 'the confessions and doctrines of early Catholicism are not the primary place to locate the most relatively adequate expression of the New Testament event'.[39] Thus doctrine is itself a corrective but as a corrective it does not play a central role in the New Testament. What doctrines do for the Church, Tracy argues revealingly, is 'to allow for the human need to find order in thought and some structure in community'. Exactly—and in so doing they domesticate the art of the Bible and thus tame and civilise prophetic, revolutionary Christianity. We manage the mysterious man Jesus by defining him in an authoritative creed that allows for no argument and that proclaims him God

---

36. Tolstoy, *What is Art?*, pp. 55-56.

37. In Eliot Deutsch, *Religion and Spirituality* (Albany, NY: State University of New York Press, 1995), p. 69.

38. Belinda Thomson, *Impressionism* (London: Thames & Hudson, 2000), p. 135 (my italics).

39. Tracy, *The Analogical Imagination*, p. 268.

because the logic of metaphysical speculation—a secondary, revisionary process subsequently canonised by the Church—demands it. Though Tracy rightly warns that 'sheer intensity without any principles of ordering can lead eventually to a self-destructive chaos' he does not fully acknowledge the danger that Christian doctrine can, and has, become the Christian gestalt. Dogma has identified what Christianity is. It has replaced the strange, unmanageable, untameable, extravagant, prophetic Gospel, and the extraordinary man who defies definition and who we dimly perceive behind it, by a dogmatic theology which all too often does not allow art—the Bible's own art—its critical and corrective place. It is now extraordinarily difficult to see the hidden order in the stories, myths, symbolic narratives and poetry—the art—of the Bible. The hidden order of this diverse material has been fragmented and re-ordered under the influence of speculative metaphysical philosophies. What happens to art has happened to the Bible because the Bible is art. To attempt to recover the hidden order of the Bible's artworks one must read them again with an undifferentiated, unfocused vision. We must live a Christian life marked by the uncertainties and insecurities—the chaos—which deserting an unthinking reliance on credal formularies both condemns us to and frees us for. This is for the imagination. We must abandon ourselves to the everyday experience of the authentic reality of the really new.

Chapter 9

Symbols of the Sublime?

Harold Rosenberg said of the painter Barnett Newman that 'painting was a way of *practicing* the sublime, not of finding symbols for it'. Practicing the sublime meant making art which was capable 'of giving someone, as it did me, the feeling of his own totality...'[1]

It is not too extravagant to say that what we experience as a revelation, religiously speaking, is the in-breaking of the sublime into our everyday, practical, lives. Can a work of art be a revelation in this sense? And if so what counts as 'the sublime'?

There is a highly subjective, personal, empathetic relationship between a work of art, the artist and the viewer/listener/reader. That there *is* a profound relationship suggests that words like 'viewer', 'listener' and 'reader' imply far too passive a role in this context. Without further qualification they suggest no participation by this third element in the creative process which is art. This is far from the case. Perhaps the theological words 'witness' or 'beholder' would be better designations, though even these words do not carry the weight I am trying to indicate.

Experiencing art—a poem or work of prose, a sculpture, a painting, a musical composition, a dance—which engages with me I have an experience which draws from me a deep response. I am not a receiver only. Hans-Georg Gadamer put it like this: 'the creation of genius can never really be divorced from the con-geniality of the one who experiences it'.[2] In paraphrasing Gadamer, Gordon Graham tells of a commonplace experience familiar to every lover of art when he says that 'appreciating a work of art requires imaginative activity on the part of the observer no less than the maker'. But there is much more to this relationship of artist, the work of art and viewer than that. As an observer my imaginative activity is of the nature of a *creative gift*. My giving is not, of course, to the art or to the

---

1. Quoted in David Sylvester, *About Modern Art* (London: Chatto & Windus, 1996), pp. 328-29.
2. Quoted in Gordon Graham, *Philosophy of the Arts* (London: Routledge, 1997), p. 15.

artist, rather it goes to the creation of that new fact which is the meeting of the artwork and me. Something happens[3] and I am an essential contributor to this happening. Without me this happening would not have happened in the way that it has happened. Others—hundreds of thousands of others—will have been contributors to unique happenings when confronted by, say, Cézanne's *Large Pine and Red Earth* but I can know nothing of those other uniquely personal events. I can know only what is happening to me. When confronted by a work of true art the happening is intensely personal, unrepeatable and unique. Any successive meetings with *Large Pine and Red Earth* would be equally unrepeatable and unique. One meeting will develop from and enrich the next. I will notice more and realise more and, perhaps, *perceive* more through my encounter with the picture. Forever, Paul Cézanne and I will be brothers.

For me this happening, this event, is of the nature of a revelation (immediate or slowly dawning). I chose the word 'revelation' advisedly and employ it in its theological sense, though not in the popular sense in which it is often used in religious discourse. Revelation suggests some kind of unveiling in which what was once concealed is now laid bare. This is true of all knowing (for good or ill). The Greek *aletheia* rendered into English as 'truth', means 'unhiddenness'. We have come to the truth when that which was concealed becomes unhidden and is brought (or brings itself) into the light. Paul Tillich said that 'revelation is not communication concerning a being, even concerning a transcendental being' but 'the self-giving of the absolutely hidden, which by the very fact of its self-giving emerges from its concealment' in a total manner.[4] This revelatory happening gives rise to a new (or refreshed) knowledge and to an enrichment of my understanding, and this in turn results in a restored sense not only of belonging to and thus rejoicing with and suffering with the human community across time and the barriers of culture, but of belonging to a limitless universe.

This is a very well known and often recorded experience. It is the experience of being profoundly at one with the work of art and through it with all things. The central historical character in A.S. Byatt's novel *Possession* is told: 'you are in love with all the human race, Randolph Ash'. He responds:

> With you, and by extension, all creatures who remotely resemble you. Which is, all creatures, for we are all part of some divine organism I do believe, that breathes its own breath and lives a little here, and dies a little there but is eternal. And you are a manifestation of this secret perfection. You are the life of all things.

3.   Richard Wollheim says that 'the spectator's activity consists in interpretation' (*Art and its Objects*, p. 87). There is much more to the spectator's role than this. It has to do with the interaction of seeing and being seen.

4.   Quoted in David A. Pailin, 'Revelation', in Alan Richardson and John Bowden (eds.), *A New Dictionary of Christian Theology* (London: SCM Press 1983), pp. 503-506 (505).

It is this experience that Byatt explores, though the theme of possession is multi-faceted in Byatt's novel. To be faced with the world of natural phenomena or man-made artefacts and to be *enchanted* by them is truly a 'possession'. It is not surprising that Kenneth Clark should use precisely the same word when he speaks of 'moments of vision'. He says

> in a moment of vision we possess, and we are possessed. It is rare to feel that anything is really ours except (as Samuel Butler said) when we eat it; and we naturally value the half second when for some mysterious reason we can do so. The element of possession is confirmed by the fact that objects which excite us in this way are so often small and apprehensible.[5]

Now Clark does not employ the word 'vision' as it is used, he says, 'by preachers, public speakers, and far-sighted men of action'. Rather, for him, a vision is 'a moment of intensified physical perception'. How incarnational that sounds, but we must resist the temptation to reduce Clark's 'moment' to the categories of Christian dogma. Now, a picture or a sculpture or a line from a poem is in this sense as apprehensible as a familiar tree. For Clark the 'collar bone of a hare, / Worn thin by the lapping of the water' in Yeats's poem was a moment of vision. A similar moment for me in provided by D.H. Lawrence's *Snake* where Lawrence describes the creature withdrawing into 'that dreadful hole', that 'horrid black hole', in the broken wall.[6] Lawrence has recognised, as had W.B. Yeats, and as does every master of an art that, as Clark says, 'an object so vividly perceived must be a symbol'. Interesting, Clark does not speculate as to what this moment of vision—this revelation—symbolises.

We can be 'possessed' in such 'moments of vision'. Clark devotes the rest of his essay to discussing just what this imaginative possession means. He touches the truth when he says that so to possess and be possessed is to discover something within us that forever and already exists. He says

> for the compulsive, all-absorbing nature of moments of vision. For an immediate self discovery, self identification: here, is seems to me, is the chief reason and unconscious self-identification does indeed 'bind our feelings even as in a chain'... In a moment of vision we are both participating with our whole being and at the same time contemplating our externalised selves with possessive delight.

In my terms, I receive a revelation. As Gadamer says so beautifully:

> In the experience of art we must learn how to dwell upon the work in a specific way. When we dwell upon the work, there is no tedium involved, for the longer we allow ourselves, the more it displays its manifold riches to us. The essence of our temporal experience is learning how to tarry in

---

5.   For the full discussion from which these quotations are taken, see Clark, *Moments of Vision*, pp. 1-17.

6.   D.H. Lawrence, *The Complete Poems* (ed. Vivian de Sola Pinto and Warren Roberts; London: Penguin Books, 1993), pp. 350-51.

this way. And perhaps it is the only way that is granted to us finite beings to relate to what we call eternity.[7]

We have noted that Friedrich von Hügel wrote of the same experience as 'engrossment', and that it was for Evelyn Underhill 'an intuition of the Real lying at the root of the visible world and sustaining its life'.[8]

This Real is 'the other', the 'transcendent', 'the beyond', the *au dela*, of which late nineteenth-century French painters spoke. It was, for von Hügel, *une affirmation ontologique*. Yet however experienced and described by the viewer or listener, it is the artist who is in actual tactile contact with the world which possesses him or her. The brush is in his hands, the clay or marble or sheet-steel under his fingers. It is her feet that leap from the floor. It is her pen that moves across the page. And this at the level of consciousness. At a deeper level it is through their fingers or voices that musicians give inarticulate inflexion to the melody by *vibrato*, *portamento*, *rubato*. Those inflexions belong to the performer's interpretation, they are spontaneous in execution, they are not instructions in the score. So it is too with a painter's distinctive brush-stroke, his unique application of paint, which, uniquely for him is his emotional and tactile response to the world.

With those last examples we move from the conscious and the articulate in art to the unconscious and the inarticulate,[9] but we should not make the distinction too precise. The artist moves from the one to the other easily and imperceptibly. At both levels of perception the artist explores the outer edges of the sublime which possesses, engrosses, viewer and practitioner alike.

There is always a gross mismatch between what one profoundly feels and seeks to express and what one's eye sees and hand does. But even for the poorest artist there are, very occasionally, moments when feeling and expression connect however partially and there is the *frisson*, the shiver of excitement of an almost physical (because perhaps it *is* a physical, adrenaline-loaded) experience. In these senses the experience I have when I paint is a mystical (albeit a profane, this-world, earth-related mystical) experience, that is, an experience the meaning of which is beyond my understanding but which I know is primordial *meditative knowing* as Martin Heidegger described it. It is certainly both an exciting and an enchanting experience and I am changed by it.

This happening gives rise also, for me, to a renewed urge to paint. Paul Valery said that 'a creator is one who makes others create'.[10] This is itself but a response to a deep need to pay attention—to give honour to—the

---

7.   H.-G. Gadamer, *The Relevance of the Beautiful and Other Essays* (Cambridge: Cambridge University Press, 1986), p. 45.

8.   Evelyn Underhill, *Mysticism*, p. 88.

9.   For a definitive discussion of 'the two kinds of attention' in art, see Ehrenzweig, *The Hidden Order,* Chapter 2.

10.   Quoted in Wollheim, *Art and its Objects*, p. 87.

world in which I live and from which I derive life itself by making something special. And this necessarily is a re-creative process. It is an interior build-ing-up—a restoration. I become whole again. Therefore, an authentic, true, creative act can be a truly salvific experience. For these reasons I claim that a truly empathetic relationship with an artwork is a genuinely spiritual experience though I fully appreciate that it is not an experience that often has much to do with conventional religion.

Now, in trying to describe this experience I have employed some sig-nificant words: relationship, witnessing, beholding, appeal, experience, response, give, revelation, happening, understanding, belonging, attentive-ness, honouring, mystical, religious, restoration, vision, wholeness/ salva-tion, excitement, enchantment, meditation. It would be too easy and facile to 'baptise' these words and the experiences, perceptions and feelings they suggest and reduce them to Christian theological categories, but we should be as opposed to reducing these experiences to those categories as we should be to the contrary reductionism which seeks to explain the truth-claims of the Christian religion solely in sociological, anthropological, bio-logical or psychological terms. Reductionism is invariably simplistic.

All we can bear witness to is the truth, the authenticity, of this experi-ence and to assert passionately that there is no substitute for it. Without this experience—the experience of art—we could not truly live. Many can (and do) live happily without dogma. Most of us could not live without art. We need to return again and again to the holy places that artists create for us.

What is taking place here? What is the nature of this experience which gives rise to these extra-ordinary reactions? One answer involves an assumption made about artists (by which I mean competent, though not necessarily great, artists). Why are we moved, delighted, enchanted, rebuked, saddened by the work that an artist does in her or his painting, music, sculpture, dance, prose or verse?

First of all, all genuine art—authentic art—reveals something to us that we *know* but have not, until that moment, *truly perceived*. We each have highly subjective moments when we do not perceive that we are appre-hending. Immanuel Kant wrote in 1798 that 'we can be mediately[11] con-scious of an apprehension as to which we have no direct consciousness'. These moments of what Kant called 'obscure apprehensions' can be of great significance for us. In fact, they are usually of much greater importance than what he calls 'clear apprehensions'. In those moments we are engrossed, we are oblivious to ourselves and our surroundings, we are transported. Now these highly subjective experiences of personal, authentic, interior knowing often have little immediate connection with the sight or sound which gave rise to them in the sense that we cease to be primarily

---

11. That is, it is an indirect, mediated, apprehension.

concerned with it. For me a painting by Paul Cézanne of an avenue of trees at Chantilly (which I have seen once and will never see again because it is now back in the American bank vault from whence it had been loaned for an exhibition in Edinburgh) had this effect—that as I looked at it I apprehended, or, better, was apprehended by, something of far greater significance that the mere composition of the picture or the direction of the artist's brush-strokes or even of Cézanne's artistic intention, all of which I could either perceive or of which I was immediately conscious. In that moment, to quote Cézanne again, his picture became 'a coloured state of grace' for me. In part this reaction has to do with the fact that, although I had never before seen this picture, not even in reproduction, I instantly recognised it as Cézanne's work. It was like recognising the hand-writing of a familiar and dear friend. I had an identical experience before Raphael's *Madonna and Child and John Baptist* thirty years earlier, as I have it on the top of Monte Baldo above Lake Garda and looking towards the Dolomites, or listening to Mozart (and, when in a less profound mood, to George Shearing) as well as when pondering the structure of a flower's form as I attempt to paint it. In saying that I am already touching upon a creation-centred spirituality which takes not only the man-made artefact but also the natural artefact with utter seriousness because it takes incarnation with utter seriousness. Whatever it is that we claim to believe that 'God' is 'he' seems evidently to be with us in and through his creation. This revelation is not by any means a religious revelation (as narrowly understood). A better word would be that word 'vision' but again, not as commonly understood by Christian believers.

A *revealing* is an uncovering of something previously hidden but which is instantly or gradually recognisable. If what was revealed was not recognisable, and therefore in some measure already known, how would we know that a revealing had taken place? That is why the word 'vision' is to be preferred. A vision is a seeing in the sense of a true perceiving.[12] It is expressed in the combination of the two Greek verbs employed in the Fourth Evangelist's account of John entering the tomb (Jn 20.8). It is a 'seeing and believing', a revelatory seeing, a *seeing the significance of*—a *discernment*.

Artists possess this gift of true vision and also possess the ability to communicate their seeing such that I am compelled to see. Kenneth Clark, certainly no conventional religious believer, wrote of this, as did R.S. Thomas and Stevie Smith and D.H. Lawrence and so very many others in very different ways. It is also the true seeing of all authentic religious traditions, the Celtic religious tradition being a particularly significant example.

---

12. Note Le Corbusier's famous distinction between *looking* (cataloguing, collecting, listening, notating) and *seeing* (which is a progress from understanding to connecting, perceiving, and, finally, to creating). See also John Berger *et al.*, *Ways of Seeing* (London: BBC; Harmondsworth: Penguin Books, 1972).

It is because I know I will be challenged truly to see that I go to art galleries with excitement but with a degree of trepidation. I know that I will be made to see and to absorb too much that is too rich. That is the problem with galleries. At the time of my visit to a superb exhibition of Impressionist and Post-Impressionist painting at the Courtauld Institute the only refreshment available in the tea room was, appropriately, rich chocolate cake! For this reason I may travel many miles to visit an exhibition of work by, say, Caravaggio or Rembrandt or Cézanne or Picasso, but be forced to leave after less than an hour! It is all too much—it is too rich! There is too much challenge—too much to have to face. I have experienced since childhood the uneasiness that the over-richness of great art prompts. Only very recently have I come across someone else who has the same feeling. Deborah, a professional photographer, who is a central character in Elizabeth George's novel *Missing Joseph* finds herself one day in the National Gallery:

> Where to go. She hadn't been inside the gallery in ages. How embarrassing, she thought, I'm supposed to be an artist. But the reality was that she had always felt overwhelmed in museums, within a quarter of an hour a hopeless victim to aesthetic-overload. Other people could walk, gaze and comment upon brushstrokes with their noses fixed a mere six inches from a canvas. But for Deborah, ten paintings into a visit and she's forgotten the first.

What I have said of man-made artefacts is also true of natural artefacts of course. What is it that I experience when I see a particular cloud formation or catch a glimpse of a kingfisher or see and hear a lark ascending, or walk by the sea along miles of deserted Northumberland beach? Much the same as in a gallery—but both more and less. More, because gallery art is just that. Paintings and sculpture in a gallery are in an artificial place. They were not produced to be deposited in large quantities in galleries. Galleries reduce art in some extraordinary way, these 'dry rooms it is difficult to breathe in' as R.S. Thomas records in his *The Earth Does its Best for Him*. For Thomas it was not that the man-made artefact in the gallery compared very unfavourably with the natural world. It was that the 'smell of dust' in the gallery compared unfavourably with 'the incense' of Lleyn. The artificial context in which the pictures had been placed and *which therefore controlled the way in which they were viewed* compared unfavourably with the sudden and unexpected givenness of nature. Yet perhaps the natural world seems to offer us less than does a work of art simply because it lacks an interpreter.

R.S. Thomas is a true artist and what artists do is to enable us see truths in the man-made and natural worlds. They open windows on these worlds. They are able to interpret the world for us or at least enable us to comprehend and appreciate, however partially, what we know intuitively but had not previously perceived.

So, one function which art performs is to enable us to see more deeply into ourselves and therefore more deeply into our relationship with the universe of people and things. But this observation merely delays facing the crucial question. What is it that we strive to see—that we intuitively know is there to be seen? Of what do artists have a vision? What is revealed to them and, as through smoked glass, to us also? Clark speaks of moments of vision as times of heightened physical perception. But what is perceived? Von Hügel placed aesthetic appreciation at a much lower level than that of mystical experience though he fully acknowledged that they shared a common source. Is it what Tillich speaks of as the ground of my ultimate concern? Is it God?

Kant speaks of 'the transcendental aesthetic'. He argues that we cannot know things in themselves, for, 'investigate the nature of objects [in the sensible world] as profoundly as we may, we have to do with nothing but appearances'. Everything is appearance. All things—that is, objects of our empirical investigation—'are mere modifications of fundamental dispositions of our sensible intuition, *while the transcendental object remains for us utterly unknown*'.[13] Yet, while the transcendental object, the substance of the transcendental aesthetic, remains for ever utterly unknown our aware-ness of it has 'an undoubted character of certainly'. We have, to put it in another Kantian way, a 'sentiment of the sublime', a Wordsworthian intima-tion of immortality.

It is of this sentiment of the sublime (or perhaps sublime sentiment) that Jean-Francois Lyotard has written so powerfully. The sublime is not to be confused with, say, beauty:

> Beauty exists if a certain 'case' (the work of art), given first by the sensi-bility without any conceptual determination, the sentiment of pleasure independent of any interest the work may elicit, appeals to the principle of a universal consensus (which may never be attained).

But the sublime is a different sentiment:

> It takes place, on the contrary, when the imagination fails to present an object which might, if only in principle, come to match a concept. We have the Idea of the world (the totality of what is), but we do not have the capacity to show an example of it... We can conceive the infinitely great, the infinitely powerful, but every presentation of an object des-tined to 'make visible' this absolute greatness or power appears to us painfully inadequate. Those are Ideas of which no presentation is possi-ble. Therefore they impart no knowledge about reality (experience)... They can be said to be unpresentable.

It is at this point that Lyotard, following Kant, touches on a truth that artists have for ever felt:

13. Kant, *Critique of Pure Reason*, p. 63 (my italics).

I shall call modern the art which devotes its 'little technical expertise' (*son 'petit technique'*), as Diderot used to say, to present the fact that the unpresentable exists. To make visible that there is something which can be conceived and which can neither be seen nor made visible.

But how is this possible? How can something which cannot be seen be made visible? Lyotard cites Kant again. Kant argued that the commandment 'Thou shalt not make graven images' was the most sublime passage in the Bible because it forbad any attempt to present the Absolute. Only in what Kant speaks of as 'formlessness, the absence of form' can there be what Lyotard calls 'a possible index to the unpresentable' sublime. For Lyotard the art of the sublime will therefore not only be non-figurative and non-representational but also completely *non*! He suggests that it will be 'white' like one of Kasimir Malevich's squares. Lyotard probably had in mind here Malevich's *Suprematist Composition, White on White* (c. 1918, Museum of Modern Art, New York). In short an art of the sublime 'will enable us to see only by making it impossible to see', that is, 'by flushing out artifices of presentation which make it impossible to subordinate thought to the gaze and to turn it away from the unpresentable'.[14]

It is worth noting that what Malevich and many of his contemporaries were attempting to do was to produce visual analogues for feelings, or, better, intuitions. They believed that the visual world could no longer be of value or use to the artist. Indeed, to seek to render the natural world is wrong: 'little pictures of fragrant roses' are mere 'dead representation pointing back to life'. What the artist must now do is to 'construct forms from nothing, discovered by Intuitive Reason'.[15] Indeed 'in copying or tracing the forms of nature we have fed our consciousness with a false understanding of art'.[16] Whether Malevich's co-Suprematists would have agreed that they were attempting to point to the existence of the unknowably sublime is a very moot point,[17] unless the Intuitive Reason is, as Idealists might claim, the channel to the sublime. Malevich himself, however, was a deeply mystical Christian believer. It seems that for him the artist's quest was the pursuit of God.

But have not all artists felt that they were struggling to find *au dela*, the beyond? Were the Impressionists merely concerned only to render the impression of light striking objects? Did not Cézanne seek to penetrate to the very heart of the landscape and through it to its ultimate meaning?

---

14. The quotations from Lyotard are all from his *Answering the Question: 'What is Postmodernism?'* in an English edition of 1983 which was reprinted as an appendix to his *The Postmodern Condition*, and is reproduced in Harrison and Wood, *Art in Theory*, pp. 1012-13.

15. Quoted from T. Anderson (ed.), *K.S. Malevich: Essays on Art 1915–1933*, I (Copenhagen, 1969), in Harrison and Wood, *Art in Theory*, pp. 168, 291.

16. Harrison and Wood, *Art in Theory*, p. 168.

17. Further to this see John Golding, *Paths to the Absolute* (London: Thames & Hudson, 2000).

When Picasso painted say, *La Vie*, the key painting of his Blue Period, or his great proto-Cubist work *Les Demoiselles d'Avignon* was he not obviously engaged in a far greater enterprise than 'merely' rendering nature? But this has been true of all great artists. The landscapes of Courbet are no mere representations. I know that Michelangelo's *David* or his *Prisoners* wrestling with the stone or his *Palestrina Pieta* connect me to the sublime. The question is whether or not he intended that they should.

The question for religious believers is: Does our religion do this? Unless, at the very least, our religion functions as art then it is dead. If it merely operates as a kind of religious philosophy, or an emotional appeal, or as a system of dogma, or as an interpretative schema or as an ethical code it may mean much, but will it connect us to God? And if these codes, schemes, dogmas and interpretations amount to a claim that God exclusively, or even primarily, chooses to reveal himself in terms of the religion, then much remains to be debated. If, on the other hand, religion is allowed to function as art and not as a scheme does this mean that, primordially (as Heidegger uses the word), religion *is* art? Probably yes. This will be challenged. From this point the debate must be held between theologians. It will be held by some that, at best, the *content* of art and religion are different even though the *methodology* is the same. It is at least worth considering whether the content, that is, the character and quality of the communicated experience—the 'revelation' or 'vision'—is, at root, the same even though the methodologies (and certainly the interpretations) are different.

Chapter 10

The Time Came and the Man

It is one thing to say that Dante's *Paradiso* or Michelangelo's pietas are revelatory. Can the same be said of modern art? Can Picasso's *Alcoholic Fallen Asleep* of 1902 or his *Weeping Woman* of 1937 or his *Still Life with Cat and Lobster* painted in 1962 be claimed to be revelatory?

What is Modern Art?

We must begin to answer this question with a definition of modern art however provisional such a definition must be. It is bound to be provisional for two obvious reasons, one historical and the other conceptual. The first is that the history of modern art is not yet complete. The second is that the idea of 'modern' is itself provisional. Are we using a merely historical, chronological designation (in which case when does the modern period begin?) or is the term 'modern', as Nikos Stangos puts it, a rubric that contains a host of ideological and programmatic, overt and concealed, presuppositions?[1] Here we will employ the term as a rubric rather than a designation, though its presuppositions are always determined by historical circumstances.

In fact the term 'modern art' is inherently confusing whether used as an historical designation or a rubric. Although 'modern' is clearly to be distinguished from 'ancient' it would be wrong to give the impression that the history of art, any more than the history of anything else, progressed in a series of linear stages, with one stage or movement neatly succeeding another. There is much overlap. We can see the genesis of a 'movement' in art concealed in that which went before—so should we include that hint or intimation in the succeeding stage? We would not regard Cézanne as a cubist, yet he is the father of cubism. Manet is not an Impressionist (he repudiated the suggestion) yet he is regarded as the father if Impressionism. Courbet would not be considered a painter of the modern period yet

1. Nikos Stangos (ed.), *Concepts of Modern Art* (London: Thames & Hudson, 1994), p. 7.

his rejection of classicist and romantic academic painting in favour of a frank realism inaugurated the modern period.

However, the notion of art 'movements', prone though it is to over-simplification does contain, as Stangos says, a conceptual orientation. Perhaps more than in any other century in the story of art twentieth-century art movements speak directly of these times—of the speed and violence of social, technological, political and ideological change during the last hundred years. The term 'modern art' and the many movements which comprise it 'crystallise underlying concepts', Stangos says. Better, they give expression to the insecurities and the freedoms (indeed the insecurities which are the result of the freedoms) as well as to the terrors, the technological advances and, perhaps most far-reaching of all, the loss of religion of this 'modern' century.

And what of postmodernism? As postmodernism is the critique of modernism so it can offer a definition of modern art, at least in negative terms. Stangos argues that postmodernism has exposed the dogmas, the 'secret tenets', of modernism for what they were:

> the separation of art and life, the emphasis on form versus content, the creation of new canons which excluded all those who might not subscribe to rigid, formalist principles or to other tyrannical party lines. Thus, modernism is now revealed to be not entirely the liberating force it had been thought to be.[2]

This offers a post-event, postmodern definition and critique of modern art, but it does not do justice to the intentions of the founding artists of the modern movement. It is a definition from the proponents of the new dogma.

Perhaps modern art can best be defined in terms of *style*. For other than the art *cognoscenti*, modern art is all art that is not realistically 'true to life'. For them it is a question of style. It might thus just include Cézanne and Matisse (though not, perhaps, Renoir and Monet), much of Picasso and all grossly distorted 'representation' and certainly all non-figurative and so-called abstract art. But a definition of modern art in those terms cannot be satisfactory because it is merely descriptive. It defines modern art, in the broadest terms, as a style of painting and sculpture which does not continue the academic traditions of the nineteenth century. Having said that the definition offers nothing more.

Nikos Stangos has defined modern art in terms of the (perhaps not always consciously recognised) *intention* of the pioneers of the modern movement. At a time of accelerating change at the turn of the nineteen and twentieth centuries when traditional value-systems were being radically challenged and every presupposition questioned it was inevitable that artists should be profoundly influenced by the mood of the times, both following it and giving it expression. Modern art could thus be defined in terms of 'the

---

2.   Stangos (ed.), *Concepts of Modern Art*, p. 8, quoting Craig Owens.

questioning and rejection of the past [which] amounted to a veritable revolution which was suitably expressed in its characterization as avant-garde',[3] noting that historically *avant-gardes* were 'explosive, expansive, trangressive; every boundary was a frontier to be crossed, a barrier to be shattered, an interdiction to be broken'.[4] As we will see, conservative Christians have reacted against modern art because it *is* revolutionary. It is seen as destructive of traditional values (rather than reflecting their destruction) and as little else.

But a definition of modern art in terms of its revolutionary questioning and rejecting of the past is also inadequate. Again, it is descriptive and not conceptual. To say merely that modern art is modern because it is revolutionary (which it is) or to say that it is modern because it is non-representational or abstract (which some modern art is) does not indicate *why* it is revolutionary or some of it is non-representational.

Herbert Read, recognising that the phenomenon of modern art is extremely complex, produced a seemingly simple criterion for selecting some artists and rejecting others for discussion in his *A Concise History of Modern Painting*. This criterion also had to do with the artists' intention, but this time in terms less of revolution than of revelation. For all its complexity, he argued, modern painting 'has a unity of intention that completely distinguishes it from the painting of earlier periods: the intention, as Klee said, not to reflect the visible, but to make visible'.[5] This definition also has its weaknesses. Read excluded twentieth-century artists like Maurice Utrillo and Jules Pascin whose aim was, he says, to reflect the visible and thus to remain true to the style of an earlier period. But does any great artist merely represent or reflect the visible? And what aspects of reality qualify as 'visible'? Does not the visible always reveal the invisible? We must leave these questions to one side here while accepting for our purpose the thrust of Herbert Read's definition, following Paul Klee. The pioneers of modern art sought to make reality visible. They did this by rejecting the fictions of the painterly conventions of the past which sought to render three-dimensional objects on a two-dimensional plane: single-source light, single-point perspective and the notions of local colour and of empty space. More of this later. Here we will consider Christian reactions to modern art written from theologically conservative positions.

Two Conservative Christian Evaluations of Modern Art

We have seen that the very complexity of modern art provokes a number of definitions of what it is. The problem with some specifically Christian evaluations of modern art is that they have more often than not assumed a

3. Stangos (ed.), *Concepts of Modern Art*.
4. Graig Owenens, cited in Stangos (ed.), *Concepts of Modern Art*, p. 9.
5. Read, *A Concise History of Modern Painting*, p. 8.

definition which tells us more about the theological presuppositions of the critics than about the art and the artists they are considering. I choose two authors, one Roman Catholic and one Protestant, who are typical of, first, a negative and, secondly, at best an ambivalent, attitude to modern art. Both see it as reflecting a decadent, Godless, contemporary society. I take first Alberto Boixados's *Myths of Modern Art*.[6] This is a not unthoughtful but nevertheless a one-sided attack not only on so-called modern art but also on many of the features of the post-Vatican II Roman Catholic Church. Its tone is set by the first sentences of its foreword by Fr Vincent P. Miceli:

> Christian civilization is in its death throes. A hurricane of revolutionary metaphysical and moral heresies is sweeping Christian nations into accepting neo-pagan ideas and hedonistic morals. This revolt against Christian truths has produced the free-thinking and sexually abandoned society, in hot pursuit of a temporal utopia. The new gospel is that 'man has come of age' and can no longer believe in the artistic and religious traditions of his classical and Christian ancestry. These ideas are simply incredible.

Boixados's little book is somewhat more balanced than this might lead his readers to expect but it sets the tone of what is to follow. *Myths of Modern Art* sets out to demolish the contemporary movements in painting, music, literature and the theatre. I take here what he has to say about modern painting and music as examples of his strictures. Boixados pleads for a recognition of, and a return to, 'the old forms'. He denigrates 'mass-pro-duced art, the product of a consumer society', for its reductionist, stylised simplicity 'does not presuppose any intellectual prowess; the banality of form only equals the triviality of content'. Further, he bitterly attacks the refusal of non-figurative artists to deal with the concrete. They should con-fine themselves, he says, to 'the framework of elemental decorative art', for, and here Boixados employs a theological idea, 'the soul is concrete and gave form to the body'. He admits that the great artists employed abstrac-tion. Indeed the measure of the greatness of a painter 'is the degree to which he possesses the power to concretize, through abstraction, the sublime internal tension of being'. But what modern non-figurative painters have done, he claims, is to cut all ties with the concrete—the concreteness of the soul—and this is a measure of the denial of the 'transcendental side' by 'the modern world'. This is a mark of the denial of spiritual values on contemporary society. Boixados is not without hope however. There are artists in every country, he says, who are following the path of Cézanne, Gauguin and Rodin, while 'the portraits of van Gogh are proof that through the right perception of the material of life a great artist can apprehend the spiritual'.

6.   Alberto Boixados, *Myths of Modern Art* (Lanham, MD: University Press of America, 1990). What follows is in substance my review of this book in *The British Journal of Aesthetics* 32.2 (1992), pp. 172-74.

Contemporary music provides Boixados with further ample evidence of the rejection of the transcendent and the spiritual in modern Western society. He pleads for a return to tonality. Atonal and discordant music, though, as Boixados admits, without much of a following even among the supposedly cultured in the population, is a denial of God-created human-ness. To compose music that is atonal or discordant is 'an extraordinary spiritual arrogance' for it denies God-given order and beauty. Perhaps because of this atonal or discordant music is bad for one's health appar-ently. Boixados quotes from the magazine *Selecta* which describes the 'rape of the audience' by the new music: 'The increase in the level of adrenaline, noradreline and hydrochloric acid provokes intestinal spasms and increases the physical production of coagulants; and the attendant circulatory risks of aggression and neurosis are detrimental to the balance of the nervous system'. And this health risk is made immeasurably worse by that 'diaboli-cal invention' stereo recording and reproduction! This desensitises the performers (under the demanding pressure of the recording studios) and results in a growing insensitivity in the listening public which 'is content to receive a series of timbres, colours, sounds, volumes, without realizing that it is succumbing to a new form of barbarism—vulgar sensuality'. It is worth noting again that this echoes Tolstoy's criticism in 1898 of 'the new composers...Liszt, Wagner, Berlioz, Brahms, and (newest of all) Richard Strauss'[7] together with the new artists and the new dramatists and poets of the time. Boixados argues that when stereo systems pump out 'powerful mind-altering—even brain-washing' polyrhythmics then listeners can be reduced to hypnotic states and even total mental derangement. He cites the Manson gang in support of this thesis and seeks to demonstrate that Charles Manson was influenced by The Beatles' *White Album* which was 'extremely revolutionary for its time, hypnotizing its listeners into a sort of ecstasy'.

The effect, indeed the purpose, of these new forms of art, Boixados believes, is to create a new humanity by destroying all that is great in our culture and civilisation. He argues for a return to a plastic art which, as in Gothic art, stimulates an inner harmony in tune with the total harmony of the world—an emotion (and here he quotes Heino Muller) 'produced as much by the aesthetic qualities of the object as by the ethical impulse which legitimized it', and a music which, as with Gregorian chant, provides 'a language [which] the soul can understand' for its power is conveyed 'through sobriety, sincerity, courtesy, and the chastity of its forms' for it 'contemplates the loftiest mysteries' and can promote authentic spiritual conversion.

This is admittedly a very conservative view, and the book's argument is easily corrupted by selective quotation. But, however extravagantly, it

7. Tolstoy, *What is Art?*, p. 97.

makes out a case which requires an answer. If the Good, the Beautiful and the True exist in any sense apart from, distanced from, the sensing organism then what is it in art, ancient or modern, which gives us hints or intimations of this ultimate ground of our being as Tillich put it? The debates, almost as old as philosophy, about what and how we know, and the battles (fought as passionately today as ever they were) between those who would dismiss mere subjectivism in favour of the spurious objectivity of popular scientism, have thrown little light upon that most exciting and perplexing issue in aesthetics which has to do with what von Hügel described as the experience of apprehending that we are perceiving 'that reality has an inside'. What is this 'inside', this principle of unity which binds the natural artefact and the man-made artefact, and what art under what conditions and constraints promotes this apprehension? Boixados does not tackle this central question. All he is sure of is that so-called modern non-figurative art and atonality in music denies that the question of what can be called the 'really real' is even worth putting. It must be admitted that much contemporary art offers evidence to support his case.

Boixados writes as a Roman Catholic. A theological consideration of modern art by a conservative Protestant art historian, H.R. Rookmaaker, was re-issued in 1994 in a new edition. Though it, too, lacks any sustained theological critique of modern art, and, like Boixados's book sees it as reflective of contemporary social decadence, it offers a much more scholarly and far from superficial Christian commentary on modern art. However, its title, *Modern Art and the Death of a Culture*, promises more than it delivers. Rookmaaker argues that contemporary artists are not merely reflecting or, worse, promoting in their work a general social decline into moral and spiritual anarchy. Rather, he sees modern art as a kind of gnosticism. Modern art rivals true religion. He recognises that much twentieth-century art is deeply mystical, but, he says, it is not a Christian mysticism which affirms the world; rather it is a gnostic mysticism which uses art as a means to escape from the world and through which artist and viewer can encounter that which is beyond. Rookmaaker argues that modern art is both gnostic and nihilist. It is gnostic because it is mystical (a typical evangelical criticism of mysticism). It is nihilist because it rejects what was held to be the pretence and superficiality and relativism of the art that it superseded and to reach for the spiritual behind the material through radically new forms of expression. In this sense, Rookmaaker acknowledges, modern art is true. It is a true rejection of superficiality. It is also a true expression of a reality: 'one in which God is dead and so man too is dying, losing his humanity, what makes him man, his personality and individuality...' Yet

at the same time it is a lie. Its portrayal of reality, of man, is not a true one. Man is not absurd. Reality is beautiful and good not only on the 'spiritual' level, but ever since the very beginning when God said it was good. We may appreciate the efforts, and even admire the greatness, of

men who have tried to find the universal, the general 'behind' appearances; yet at the same time their quest was doomed to fail, for all
universals break down as soon as the Creator, He who made man in His
image, is denied or left out of account. It was doomed to fail because
men started solely from their senses and their own brains, not accepting
any reality beyond them.[8]

This is as far as Rookmaaker's theological analysis goes. His acceptance
that contemporary artists truly represent the falsity and sinfulness of contemporary culture enables him to acknowledge the greatness of the major
figures in twentieth-century art, and by far the best chapters of his book
contain his summary analysis of the modern movement in painting and
sculpture. He asserts that the best works of Kandinsky are 'the works of a
genius'[9] and that Picasso's *Les Desmoiselles d'Avignon* is 'an unsurpassed
masterpiece'.[10] Rookmaaker's brief discussion of Picasso's proto-cubist *Les
Desmoiselles*, painted in 1907, illustrates his ambivalent attitude to modern
art. He readily acknowledges the greatness of the painting and its pivotal
place in the history of art. Although it portrays prostitutes in a brothel,

> the picture is completely a-moral; it is neither moral nor immoral. Moral-
> ity has nothing to do with it. Even if its starting-point is a brothel...the
> painting is neither propaganda for this type of sexual activity nor does it
> show any indignation or say how awful prostitution is. It is simply a
> picture, as such still in the old humanist tradition, a picture of a number
> of nude figures, standing in this way for humanity and timeless reality
> and truth. It is not a question of moral or other standards, but of the
> quest for the universal.[11]

This artistic quest for a humanist universal is what Rookmaaker the art
historian admires, for this painting is 'an unsurpassed masterpiece', but it is
also what Rookmaaker the evangelical Christian condemns. Like so many
Protestant theologians Rookmaaker blames the eighteenth-century
Enlightenment for twentieth-century decadence, for 'the principle of the
Enlightenment excludes the possibility of true norms or basic principles. So
good and evil have to be put aside as part of real reality—they can best be
considered subjective human evaluations of behaviour'.[12] Thus

> man became 'natural' and lost his particular place in the cosmos. He lost
> his humanity. What does that mean? If man is just another animal, for
> instance, then what is 'love'? After a long development the answer came
> out loud and clear: Libido, Lust, Love is *really* only sex. All that seems to
> be more is 'in fact' sublimation, a nice kind of facade to hide the real
> drives. Sex one can see and experience. But love?[13]

8.   Rookmaaker, *Modern Art*, p. 132.
9.   Rookmaaker, *Modern Art*, p. 112.
10. Rookmaaker, *Modern Art*, p. 114.
11. Rookmaaker, *Modern Art*, p. 116.
12. Rookmaaker, *Modern Art*, pp. 45-46.
13. Rookmaaker, *Modern Art*, p. 46.

This is a typical example of Rookmaaker's style and the quality of his argument when he writes not as a professional art historian but as a conservative evangelical theologian, and it is against this evangelical denunciation of the Enlightenment that he sets, uneasily, his professional evaluation of modern art. Thus modern art expresses the consequences of the basic principles of the Enlightenment.[14] This uneasy combination of evangelical conviction and professional detachment leads Rookmaaker inevitably to confuse his readers. Rookmaaker the evangelical theologian claims that the four great post-Impressionist masters of the early years of the modern movement, Cézanne, Seurat, van Gogh and Gauguin, were mistaken in seeking to make sense of the universe through the application of human rationality by bringing together 'the two great principles of the modern post-Enlightenment world; the principle of starting from sense-perception in order to gain knowledge of the universe; and the other great principle of human freedom, the search for a humanist humanity'.[15] They were doomed to fail in their search for 'the deeper universal' supposedly hidden in these principles, because, so Rookmaaker argues, this universal was of man and not of God. It was a universal to be *discovered* and had nothing to do with God's *revelation*. Yet, Rookmaaker the art historian acknowledges, they nevertheless achieved a synthesis. They overcame the naturalism of the art of the immediate post-Enlightenment period and pointed to a fuller and richer art by refusing to be bewitched either by mere sense-impressions on the one hand or by the attractions of mere fantasy and of the 'vaguely mystical' on the other. The successors of the great post-Impressionist group, those who moved art towards eventual non-figuration and abstraction, also included men of genius, Rookmaaker the art historian acknowledges, but, men of genius though they were, their attempt to force a way through the deadness of early nineteenth-century art to discover the truly human could not succeed, Rookmaaker the evangelical claims, because it was a humanist way—it left God out of account.

Even as an art-historical perspective how adequate an analysis is this? Take Cézanne. While acknowledging his greatness Rookmaaker claims that together with the other post-Impressionist masters Cézanne tried, unsuccessfully, 'to create a rational universe from what could be perceived by the senses'. But does this attempt preclude religious conviction *a priori* as Rookmaaker seems to claim? It is clear that Cézanne, morose and lonely and self-pitying as he may have been, remained a faithful Catholic until the end of his days. In the famous passage from a letter to Emile Bernard, which Rookmaaker quotes as crucially influential for the generation of painters which followed him, Cézanne bids the young painter to 'treat nature by means of the cylinder, the sphere, the cone, everything brought into proper perspective so that each side of an object or plane is directed

14. Rookmaaker, *Modern Art*, pp. 62-63.
15. Rookmaaker, *Modern Art*, p. 96.

towards a central point'. But in the next sentence, crucially not quoted by Rookmaaker, Cézanne continues: 'Lines parallel to the horizon give breadth, whether it is a section of nature or, if you prefer, of the show which the *Pater Omnipotens Aeterne Deus* spreads out before our eyes'.[16] In his correspondence there are other indications of his religious convictions. Of the saints, 'St. Vincent de Paul is the one to whom I must recommend myself most'.[17] Cézanne gave up going to mass in the last year of his life merely because 'the idiot' of an abbé 'works the organ and plays it wrong. In such a manner that I can no longer go to mass, his way of playing music makes me positively ill.'[18] These and other references do not necessarily contradict Rookmaaker's claim that Cézanne was a children of the Enlightenment, but they do suggest he did not see the practice of his art and the perceptions of reality to which he arrived by the end of his life as at all at variance with orthodox Catholic religious convictions. As we have noted several times, for Cézanne a painting could be a 'coloured state of grace'. Is art, Cézanne writes despairing, 'a priesthood that demands the pure in heart who must belong to it entirely?'[19] That Cézanne's art had a profound religious significance was recognised by a perceptive contemporary Joachim Gasquet who wrote (admittedly effusively) of Cézanne's Provencal landscapes that they possessed a 'luminous saintliness', filling the viewer 'with a sense of religion' and indicating that 'as in biblical times, trees and stones will speak, that all are awaiting a saviour, that the world wants a master, that the soul of Provence will descend in the shape of some human being...'[20] Cézanne was deeply moved by these sentiments and waited several weeks before writing a letter of thanks to Gasquet.[21]

So it is that Rookmaaker fails to convince us that post-Enlightenment painting is *a priori* God-denying art. He acknowledges the greatness of the artists of the modern movement. They truly revealed, *while fully sharing in,* the falsity and untruth, crisis, alienation and absurdity, the squalor and the destruction (his words) of the modern human condition—the condition of a humankind that has rejected God. On this analysis the best that can be said of Cézanne, Seurat, van Gogh, Gauguin, Picasso, Kandinsky and so many great painters of the modern period is that they were heroic failures. They were looking for truth in the wrong place. But, at least for Cézanne the father of the modern movement, this was not true. In attempting to penetrate the significance of the landscape he seems in no way to have left the *Pater Omnipotens* out of account—rather the reverse.

16. Rewald, *Cézanne Letters*, p. 301.
17. Rewald, *Cézanne Letters*, p. 317.
18. Rewald, *Cézanne Letters*, p. 322.
19. Rewald, *Cézanne Letters*, pp. 293-94.
20. From a book review by Gasquet of Charles de Ribbe's work 'La Société provençale à la fin du Moyen-âge' published in Gasquet's journal 'Les Mois Dorés' in March/April 1898 and quoted in Rewald, *Cézanne Letters*, pp. 264-65.
21. Rewald, *Cézanne Letters*, pp. 265-66.

Given Rookmaaker's fundamental theological stance, namely that modern art is symptomatic of a fallen world (but, on this assumption, is this not true of art in any age?) what is a truly Christian art? Rookmaaker says that it must be an art that is true, honourable, just, pure, lovely, gracious, excellent and worthy of praise (Phil. 4.8). He applies these criteria to art in, frankly, a somewhat naive way. Take his treatment of *honesty* in art. He rightly says that the artist must be honest, never concealing his true intentions and never indulging in 'a sort of make-believe'. An artist 'must show his own insight, his own vision, his own understanding'. Christian art is honest art. But is Picasso honest and if so is his art Christian art? Yes, Rookmaaker says, Picasso is honest but his art is not Christian. And this is because Picasso, while honest, is honest to false criteria!

> [Picasso] gives a clear and consistent statement of his nihilistic view of reality. He is honest to this extent: but does he really show reality in truth? Truth does not mean to be conceptually in accordance with reality—this is a rationalistic view of truth. The Bible speaks of *doing* the truth, acting in love and freedom, according to the relationships God wants for man. So in a way art *does* the truth often more than it *is* true in the sense that it portrays reality according to its conceptual reality. Art does the truth in its own artistic way.[22]

Now this is a crucially significant theological statement for Rookmaaker. Of course truth 'does not [merely?] mean to be conceptually in accordance with reality' (though one would have supposed that it must *at least* be in accordance with reality, because if it is not what is the truth true to?) and of course one must 'do' the truth, but Rookmaaker seems to claim that Picasso's art cannot 'do' the truth because, in Rookmaaker's view, Picasso is a nihilist! Thus, *a priori*, Picasso's 'unsurpassed masterpiece' *Les Desmoiselles d'Avignon* cannot 'do' the truth even though the painting stands 'for humanity and timeless reality and truth...[in its] quest for the universal'.[23]

At best this is confusing. Where does Rookmaaker really stand in relation to modern art and, given this apparent confusion, what guidance can Rookmaaker offer to the contemporary Christian artist? As to the latter, Rookmaaker suggests that, ideally, art with 'true Christian content' must offer 'testimony',[24] exegesis, confession and credal statement.[25] It must possess the power to convert. But, confusingly, this does not mean that Christian art must necessarily use biblical or other Christian themes. Rather 'what is Christian in art lies...in the spirit of it, in its wisdom and the understanding of reality it reflects'. It is 'sound, healthy and good art. It is art that is in line with the God-given structures of art, one which has a loving and free view of reality, one which is good and true'. In saying this

22. Rookmaaker, *Modern Art*, p. 238.
23. Rookmaaker, *Modern Art*, p. 116.
24. Rookmaaker, *Modern Art*, p. 71.
25. Rookmaaker, *Modern Art*, p. 75.

Rookmaaker acknowledges that there is no specifically Christian art; there is only good art and bad art, art that is 'sound and good' and art that is 'false and weird in its insight into reality'.[26] But what is 'reality'? And what determines truth from falsehood in the 'insights' of art? In assuming answers to these questions Rookmaaker the evangelical seems ill at ease with Rookmaaker the art historian. According to these criteria Picasso and Braque were 'Christian' artists. Far from being nihilist and a child of the Enlightenment they returned to early (and certainly pre-Enlightenment) Iberian and African and also Egyptian artefacts in their search for reality. They had no interest in rendering the merely *immediate and particular*, not even in portraiture. For Braque (as for Picasso) African art opened a 'new horizon. It permitted me to make contact with instinctive things, with direct manifestations, which were in opposition to the false traditionalism which I abhorred.' He said of his *Nude*, painted in 1907–1908, that 'I wanted to expose the Absolute, and not merely the factitious woman'.[27] Is not this incarnational? A theology of the incarnation is certainly concerned with the immediate and the particular. Yet it is concerned for the immediate and the particular because it reveals the Absolute, for the Christian the *Pater Omnipotens Aeterne*.

The Problem of the Enlightenment

At the heart of this uneasiness is Rookmaaker's evangelical understanding of the Enlightenment. The Enlightenment was the age of rationalism. It resulted in 'the denial to God of the place that He deserves as Creator and Lawgiver'.[28] Rookmaaker here makes a distinction between rationality and rationalism:

> The Reformation had never asked man to accept faith as a leap in the dark: for the Bible itself points to facts. Faith and rationality do not exclude each other. But rationalism is something different: it means that there is nothing more to the world but what the senses can perceive and reason apprehend. There is nothing but scientific fact—or fancy. And God? God is amenable neither to sense perception nor to reason. So God is left out...[29]

The effect of rationalism on man's understanding of himself was disastrous: 'Man became "natural" and lost his place in the cosmos. He lost his humanity... Life became nothing more than biological life, the beating heart and sexual urges and quest for food and drink'.[30] Man placed himself in a box—

---

26. Rookmaaker, *Modern Art*, p. 228.

27. Cited in Douglas Cooper, *The Cubist Epoch* (Oxford: Phaidon Press, 1970), pp. 27-28.

28. Rookmaaker, *Modern Art*, p. 50.

29. Rookmaaker, *Modern Art*, p. 46.

30. Rookmaaker, *Modern Art*, p. 47.

in a world that was no longer open to a transcendent God. 'The content of the box was the only true reality allowed by the men of the Age of Reason, the things that can be understood by rationalist reason and mechanistic science, together with the dream of the new world they had begun to build'.[31]

This understanding of the Enlightenment can be attacked from many sides. The great figures of the Enlightenment are mentioned only in passing. While Rookmaaker admits that the eighteenth-century philosophers in general sought for a unity to the deeper problems of the nature of reality (Kant, for example,[32] though Rookmaaker admits of no God in Kant's philosophy) nevertheless the longer term result of the Enlightenment was that man not only learned to live without God but that he came to believe that God did not exist. Man thus effectively became trapped in the box or prison of his own humanistic definition of himself—a prison from which he has been seeking to free himself ever since through existentialist philosophy, through drugs, through fringe and non-Christian religions, and through modern art—all of them the longer-term results of the disaster of the Enlightenment.

Now there is, of course, some truth in Rookmaaker's definition and analysis of the Enlightenment. However many *philosophes* found a place for God in their systems there was only one Enlightenment, as Peter Gay points out. This one Enlightenment he defines as 'the dialectical interplay of their [the *philosophes*] appeal to antiquity, their tension with Christianity, and their pursuit of "modernity"'. The Enlightenment was thus 'a volatile mixture of classicism, impiety, and science: the philosophes, in a phrase, were modern pagans... [As] Hume makes plain...since God is silent, man is his own master.'[33] Man had indeed come of age, but Rookmaaker asserts that with his coming to adulthood Western man had rejected that reality, that meaning or purpose, that Absolute that, on the far side of all dogma and all definition, we label 'God'.

While that is not true there can be no going back to a culture where God is centre-stage, though Rookmaaker seems to believe that that is the only cure for the ills of the contemporary world. To consider this huge issue, however briefly, would take us well away from our specific theme. In any case how relevant would such a consideration be? Is it true that, as Rookmaaker says, 'to look at modern art is to look at the fruit of the spirit of the avant-garde; it is they who are ahead in building a view of the world with no God, no norms'?[34] Is it true that the masters of the modern movement in art are among those who are leading the world away from God?

31. Rookmaaker, *Modern Art*.
32. Rookmaaker, *Modern Art*, p. 203.
33. Peter Gay, *The Enlightenment: An Interpretation* (New York: Knopf, 1967), pp. 8, 419, quoted in Martland, *Religion as Art*, p. 5.
34. Rookmaaker, *Modern Art*, p. 222.

Even if it is, is it true that the blame for this apostasy must be laid at the door of the 'modern pagans' of the Enlightenment? One would have supposed that the development of human perceptions and ideas, cultural, intellectual and religious change and the evolution of knowledge were far more complex and interrelated than the simple, causal connections of Rookmaaker's critique would lead us to assume. As many radical theologians have been asserting for many years, there must be a better, indeed a more truly biblical and theological, way for Christian believers to engage with the contemporary world than merely to wish that it was not as it is. Ronald Gregor Smith said more than fifty years ago that a truly biblical theology must be done with the stuff of the secular, and this includes modern art. Is it possible to speak of art theologically in a theologically value-free way, that is in a way that is free of any theological/doctrinal assumptions whatever? Can theology be done outside the traditional framework and language of theology? For example, can theology be done in the same spirit as the cubists painted?

The Possibility of a Cubist Theology

We have already suggested that Cézanne was not the creator of 'a rational universe out of what can be perceived by the senses'—a rational universe that had no place for God. Perhaps it would have been more difficult to defend Picasso against the charge of rationalism. Did not he, for all his greatness, come to paint 'absurd man, absurd reality; man made up of some planks; man as non-man' as Rookmaaker says?[35] Is not Picasso the archetypal modern artist, the artist as destroyer? Rookmaaker properly acknowledges that Picasso was much more than this. What Picasso attacked with such savagery was, Rookmaaker affirms, 'the trite individualism and superficial naturalism of the previous period'. Picasso was reacting against the superficiality and emptiness at the heart of modern man caused by the Enlightenment, so Rookmaaker claims, but in so doing art loses a humanist humanity and becomes (confusingly) both extremely intellectual and irrational.[36] How sound is this judgment? Were Picasso and Braque the epitome of the godless *avant-garde*—the latter-day disciples of the pagan philosophers of the Enlightenment? To answer that question we must briefly discuss the genesis of cubism.

Gertrude Stein knew Picasso well. In 1938, decades before Picasso's death and when he was well able to contradict her, she offered three reasons for the making of cubism. These were each reflective of the time—the end of the first decade of the twentieth century in Europe—in which Picasso and Braque worked together. The reasons were:

35. Rookmaaker, *Modern Art*, pp. 151-52.
36. Rookmaaker, *Modern Art*, p. 117.

> First. The composition, because the way of living had changed the composition of living had extended and each thing was as important as any other thing. Secondly, the faith in what the eyes were seeing, that is to say the belief in the reality of science, commenced to diminish. To be sure science had discovered many things, but the principle which was the basis of all this was completely understood, the joy of discovery was almost over. Thirdly, the framing of life, the need that a picture exist in its frame was over. A picture remaining in its frame was a thing that always had existed and now pictures commenced to want to leave their frames and this also created a necessity for cubism. The time had come and the man.[37]

The extension of the composition of living, the diminishing authority of science, the desire to leave the traditional frames of life: Gertrude Stein here sets out not merely the reasons for cubism, she delineates also the foundations of the postmodernism of the latter half of the century. But these are not merely or primarily intellectual foundations; rather they have to do with feelings, with emotions, with the yearning to be free from the constraints of the old ways, all revealed, as Apollinaire wrote in 1912, not through the reality of sight but through the reality of *insight*.[38]

Cubism was thus a product of the time, it did not create it. Picasso painted the shape of the time in which he lived, and that shape was cubist. He did not invent it *ex nihilo*. Life had become multi-dimensional but, more importantly, its dimensions, its forming templates (or, better, its cubist facets), were now seen to be of equal or at least complementary importance. This is what Stein means by 'the composition of life'. She tells of the founding of the abbey of Hautecombe. The first site was on a hill near a very frequented road. But, Stein asks, what was a 'very frequented road' in the fifteenth century? Did it mean that people passed once a day or once a week? Stein uses this road as a metaphor. She continues:

> The composition of each epoch depends upon the way the frequented roads are frequented, people remain the same, the way their roads are frequented is what changes from one century to another and it is that that makes the composition that is before the eyes of every one of that generation and it is that that makes the composition that a creator creates.[39]

Stein applies this insight to the first world war:

> Really the composition of this war, 1914–1918, was not the composition of all previous wars, the composition was not a composition in which there was one man in the centre surrounded by a lot of other men but a composition that had neither a beginning nor an end, a composition of which one corner was an important as another corner, in fact the composition of cubism.[40]

37. Gertrude Stein, *Picasso* (New York: Dover Publications, 1984), p. 12.
38. In 'Les Peintres Cubistes', reproduced in part in H.B. Chipp (ed.), *Theories of Modern Art* (Berkeley: University of California Press, 1968), pp. 221-48 (227) (my italics).
39. Stein, *Picasso*, p. 11.
40. Stein, *Picasso*.

If there is any truth in this insight then it should be possible to do theology similarly. If the first world war was a cubist war because the prevailing world-view was, and remains, essentially cubist, then a contemporary theology must also be multi-faceted.

Cubism and the Postmodern Condition

I say 'remains essentially cubist' because although the cubism epoch ended effectively in 1921, cubism marks the beginning of non-figuration in art. However anticipated in the work of the post-Impressionist masters it marks if not the beginning then a revolutionary stage in the development of modern art. Jean-Francois Lyotard has made the illuminating suggestion (and here he is referring directly to the pioneers of the modern movement in art) that 'a work can become modern only if it is first postmodern. Post-modernism thus understood is not modernism at its end but in the nascent state, and this state is constant'. Seen in this way, cubism is postmodern. Supremely in art, though here Lyotard is speaking of the postmodern in general, it 'put forward the unpresentable in presentation itself'. Cubism was a new—a revolutionary—presentation, not to be enjoyed in itself 'but in order to impart a stronger sense of the unpresentable.[41] Picasso and Braque worked outside the conventional and familiar rule and categories in order to discover the rules and categories of what they had done! As such their work, as Lyotard says of postmodern artists and writers in general, came always too late for their creators. In that sense their work was always provisional. There was constant change, constant readjustment. Picasso and Braque were always in front of the future.

What was Cubism?

We will be concerned here with the first phase of cubism, the period of analytical or 'pure' cubism.[42] Picasso painted his proto-cubist *Les Desmoiselles d'Avignon* in 1907. The generation of French Impressionist painters before him had, in the main, been concerned to render the subjective effect of light falling on objects in space. This was a huge advance in itself. Their studies in colour and of the effect of light had led them to realise that the appearance of an object in space was in fact nothing more than the appearance of light falling on it. All that can be seen is the effect of light and this they sought to capture. Their great forerunner Courbet, had, like the Impressionists, painted scenes from everyday life, but he had done so with regard to their tangible reality. All painting is a fiction, but Courbet was concerned to represent the reality through the fiction of painting. Most

41. Lyotard, *The Postmodern Condition*, pp. 79-81, reproduced in Harrison and Wood, *Art in Theory 1900–1990*, p. 1014.
42. See Cooper, *The Cubist Epoch*.

current art historians would claim that the Impressionists were concerned with colour and with the ephemeral effects of changing light—with what Douglas Cooper describes as 'the cult of the immaterial'. In this they had lost sight of Courbet's concern with the tangible reality. The post-Impressionist masters, van Gogh, Gauguin and, supremely, Cézanne were concerned not merely with the solid reality of things but with the structures beneath that solid reality and revealed through it. In this Gauguin and Cézanne anticipated (and Cézanne partly solved) the conceptual and technical problems that Picasso and Braque recognised and cubism solved. The principal problem, as their contemporary the critic Jacques Rivière observed, was how to construct the object *as it is* rather than as the painter *sees it*, 'that is to say, in the form of geometrical volume, set free from lighting effects'.[43] Rivière noted further that it required the painter to eliminate perspective also (what Cooper rightly calls 'the eye-fooling illusion of three-dimensional seeing'). The effect of light is transitory, it is but an indication of time. Illusional perspective tells us only of the equally temporary position in space of the observer. Neither the light nor the observer's position as indications of time and of space tell us anything about the tangible reality of the object in itself. Cézanne rendered this tangible reality by largely ignoring light effects and wholly ignoring linear perspective. Writing is 1912 the cubist painters Albert Gleizes and Jean Metzinger said of Cézanne that 'if he did not himself reach those regions where profound realism merges insensibly into luminous spirituality, at least he dedicated himself to whoever really wants to attain a simple yet prodigious method'.[44]

The rendering of 'profound realism' (to be contrasted to the 'superficial realism' of the Impressionists) was the mission of the cubists. They sought to do this by rejecting the single perspective view and the other optical illusions, together with the merely sensual, in order to express what their contemporary Apollinaire called 'the grandeur of metaphysical forms'. In this, he said, 'contemporary art, even if it does not directly stem from specific religious beliefs, nonetheless possesses some of the characteristics of great, that is to say, religious art'.[45] This is not to imply that Picasso and Braque renounced rationality. Far from it. André Salmon, a friend of Picasso in these early years, wrote that Picasso was greatly attracted to African sculpture because it seemed to him to be 'rational' by which he meant the rejection of the merely sentimental. Picasso was, Salmon says, 'struck by the fact that Negro artists had attempted to make a true representation of a human being, and not just to present the idea, usually sentimental, that we have of him'.[46]

---

43. Quoted in Harrison and Wood, *Art in Theory*, p. 183.
44. Harrison and Wood, *Art in Theory*, p. 189.
45. Chipp (ed.), *Theories of Modern Art*, p. 224.
46. Cooper, *The Cubist Epoch*, pp. 31-32.

There is much more that can be said, but I am concerned here not to describe the cubists' methodology or even to discuss whether they achieved their aims but merely to indicate what they set out to achieve. If these were 'rational' aims, then that rationality, as their friend the poet Apollinaire observed, was fundamentally religious. It had to do with the ground of the being revealed in the face and body of the person or in the still-life or the landscape.

A Cubist Theology?

What follows here is no more than a superficial outline sketch—a mere indication of a path to explore. A theology that has learnt from cubism would be:

- a theology that is done outside the boundaries and constraints of a merely formalised past. Our credal beliefs and their formulations must be made open to fresh expressions and new interpretations deriving from, and thus appropriate to, today's world,
- a theology that must be provisional. It must search for its underlying rules and procedures as it proceeds and not impose rules and procedures as a condition for doing theology before it begins its work,
- a theology that must recognise that no one feature or factor in the world is more significant or important than any other, least of all the particular, one-sided, perspective of the theologian,
- a theology that must always keep contact with and use the stuff of the everyday world (as Picasso and Braque incorporated actual everyday objects into their work) as intrinsic to theology and not alien or subservient to it,
- a theology that must always be true to what actually is, and never employ mind-fooling religious perspectives and tricks which pretend to open a door on so-called reality. It must be revelatory and never illusory.
- a theology that must offer clues or keys as touchstones of a reality that men and women must discover for themselves, and not impose unchallengeable dogmas or authoritative statements which forbid any questioning,
- a theology that must reflect the truth that we live in what Picasso recognised as 'a strange and not very reassuring world' and not pretend to a confident certainty that we cannot have. As Herbert Read observed: 'Our age has demanded...a new vision to express a new dimension of consciousness—not only harmony, but the truth which is, alas, fragmentary and unconsoling'.[47] It will be a theology which is also inevitably fragmentary and often seemingly unconsoling,

47. Read, *A Concise History of Modern Painting*, p. 81.

- a theology that must make demands upon men and women radically to change their viewpoint on, or perception, of reality, to return to it if they must, but at least honestly to attempt to approach the truth of things from different and unfamiliar directions,
- a theology that must recognise that truth is to be found in unity and not in separation or distinction, that is, the locus of unity is not in a particular object or person, however sacred, but in the relationships between entities. There is no such thing as 'empty space' in a cubist theology. Nothing is unimportant or unworthy.
- a theology that must seek the truth, the idea, behind the appearance through paying the utmost attention to that which engages our senses in the material.

Can a theology of the incarnation be otherwise? Apollinaire argued in his *Les peintres cubistes* in 1913 that his young friends, in discarding the old art of optical illusion and local proportion, were seeking to express 'the grandeur of metaphysical forms'. That is why the best contemporary art, even if it does not directly stem from specific religious beliefs, nonetheless possesses some of the characteristics of great, that is to say truly religious, art.

If this analysis has any value one of its implications for our understanding of God would be that there is no one 'true' perspective from which we can (least of all must) see and be seen by him. A realist/objective and an expressionist/subjective understanding of God are either of equal value or they are equally valueless in providing us with clues as to what or who 'God' is.

Chapter 11

A Glimpse of the Cosmic Dance

The theological theme of this book (if it can be said to have had one at all) has been very simple and very obvious. It is that salvation is not to be found in escape from or denial of the world.[1] We are not saved from a world which is by its very essence and character corrupting. Such a notion is not found in the Hebrew tradition, though it has had to struggle to be recognised in the Christian. Rather, we are saved in a cosmos which is shot through and through with practical, material, enfleshed, enduring love—the love that is the nature and very essence of God. It is this God who created and sustains this cosmos.

We have noticed that the New Testament word that we translate by the metaphor 'to save' means to make whole. It tells of the restoration of a lost integrity and authenticity in every sphere of our experience of ourselves, each other and the world, physically, mentally, emotionally and (if this sphere can be separated from others) spiritually. The significance of Jesus, the word of God made flesh, in the New Testament—that same word of God which 'runneth very swiftly'[2] on every page of the Old—is not that he showed us what God is like in the sense of revealing a metaphysical truth previously unknown, but rather that he showed men and women what it means to be authentically human, thus exposing, as Jose Comblin said memorably, 'the self-satisfaction and superficiality of humanistic definitions of being human',[3] for to be authentically human is to be made in the image and likeness of God. The writers of the Bible never indulge in metaphysical speculations. They never theorise about the internal dynamics of the God-head. Their announcement of the truth that is in Christ is never an indulgence in mere ideas. When they speak of the Word of God made flesh they speak always of salvation. The New Testament teaches us that in enabling us to be authentically human Jesus did that great work of the Father for

---

1.   This chapter draws in part from an article of mine 'Art et salut' published in Edward Bailey (ed.), *Religion Implicite* (Religiologiques, 14; Université du Québec à Montréal, 1996), pp. 101-14.
2.   Ps. 147.15 (Authorized Version).
3.   Jose Comblin, *Sent from the Father* (Dublin: Gill & Macmillan, 1979), p. 3.

which he was sent—he restores to us our wholeness. The New Adam, he renews the face of every Adam and Eve. As he did and does this saving work of the Father Jesus is his son. He is son because he is saviour. He is not saviour because he is son.

Thus salvation is focused in this universe. As such it is essentially earthed and practical in today's world. Salvation is making peace where there is conflict, it is bringing judgment where there is sin, it is bringing reconciliation where there is alienation, healing where there is disease, wholeness where there is brokenness, liberty where there is captivity, resurrection where there is crucifixion, life where there is death. That is what salvation means. Salvation for the Old Testament writers is invariably a this-world experience. The Exodus is practical deliverance, and it continues to be a paradigm for deliverance throughout the Old Testament and in the history of the oppressed to this day—black and gay, the poor and the mentally disturbed, the alienated and the oppressed. In the stories of the wilderness wanderings of the Hebrews wherever God 'caused his name to dwell' is invariably a place of peace, rest, water, food and safety—a place of practical salvation. In the New Testament salvation is never an other-worldly or spiritualised or merely interior experience. Very much the reverse. Salvation *is* the sighted and the unsighted blind receiving their sight, the lame running, the deaf hearing, lepers being cleansed, demoniacs being released, those who are oppressed being set at liberty from the million prisons in which they are held, and the dead being raised from the million deaths they die.

That is a rather breathless resume which raises at least as many questions as it makes claims. It is by no means an adequate summary of what salvation signifies in the Bible. It serves only to indicate the this-worldly, practical nature of salvation. What those of us who profess Christian discipleship must do (with what Reinhold Niebuhr once called 'secular urgency') is to take that biblical, world-focused Gospel as practical making-whole with profound seriousness in our contemporary world. To do so we must continue to struggle to free ourselves from presuppositions and dogmas, however sacred they may be, *if* these assumptions and definitions hold us captive in the safe and comfortable prison of a spiritualised, world-fearing, flesh-denying, life-renouncing religion.

That central truth of salvation—that it is practical earthed love by a God whose very nature is love—is celebrated from strikingly different viewpoints by two of the most imaginative theologians of the twentieth century, Thomas Merton and Teilhard de Chardin.

The last page of the final meditation in Thomas Merton's *Seeds of Contemplation* has these words:

> What is serious to me is often very trivial in the sight of God. What in God might appear to us as 'play' is perhaps what He Himself takes most seriously. At any rate the Lord plays and diverts Himself in the garden of

His creation, and if we could let go of our obsession with what we think is the meaning of it all, we might be able to hear His call and follow Him in His mysterious, cosmic dance. When we are alone on a starlit night; when by chance we see the migrating birds in autumn descending on a grove of junipers to rest and eat; when we see children in a moment when they are really children; when we know love in our hearts; or when, like the Japanese poet Basho, we hear an old frog land in a quiet pond with a solitary splash—at such times the awakening, the turning inside out of all values, the 'newness', the emptiness and the purity of vision that make themselves evident, provide a glimpse of the cosmic dance.[4]

Thomas Merton was a Trappist monk, and thus a member of a world-renouncing religious Order. Monica Furlong, one of the best because one of the least hagiographical of his biographers, suggests that Merton was drawn to the disciplines of his order because he was so personally susceptible (as was Augustine of Hippo) to the attraction of people and the world. Perhaps so, but he never lost his warm love of either. On the contrary, from the security of his faith and religious tradition he actively engaged with the world in all its political and religious diversity. He died in Bangkok on one of his journeys of exploration into Eastern spirituality of which he wrote with so much theological openness. He was supremely a man of this world.

Teilhard de Chardin, a member of another religious Order, the Jesuits, was one of the finest palaeontologists of his age. One day, while on a scientific expedition in the Ordos Desert, he found himself unable to say mass. It was the Feast of the Transfiguration—a special feast for this gentle priest. What this denial called forth from him was *The Mass on the World* in which he celebrates the real presence of the risen Christ in the whole universe. The Offering contains these words:

> Over there, on the horizon, the sun has just touched with light the outermost fringe of the eastern sky. Once again, beneath this moving sheet of fire, the living surface of the earth wakes and trembles, and once again begins its fearful travail. I will place on my paten, O God, the harvest to be won by this renewal of labour. Into my chalice I shall pour all the sap which is to be pressed out this day from the earth's fruits.
>
> My paten and my chalice are the depths of a soul laid widely open to all the forces which in a moment will rise up from every corner of the earth and converge upon the Spirit. Grant me the remembrance and the mystic presence of all those whom the light is awakening to this new day...[5]

Those are just brief passages from the pens of these two men. What poetry they contain, and what a passionate affirmation of the reality of the heart of love which beats at the centre of all things. They were poets with a breadth of vision deriving from a Christian faith illuminated by the

4.   Thomas Merton, *Seeds of Contemplation* (Wheathamstead: Anthony Clarke, 1961), p. 230.
5.   Teilhard de Chardin, *Hymn to the Universe* (New York: Harper & Row, 1961), p. 19.

imagination. They expressed themselves simply, but, as the Austrian writer Hugo Hofmannsthal has said, powerful imaginations are always conserva-tive.[6]

Merton's vision saw the hand of redeeming, saving love in the micro-cosm. Everything that is, he said, is holy: 'The pale flowers of the dogwood outside this window are saints. The little yellow flowers that nobody notices on the edge of that road are saints looking up into the face of God...'[7] In a way that is far from being sentimental, Merton proclaims the individual sanctity of even the tiniest and least regarded things in the cosmos. Teilhard de Chardin's vision saw the hand of redeeming, saving love in the macro-cosm. In his passionate 'Hymn to Matter' he does not call on all creation to bless the Lord as in a *Cantate Domino* but rather he pronounces all creation itself blessed by God: 'Blessed be you, universal matter, immeasurable time, boundless ether, triple abyss of stars and atoms and generations: you who by overflowing and dissolving our narrow standards of measurement reveal to us the dimensions of God'.[8]

We have in these two poet mystics a still remarkably daring theology, at least in the West and at the beginning of the twenty-first century. It is daring because it rebukes that still strong Christian puritan tradition, owing much to alien Greek notions of the corruptibility of matter, that sees all matter and especially all flesh, as essentially and originally sinful. We have seen this strong tendency in Christian attitudes to the arts. Because it is biblical to the core it is remarkable that the notion that flesh is God-created and redeemed is regarded as suspect by many Christians. Almost wherever one looks in the earlier strata of the Old Testament writings one finds reflected the assumption that God is everywhere present, alive and active in his creation in saving love. This last point must be emphasised. God was known as saviour before he was recognised as creator. His creative work is predicated on his saving action. The theological watershed of the Exodus floods forward into all subsequent Hebrew history as it washes back into the pre-Exodus history, and indeed into pre-history to the moment of crea-tion itself as the Bible portrays it. Knowing God as saviour, those who compiled the creation narratives in Genesis spoke of God as saviour-creator. And so it is throughout the Old Testament and into the New.

But if speaking about salvation in and through the natural order is easy, however controversial it still is for some Christians that the truth of our original bliss has primacy over later notions of our original sin, it is much more difficult to be convincing when one comes to tell of salvation in art—in not the natural but the man-made artefact. Merton speaks of an art-form

6.   Quoted in *The Independent* (23 March 2004).
7.   Thomas Merton, 'Things in their Identity', in *idem*, *Seeds of Contemplation*, p. 24.
8.   From Teilhard de Chardin, 'Hymn to Matter', in *idem*, *Hymn to the Universe*, pp. 63-64.

when he tells of God. He tells of God at play in his universe and of the cosmic dance. But what of my play and of my dance? Can these be equally salvific? Can they tell of the practical, earthed love of God in judgment and redemption?

This book has told of the struggle of many artists to stay within the constraints of their art but to move beyond it to the truths in which, they seem to believe, it partakes. Lionello Venturi said of Cézanne that he was a seer who could see in a peasant, in the surface of the sea, in some fruit, eternal and universal truths beyond the confines of any formal religion. Hence, he said, the incomparable greatness of Cézanne's art. As he came to the end of his life Cézanne himself proclaimed to the poet Leo Larguier: 'Art is a religion, its goal is the elevation of truth'. As we have seen, this capacity in Cézanne and all great artists to move beyond the confines of their art gives to it what Venturi called 'moral beauty'. We have seen, too, that in his depiction of real agony, distress, evil and sorrow in his *Guernica* and his *Woman Weeping* and other work Picasso produces incomparable art which judges us. *Guernica* and Picasso's pictures of women mirror our own actions. Francis Bacon's demented and scarcely human beings screaming in cages mirror with astonishing and profoundly disturbing truth our own inhumanity. Can it possibly be claimed that such art is salvific? Insofar as these pictures mirror ourselves they judge us. There is no salvation without judgment. The light which opens blind eyes in the Fourth Gospel is the same light which shines in the dark places of the world and shows up evil men for what we are. Picasso's art, and Bacon's art, Manet's and Michelangelo's art serve my restoration and wholeness by compelling me to face up to my ambivalence, my two-facedness, my hypocrisy. The light illuminates my wickedness.

The great humanist painters and sculptors of the Renaissance reflected in their work Christian and classical values about man. What many twentieth-century artists reflected was the cry of despair that we have lost that freedom and that greatness and that it is impossible now to be authentically human. How can a Christian possibly claim that the expression of such agony and despair is salvific? Indeed how can the work of such a despairing atheist as Francis Bacon possibly be religious?

We have noted that Paul Tillich argued with passion that what the authentic artist creates are revelations. What great artists do, even confessed atheists (perhaps most of all confessed atheists for they struggle to disengage, not always successfully, from the interpretative categories of religion) is to reveal to us a dimension of reality. They are seers, as Venturi said of Cézanne. What Bacon saw was the futility, the pain and the despair of Western civilisation after Christianity. He was a brother of Samuel Beckett in this regard. The overwhelming majority of those who live in the West have become not merely estranged from religion but quite indifferent to the claims that religion makes. To them, if they give it any thought at all, religion belongs to a very alien and irrelevant world of personal superstition, unless at moments of personal and national tragedy the beauty and solemnity of its language serves as a necessary vehicle for the expression of otherwise inarticulate but powerful emotions. In this, liturgy operates more as an art-form than as an expression of personal faith for so very many. The truth is that the salvation which Christianity proclaims is ignored by most people. Christians must face squarely the fact that very large numbers of men and women live courageously without the hope that the Gospel promises. Many live with emptiness and despair as not only the ultimate reality but as daily companions. To be confronted with this truth is to be jolted out of a cosy Christian complacency. Very many people are indifferent to the claims of Christianity because these claims seem to them to lack meaning in the world that they inhabit. The Gospel does not touch them.

It is of this authentic world—a world largely without conventional religion—that the great artists of the twentieth century have written and painted. To see this world for what it is in its essential integrity is to be set free from complacency. We are shown the truth by these men and women. The truth sets us free, and to be set free is to be saved.

I have chosen to speak of the darker perspectives of great modern art because it is that perspective which it is hard to defend as salvific. Yet, because it has moral beauty it must be so. It is less difficult to defend great art as salvific in its heavenward-facing aspect. Art is life-giving. Henry Moore once said that 'to be an artist is the opposite of being in a state of despair. To be an artist is to believe in life' and again, 'if you can get into the right kind of receptive and appreciative—creative—way of seeing, then the whole world is full of new ideas and possibilities'. Here again is the artist as seer. I say 'seer' and not 'visionary' because the artist does not see visions. He sees the ordinary everyday truths to which most of us are blind. Nevertheless, the word 'vision' has cropped up in this book. It has been said that poetry stretches the ordinary use of language. That is true of all authentic art be it poetry or prose, painting, sculpture, dance or music. The artist gives 'memorable expression' by stretching the ordinary use of the medium to the limits and even beyond. His or her art gives us life by enabling us to see and therefore to know, through 'stretched' paint or clay or movement or sound. Theologically, what more biblical and, specifically Johannine, understanding of salvation can one hope for? In the Fourth Gospel we *see* and *know* through the life and death of the Poor Man from Nazareth, whose 'stretched' humanity is his and our true divinity.

But there is mystery in truly seeing and knowing. If truly we see and know then what we see and know is that we glimpse but the nearer edge of a wondrous vista as Kant reminded us. That is why authentic art is essential mysterious. The Irish sculptor F.E. McWilliam produced pieces which, he said, combine 'surreal illogicality with the logic of design'. He demanded of himself that his works embody mystery because, he said, 'if you take the mystery out of art you're left with nothing but design or illustration'.

What this book has attempted to do has been no more than to allow artists to speak in their own ways to men and women of religious belief. It has noted the following truths about authentic artists: they produce work of moral beauty, they embody or incarnate truth, they enable us to see and to know, they are life-givers, they bring us to judgment, they sow seeds which germinate secretly within us, they bring us to the edge of a mystery which is as vast and as exciting for them as it is for the rest of us yet they seem to know the way to it and can lead us there. It is little wonder that not only have art and religion been confused but that for so many art has replaced conventional religion. The gallery has become the place of pilgrimage.

That is as far as I am ready to take any analysis of the relationship of art and religion. Any more would be even more pretentious and, more seriously, potentially destructive of the integrities of both art and faith. Verbalisation about both art and religion can so easily destroy vision by substituting opinion for true insight. Superior intellectual opinions about the work of, say, that gentle visionary painter Samuel Palmer can separate us from him. I want him, as it were, to hold my hand and take me to lie with my lover in a sheepfold on a moonlit night beneath the magic apple-tree. His place in the development of nineteenth-century English art may one day be of interest to me, but what I need now is to be made whole, and that wholeness will not come by assault from the doctrines and historical theologies of aesthetics. If, however, we want an unpretentious summary of what we have tried to explore in this book (unpretentious because written by a fine artist of the written word) then listen to Iris Murdoch. In her *The Fire and the Sun* published in 1977 she said this from a position quite outside a confessional religion:

> Good art...provides a stirring image of pure transcendent value, a steady visible enduring higher good, and perhaps provides for many people in an unreligious age without prayer or sacraments, their clearest experience of something grasped as separate and precious and beneficial and held quietly and unpossessively in the attention. Good art which we love can seem holy and attending to it can be like praying.

For Hildegard (1098–1179) 'art is a half-effaced recollection of a higher state from which we have fallen since the time of Eden'. Hannah Arendt in *The Human Condition* echoes this. She notes that a work of art is a thing in the world yet it possesses 'outstanding permanence'. It is as if, she says,

> worldly stability has become transparent in the permanence of art, so that a premonition of immortality, not the immortality of the soul or of life but of something immortal achieved by mortal hands, has become tangibly present, to shine and to be seen, to sound and to be heard, to speak and to be read.[9]

9.   Arendt, *The Human Condition*, p. 168.

It is too much to say that the truth spoken of here can be incarnation and salvation? If not, then at least for me, and for very many others I dare say, a work of true art can tell of

> that which was from the beginning, which we have heard, which we have seen with our eyes, which we have looked upon and touched with our hands, concerning the word of life—the life was made manifest, and we saw it, and testify to it... (1 Jn 1.1-2)

Bibliography

Ackroyd, Peter, *T.S. Eliot* (London: Penguin Books, 1993).

Alexander, Sidney, *Marc Chagall: An Intimate Biography* (St Paul, MN: Paragon House, 1989).

Anderson, T. (ed.), *K.S. Malevich: Essays on Art 1915–1933*, I (Copenhagen, 1969).

Arendt, Hannah, *The Human Condition* (California: University of California Press, 1958).

Arnheim, Rudolf, *Art and Visual Perception* (Berkeley: University of California Press, 1974).

—*Picasso's 'Guernica'* (London: Faber & Faber 1964).

—*To the Rescue of Art* (Oxford: University of California Press, 1992).

Austin, M.R., 'Art and Religion as Metaphor', *The British Journal of Aesthetics* 35.2 (1995), pp. 145-53.

—'Art et salut', in Edward Bailey (ed.), *Religion Implicite* (Religiologiques, 14; Université du Québec à Montréal, 1996), pp. 101-14.

—'As the Bird Sings', *Modern Believing* NS 36.2 (1995), pp. 12-18.

—'Derrida's Kind of Salvation', *Implicit Religion* 5.1 (2002), pp. 49-59.

Badt, Kurt, *The Art of Cézanne* (London: Faber & Faber, 1965).

Balthasar, Hans Urs von, *The Glory of the Lord*. I. *Seeing the Form* (ed. J. Fessio and J. Riches; trans. E. Leivà-Herikakis; Edinburgh: T. & T. Clark, 1982).

Barth, Karl, *Church Dogmatics*, III, Part 3 (Edinburgh: T. & T. Clark, 1978).

—*Dogmatics in Outline* (London: SCM Press, 1949).

—'The Gift of Freedom: Foundation of Evangelical Ethics', in *idem*, *The Humanity of God*, pp. 70-96.

—*How I Changed my Mind* (Edinburgh: St Andrew's Press, 1969).

—*The Humanity of God* (Atlanta: John Knox Press, 1960).

—*Wolfgang Amadeus Mozart* (Grand Rapids: Eerdmans, 1986).

Berger, John, *Success and Failure of Picasso* (London: Granta Books, new edn, 1992).

Berger, John *et al.*, *Ways of Seeing* (London: BBC; Harmondsworth: Penguin Books, 1972).

Boixados, Alberto, *Myths of Modern Art* (Lanham, MD: University Press of America, 1990).

Bonhoeffer, Dietrich, *Ethics* (London: SCM Press, 1955).

Brown, Raymond E., *The Gospel according to John* (London: Geoffrey Chapman, 1971).

Busch, Eberhard, *Karl Barth* (London: SCM Press, 1976).

Caird, G.B., *The Language and Imagery of the Bible* (London: Gerald Duckworth, 1980).

—*The Revelation of St John the Divine* (London: A. & C. Black, 1984).

Calvino, Italo, *Six Memos for the Next Millennium* (London: Random House [Vintage], 1996).

Campbell, Joseph, *The Power of Myth* (New York: Doubleday, 1989).

Carpenter, Rhys, *The Esthetic Basis of Greek Art* (Bloomington: Indiana University Press, 1959).

Casey, Maurice, *From Jewish Prophet to Gentile God* (Cambridge: James Clarke, 1991).

Cecil, David, *Visionary and Dreamer* (London: Constable, 1969).

Chave, Anna C., *Mark Rothko* (New Haven: Yale University Press, 1989).

Chipp, H.B. (ed.), *Theories of Modern Art* (Berkeley: University of California Press, 1968).

Clark, Kenneth, *Moments of Vision* (London: John Murray, 1981).

Collingwood, R.G., *The Principles of Art* (Oxford: Oxford University Press, 1938).

Comblin, Jose, *Sent from the Father* (Dublin: Gill & Macmillan, 1979).

Cooper, David (ed.), *A Companion to Aesthetics* (Oxford: Basil Blackwell, 1995).

Cooper, Douglas, *The Cubist Epoch* (Oxford: Phaidon Press, 1970).

—*Nicholas de Staël* (New York: W.W. Norton, 1961).

Crompton, Susan, *Chagall: Love and the Stage 1914–1922* (London: Royal Academy of Arts/Merrell Holberton, 1998).

Cupitt, Don, *Radicals and the Future of the Church* (London: SCM Press, 1989).

Daab, Zan Schuweiler, 'For Heaven's Sake: Warhol's Art as Religious Allegory', *Religion and the Arts* 1.1 (1996), pp. 14-31.

Dante Alighieri, *The Divine Comedy*. II. *Purgatory* (trans. and ed. Dorothy L. Sayers; Harmandsworth: Penguin Books, 1974).

Denis, Maurice, 'From Gauguin and van Gogh to Neo-Classicism', in *L'Occident* (Paris, May 1909), reprinted in Harrison and Wood, *Art in Theory*, pp. 47-53.

Deutsch, Eliot, *Essays on the Nature of Art* (Albany, NY: State University of New York Press, 1996).

—*Religion and Spirituality* (Albany, NY: State University of New York Press, 1995).

Dewey, John, *Art as Experience* (New York: Capricorn, 1934).

Dixon, John W., *Art and the Theological Imagination* (New York: Seabury Press, 1978).

Ehrenzweig, Anton, *The Hidden Order of Art: A Study in the Psychology of Artistic Imagination* (London: Weidenfeld, 1993 [1st edn Berkeley: University of California Press, 1967]).

Elgar, Frank, *Cézanne* (London: Thames & Hudson, 1969).

Evans, Richard J., *In Defence of History* (London: Granta Books, 1997).

Findlay, J.N., *Ascent to the Absolute* (London: Allen & Unwin, 1970).

Fischer, Ernst, *The Necessity of Art* (London: Penguin Books, 1963).

Flam, Jack D., *Matisse on Art* (Oxford: Phaidon Press, 1973).

Ford, D.F. (ed.), *The Modern Theologians*, I (3 vols.; Oxford: Basil Blackwell, 1989).

Gadamer, H-G., *The Relevance of the Beautiful and Other Essays* (Cambridge: Cambridge University Press, 1986).

Gauss, Charles Edward, *The Aesthetic Theories of French Artists from Realism to Surrealism* (Baltimore: The Johns Hopkins University Press, 1949).

Gay, Peter, *The Enlightenment: An Interpretation* (New York: Knopf, 1967).

Gedo, Mary Mathews, *Looking at Art from the Inside Out: The Psychoiconographic Approach to Modern Art* (Cambridge: Cambridge University Press, 1994).

George, Waldemar, and Genevieve Nouaille-Rouault, *Rouault* (London: Pall Mall Press, 1971).

Golding, John, *Paths to the Absolute* (London: Thames & Hudson, 2000).

Gombrich, E.H., *Art and Illusion* (Oxford: Phaidon Press, 1977).

—'Art and Self-Transcendence', in *idem*, *Ideals and Idols*, pp. 123-30.

—'Canons and Values: A Correspondence with Quentin Bell', in *idem*, *Ideals and Idols*, pp. 167-83.

—*Ideals and Idols* (Oxford: Phaidon Press, 1994).

—*The Story of Art* (Oxford: Phaidon Press, 15th edn, 1989).

Gore, Charles, 'The Holy Spirit and Inspiration', in *idem* (ed.), *Lux Mundi* (London: John Murray, 1889), p. 231.

Graham, Gordon, *Philosophy of the Arts* (London: Routledge, 1997).

Guillemot, Maurice, 'Claude Monet', *La Revue Illustrée* (15 March 1898), reproduced in Charles F. Stuckey (ed.), *Monet: A Retrospective* (New York: Hugh Lauter Levin Associates, 1985), pp. 195-201.

Hamilton, George Heard, *Painting and Sculpture in Europe 1880–1940* (New Haven: Yale University Press, 1993).

Hamilton, James, *Turner: A Life* (London: Hodder & Stoughton, 1997).

Hamlyn, D.W., 'History of Metaphysics', in Ted Honderich (ed.), *The Oxford Companion to Philosophy* (Oxford: Oxford University Press, 1995), p. 556.

Harrison, Colin, *Samuel Palmer* (Oxford: Ashmolean Museum, 1997).

Harrison, C., and P. Wood, *Art in Theory 1900–1990* (Oxford: Basil Blackwell, 1993).

Hügel, Friedrich von, *The Mystical Element of Religion as studied in Saint Catherine of Genoa and her Friends* (London: Dent, 1908).

—*The Mystical Element of Religion* (2 vols.: London: Dent, 1923).

Hughes, Robert, *The Shock of the New* (New York: McGraw–Hill, 1980).

Inwood, Michael, *A Hegel Dictionary* (Oxford: Basil Blackwell, 1992).

Jalard, M.-C., *Post-Impressionism* (London: Heron, 1968).

James, William, 'Reflex Action and Theism', in *idem*, *The Will to Believe* (London: Longmans Green, 1897), pp. 111-14.

—*The Varieties of Religious Experience* (London: Longmans Green, 1902).

Jung, C.J., *Man and His Symbols* (London: Aldus, 1964).

Kadowaki, J.K., *Zen and the Bible* (Routledge & Kegan Paul, 1982).

Kandinsky, Wassily, *Concerning the Spiritual in Art* (New York: Dover Publications, 1977).

Kant, Immanuel, *Critique of Judgment* (Oxford: Oxford University Press, 1973).

—*Critique of Practical Reason* (London: Dent, 1993).

Kelsey, David H., *The Uses of Scripture in Doctrine* (Philadelphia: Fortress Press, 1975).

Kenner, Hugh, *The Pound Era* (London: Faber & Faber, 1972).

Kierkegaard, Søren, *The Last Years: Journals 1853–1855* (London: Collins, 1968).

Kung, Hans, *Art and the Question of Meaning* (trans E. Quinn; London: SCM Press, 1981).

—*Mozart: Traces of Transcendence* (London: SCM Press, 1992).

Kupfer, Joseph, 'Aesthetic Experience and Moral Education', *Journal of Aesthetic Education* 12.3 (1978), pp. 13-22.

Langer, S.K., *Feeling and Form* (London: Routledge, 1953).

—*Problems of Art* (London: Routledge & Kegan Paul, 1957).

Lawrence, D.H., *The Complete Poems* (ed. Vivian de Sola Pinto and Warren Roberts; London: Penguin Books, 1993).

—*Selected Essays* (London: Penguin Books, 1950).

—'Whistling of Birds', in *idem, Selected Essays*, p. 112.

Lewis, H.D., *Our Experience of God* (London: Collins, 1970).

Lorca, Federico Garcia, 'Snail', in *idem, Songs and Ballads* (Montreal: Guernica Editions Inc., 1997), p. 15.

Lynton, Norbert, 'Expressionism', in Stangos (ed.), *Concepts of Modern Art*, pp. 30-49.

Mallarmé, Stéphane, 'The Impressionists and Edouard Manet', *The Art Monthly Review* (London, 30 September 1876).

Malraux, André, *Voices of Silence* (St Albans: Paladin, 1974).

Martland, Thomas, *Religion as Art* (Albany, NY: State University of New York Press, 1981).

Marxsen, Willi, *The Beginnings of Christology* (Philadelphia: Fortress Press, 1979).

Masini, Lara Vinca, *Van Gogh* (London: Thames & Hudson, 1967).

McIntyre, John, *Faith, Theology and Imagination* (Edinburgh: The Handsel Press, 1987).

McMullen, R., *The World of Marc Chagall* (London: Aldus, 1968).

Merton, Thomas, *Seeds of Contemplation* (Wheathamstead: Anthony Clarke, 1961).

—'Things in their Identity', in *idem, Seeds of Contemplation*, p. 24.

Milner, M., *On Not Being Able to Paint* (London: Heinemann Educational, 1971).

Mitchell, Basil, *The Justification of Religious Belief* (London: Macmillan 1973).

Murray, P., and L. Murray, *A Dictionary of Art and Artists* (London: Penguin Books, 1972).

Nietzsche, Friedrich, *Human, All Too Human* (Leipzig: E.W. Fritzsch, 2nd edn, 1886).

Novak, Philip, *The Vision of Nietzsche* (Shaftesbury: Element Books, 1996).

Pailin, David A., 'Revelation', in Alan Richardson and John Bowden (eds.), *A New Dictionary of Christian Theology* (London: SCM Press 1983), pp. 503-506.

Palmer, Michael F., *Paul Tillich's Philosophy of Art* (Berlin: W. de Gruyter, 1983).

Panofsky, Erwin, *Meaning in the Visual Arts* (Garden City, NY: Doubleday, 1955).

Parrinder, G., *Mysticism in the World's Religions* (Oxford: Oxford University Press, 1976).

Pattison, George, *Art, Modernity and Faith* (Basingstoke: Macmillan, 1991).

Pattison, George (ed.), *Kierkegaard on Art and Communication* (Basingstoke: Macmillan, 1992).

Polka, Brayton, 'Aesthetics and Religion...', in Pattison (ed.), *Kierkegaard on Art*, pp. 23-54.

Pool, Phoebe, *Impressionism* (London: Thames & Hudson, 1967).

Popper, K.R., *Objective Knowledge: An Evolutionary Approach* (Oxford: Oxford University Press, 1972).

Ramachandran, V.S., 'Sharpening Up "The Science of Art": An Interview with Anthony Freeman', *Journal of Consciousness Studes* 8.1 (2001), pp. 9-29.

Ramachandran, V.S., and William Hirstein, 'The Science of Art', *Journal of Consciousness Studes* 6 (1999), pp. 15-51.

Read, Herbert, *A Concise History of Modern Painting* (London: Thames & Hudson, rev. edn, 1968).

—*The Meaning of Art* (London: Faber & Faber, 1951).

—*The Philosophy of Modern Art* (London: Faber & Faber, 1964).

Reid, L.A., *Meaning in the Arts* (London: Routledge & Kegan Paul, 1969).

Rewald, John (ed.), *Paul Cézanne: Letters* (Oxford: Bruno Cassirer, 1976).

Riches, John (ed.), *The Analogy of Beauty* (Edinburgh: T. & T. Clark, 1986).

Rookmaaker, Hans, *Modern Art and the Death of Culture* (London: Intervarsity Press, 2nd edn, 1973).

Rubin, James H., *Manet's Silence and the Poetics of Bouquets* (London: Reaktion Books, 1994).

Saramago, Jose, *The Gospel according to Jesus Christ* (London: Harvill, 1993).

Sheppard, Anne, *Aesthetics: An Introduction to the Philosophy of Art* (Oxford: Oxford University Press, 1987).

Stangos, Nikos (ed.), *Concepts of Modern Art* (London: Thames & Hudson, 1994).

St Augustine, *Confessions* (London: Penguin Books, 1961).

Stein, Gertrude, *Picasso* (New York: Dover Publications, 1984).

Steiner, George, *No Passion Spent* (London: Faber & Faber, 1996).

Stuckey, Charles F. (ed.), *Monet: A Retrospective* (New York: Hugh Lauter Levin Associates, 1985).

Sylvester, David, *About Modern Art* (London: Chatto & Windus, 1996).

Taylor, Mark C., *Disfiguring: Art, Architecture, Religion* (Chicago: University of Chicago Press, 1992).

Teilhard de Chardin, Pierre, 'Hymn to Matter', in *idem, Hymn to the Universe*, pp. 63-64.

—*Hymn to the Universe* (New York: Harper & Row, 1961).

Thomson, Belinda, *Impressionism* (London: Thames & Hudson, 2000).

Tillich, Paul, 'Religion and Secular Culture', *The Journal of Religion* 26.2 (1946), pp. 79-86.

Tolstoy, Leo, *What is Art?* (London: Walter Scott, 1898 [Ward Lock Reprints, 1970]).

Tracy, David, *The Analogical Imagination* (London: SCM Press, 1981).

Tucker, Paul Hayes, *Monet in the 90s: The Series Paintings* (Boston: Museum of Fine Arts, Boston, in association with Yale University Press, 1989).

Underhill, Evelyn, *Mysticism: A Study in the Nature and Development of Man's Spiritual Consciousness* (London: Methuen, 1911).

Walker, Ralph C.S., *Kant* (Routledge & Kegan Paul, 1978).

Walsh, Sylvia, 'Kierkegaard: Poet of the Religious', in Pattison (ed.), *Kierkegaard on Art*, pp. 1-22.

Whelan, J.P., *The Spirituality of Friedrich von Hügel* (London: Collins, 1971).

Wollheim, Richard, *Art and its Objects* (Cambridge: Cambridge University Press, 1992).

Index of Authors and Subjects